Biography of Dr. Ambedkar

Biography of DR. AMBEDKAR

Dr. Ajay Deewan

Corporate Office:
EMPTY CANVAS PUBLISHERS$_{TM}$
2/42, First Floor, Ansari Road, Daryaganj
New Delhi-110002
Email: emptycanvaspublishers@gmail.com
www.emptycanvaspublishers.com

Edition : 2026

ISBN: 978-93-90594-56-6

DR. AMBADKAR - BIOGRAPHY
AUTHOR: DR. AJAY DEEWAN

Published by:
EMPTY CANVAS PUBLISHERS$_{TM}$
New Delhi-(India)

Printed and Bound in India

Preface

Dr. Bhimrao Ambedkar was a great visionary who lived in India in the 20th century. Architect of the Indian Constitution, his work liberated millions of people and he is venerated within the Dalit (ex-untouchable) caste of people. But his vision is relevant to all communities of people all over the world.

As a leading Indian scholar, Ambedkar had been invited to testify before the South borough Committee, which was preparing the Government of India Act 1919. At this hearing, Ambedkar argued for creating separate electorates and reservations for Dalits and other religious communities. In 1920, he began the publication of the weekly Mooknayak (Leader of the Silent) in Mumbai. Attaining popularity, Ambedkar used this journal to criticize orthodox Hindu politicians and a perceived reluctance of the Indian political community to fight caste discrimination. His speech at a Depressed Classes Conference in Kolhapur impressed the local state ruler Shahu IV, who shocked orthodox society by dining with Ambekdar. Ambedkar established a successful legal practice, and also organised the Bahishkrit Hitakarini Sabha to promote education and socio-economic uplifting of the depressed classes.

In 1935, Ambedkar was appointed principal of the Government Law College, Mumbai, a position he held for two years. Settling in Mumbai, Ambedkar oversaw the construction of a house, and stocked his personal library with more than 50,000 books. His wife Ramabai died after a long illness in the same year. It had been her long-standing wish to go on a pilgrimage to Pandharpur, but Ambedkar had refused to let her go, telling her that he would create a new Pandharpur for her instead of Hinduism's Pandharpur which treated them as untouchables. Speaking at the Yeola Conversion Conference on October 13 near Nasik, Ambedkar announced his intention to convert to a different religion and exhorted his followers to leave Hinduism. He would repeat his message at numerous public meetings across India.

Upon India's independence on August 15, 1947, the new Congress-led government invited Ambedkar to serve as the nation's first law minister, which he accepted. On August 29, Ambedkar was appointed Chairman of the Constitution Drafting Committee, charged by the Assembly to write free India's new Constitution. Ambedkar won great praise from his colleagues and contemporary observers for his drafting work. In this task Ambedkar's study of sangha practice among early Buddhists and his extensive reading in Buddhist scriptures were to come to his aid. Sangha practice incorporated voting by ballot, rules of debate and precedence and the use of agendas, committees and proposals to conduct business.

In 1954 he twice visited Burma, the second time in order to attend the third conference of the World Fellowship of Buddhists in Rangoon. In 1955 he founded the Bharatiya Bauddha Mahasabha or Indian Buddhist Society and installed an image of the Buddha in a temple that had been built at Dehu Road, near Poona. Addressing the thousands of Untouchables who had assembled for the occasion, he declared that henceforth he would devote himself to the propagation of Buddhism in India.

This is a reference book. All the matter is just compiled and edited in nature, taken from the various sources which are in public domain.

The book, which provides a rare opportunity to debate and discuss the contribution of Dr. Ambedkar in nation-building, will be great interest to all sections of people.

—Editor

Contents

1

Introduction

Dr. Bhimrao Ambedkar was a great visionary who lived in India in the 20th century. Architect of the Indian Constitution, his work liberated millions of people and he is venerated within the Dalit (ex-untouchable) caste of people. But his vision is relevant to all communities of people all over the world.

He has long been a spiritual hero of mine. Dr. Ambedkar proved that one person can make an enormous difference to millions of people's lives.

Born as an untouchable with no rights to be an equal in Indian Society, Dr. B.R. Ambedkar educated himself as the most qualified person of his time, inspired untouchable castes to reject Brahmanical Social Order (BSO) that kept them socially degraded, economically poor, culturally despised, politically powerless, and denied them the " basic human rights". He challenged the leadership of his time by exposing follies of their proposition of freeing India without freeing millions of untouchables, tribals and socially and educationally backward classes living in sub--human conditions under the Socio-Economic Raj of the Hindus. As the Chief Architect of free India's New Constitution, he abolished all forms of discriminations and inequalities based on caste, gender, race or status. But, what was his vision to uplift the Dalits?

Leadership has always been associated with many attributes. These attributes range from individual persona of the leader to a number of skills such as self-confidence, strong convictions, poise, ability to speak and present his concerns, and influence others' thought and actions. But it is the articulation of vision in the leadership that taps the conscious or unconscious needs, values, aspirations and feelings of followers such that the leadership enthuse them with shared ideological goal. This paper attempts to define the terms vision and leadership, and then establishes the linkages between the two. Before exploring actions, programmes of Dr. B. R. Ambedkar and vision behind them, attempt has been made to explore the source of his vision.

CHILDHOOD & YOUTH

BRAs Family

Ambedkars come from Konkan. BRA's ancestral village is Ambavade, five kms from Mandangad, a small town in the Ratnagiri district. The family had some prestige in the village. BRA's grandfather Maloji Sakpal came of a good Mahar family. Of all the untouchables the Mahars are the most robust, adaptable, fighting, brave and leading community. It is believed that the Mahars were the original inhabitants of Maharashtra which they say was Mahar –Rashtra! Yet the origin of the word Mahar is said to be Maha-Ari, the great enemy! They were the first to come into contact with the Europeans. They formed a part of the Bombay Army of the East India Co just as the Dusads of Bihar.

Maloji was a retired military man. BRA's father was Ramji & mother Bhimabhai. The family belonged to the devotional Kabir school of thought. Thus Bhakti school found consolation in the human attributes like love, compassion and resignation to God. These devotees sought & found moral/spiritual food in Lord Krishna/Ram. But the most important effect upon the mind of the followers of this school was that they had abolished the rigidity of the caste system as Kabir had condemned it.

An uncle of BRA'S conferred a boon on Ramji that soon would a boy be born who would leave his mark on history. Entranced with the belief, Ramji and wife intensified their religious observances. The boon took effect at Mhow, on April 14, 1891 & so was born Bhim. BRA's mother Bhimabai came of the Murbadkars, an untouchable Hindu family. They were a rich family from the village of Murbad in Thane district. Fair by complexion, she had a broad forehead, curly hair, round glowing eyes & short nose.

BRA's father secured a job in Bombay in the military quarters at Satara. His mother passed away when BRA was six. Being the youngest of five children now his married sisters looked after him turn by turn. Besides his father's sister Mirabai was there to take care of the family. Soon BRA became her favorite. BRA's father Ramji Sakpal lived a very industrious & intensely religious life. He offered prayers morning & evening. He read & recited to his children the Ramayana & Mahabharata, the two unfailing sources of divine inspiration. He also sang spiritual songs from the Marathi saint-poets like Moropant, Mukteshwar and Tukaram. Constant recitals of these songs provided his children with a certain toning & command over language at an early age. For 14 years Ramji served as headmaster in military schools & had attained rank of Subedar-Major. He was a teetotaler and never touched meat. A friend & admirer of Phule he was aware of the social problems faced by his community. When the British banned the recruitment of the Mahars in the Indian Army, Ramji took a lead in protesting, approached the ever helping Ranade to draft a petition appealing to the British to rescind the orders. No wonder BRA had derived from his father his painstaking spirit, forceful mental energy and intense interest in the welfare of his society.

Early Education

At Satara BRA completed his primary education. During his school days BRA realized painfully what the stigma of untouchability meant. Once he & his brother took a train for Goregaon. Since their father had not come to the station they took a bullock cart for Goregaon. When the god-fearing caste Hindu cartman came to know that the two brothers were untouchables he asked the brothers to get off the cart, took them back only after they had paid him double the fare. After that the caste Hindu walked behind the cart with BRA's brother driving it. This was the first rude & shattering shock to the budding mind of Bhim. A few days the earlier impression got confirmed when he was drinking water stealthily at a public watercourse, got caught, and was beaten black & blue. The barber refused to cut his hair so his sisters cut his hair.

What an indelible impression these cruel disabilities must have made on Bhim's young mind that was so strong, so sensitive & yet too resolute. Such insults must have engendered in him a burning hatred for Hinduism. Bhim was pugnacious, resourceful & fearless. He could defy anybody and anything that dictated rules of conduct & discipline.

A Brahmin teacher by the name Ambedkar loved Bhim very much. He dropped part of his meal into the hands of Bhim every recess. This teacher has left his impress on the life of his pupil. The original name of Bhim father was Sakpal. Bhim drew his surname Ambavadekar from his native village Ambavade, as Maharashtrian surnames are often derived from the names of the ancestral villages. 'Friends it happens in other parts of India like Punjab's ex-CM Parkash Singh Badal came from the village Badal. Sachin Tendulkar's village is Tendu'. The teacher took so much fancy to the Bhim that he changed his surname from Ambavadekar to Ambedkar in the school records. Despite those oases of warmth, Bhim & his brother were not treated well at school.

He was a playful child who was not keen on studies but liked to indulge in all sorts of hobbies, fancies and gardening. When Ranade died in 1901 he was happy to enjoy the holiday not knowing who Ranade was. Sometime before this, Bhim's father married again. Bhim did not like this and so decided that he must earn his own livelihood. He had heard from his sisters that boys from Satara had found jobs in mills in Bombay, thus, he decided to be a winding boy in a Bombay mill. Unable to arrange the money for fare to Bombay he decided to give up his truant habits, study hard, get through his exams as fast as possible so that he could be independent of his father. This marked a turning point in his life because he became so diligent that his teachers urged his father to give him the best possible education.

Then Ramji & family moved to Mumbai, stayed at Dabak chawl in Lower Parel. He got his sons admitted into the Maratha school. Under his father Bhim did the translation of Howard's English Reader & the three famous translation books by Tarkhadkar. This improved Bhim's English tremendously. Bhim like Tilak & Savarkar developed in his youth a passion for reading. His desire to possess books was insatiable. A wide reading, deep knowledge & historical perspective bestow upon their growing lives a certain prestige & toning, Bhim was no exception. Ramji borrowed money to ensure that his son was supplied with new books. It was his ardent desire that his son should become a man of letters & light.

After a few months, Bhim was sent to the Elphinstone High School a leading school. Bhim studied hard, read at night – early morning under a kerosene oil-lamp. Inspite of being a govt school there were the same prejudices. By virtue of living in a labor class locality i.e. Parel he had the opportunity of observing the conditions of the labor class. In this environment three years glided by. By dint of hard work he got through his exams.

Yet the school life of Bhim was to receive its unkindest cut that was so deep which all his life he remembered with strongest aversion. Both Bhim & his brother were not allowed to take up the study of Sanskrit – a key to the study of the Vedas, but were forced to take Persian instead against their will. Afterwards BRA studied Sanskrit partly by himself & sometimes with the help of some pandits & himself became a pandit. "In his opinion, Persian stands no comparison with Sanskrit as the latter, observes he, is the golden treasure of epics, the cradle of grammar, politics & philosophy and the home of logic, dramas & criticism". Quote from Hudilkar, Prof Satyabodh. BRA praises Sanskrit.

Notwithstanding the ills & intolerable insults inflicted upon him and stimulated by his father to rise to a high position on life, encouraged by broad-minded men, Bhim passed the Matriculation exams in 1907 from Elphinstone High School. Bhim obtained 282 out of 750. This scoring of average marks is not uncommon in case of ambitious boys whose minds are absorbed in subjects other than texts and who become great in the future. But these marks were uncommon for an Untouchable. The community under the presidentship of S.K. Bole, a well-known social reformer, decided to honor Bhim. At this meeting well-known author & social reformer Krishnaji Arjun Keluskar took a fancy to Bhim & presented him with a copy of his new book, Life of Gautama Buddha.

A short time after the exams Bhim in abeyance to his father's wishes got married in an open shed of the Byculla market in Bombay. Bhim was hardly 17 and his wife 9, name Rami she was renamed as Ramabai.

By now the problem of Untouchables had made headway. From among them emerged Shivaram Janba Kamble who convened the first Conference of Untouchables in India. He sent a memorandum to the British govt in 1910 appealing to them to enlighten & elevate the Untouchables 'by allowing them to remain followers of their own ancestral faith'. Another stalwart from the Maratha community V.R. Shinde, educated at Oxford, started in 1906 the Depressed Classes Mission of India. It opened branches in other cities too.

Encouraged by his father Bhim studied further, completed his Inter Arts after which his father ran out of funds, approached Keluskar for help who called the Maharaja of Baroda reminding him of the announcement he had made a few days earlier at a Townhall meeting in Bombay, promising to help any Untouchable in the pursuance of higher studies. Mahaja Sayajirao Gaekwad asked Bhimrao some questions, satisfied, he granted him a scholarship of 25 rupees per mensem.

AIM. BRA studied now with a view to passing the exam. But reading was the greatest joy in life. It was directed to some purpose in life. It was his aim to arm himself with every possible missile, make himself master of a repository of knowledge & develop the power of his mind to prepare himself for higher attainments & a new life that was to open the portals & possibilities of a great career.

BRA passed his B.A. exams in 1912. It was during this period that the rights of Indians were totally suppressed by the British govt. This gave rise to a whirlwind of discontent. Tilak's deportation to Mandalay & Savarkar's brother's revengeful transportation to the Andamans, imprisonment of several others shook Maharashtra violently. This state of repression must have agitated the strong currents of BRA's mind.

The repercussions of these events were seen on his mind when he wrote his famous thesis, The Evolution of Provincial Finance in British India. The patriot in BRA describes in it how the Brits resorted to repressive measures and indicts the British administration in India with these words, 'Not satisfied with the aid of power with which the Executive was endowed by the provisions of the Criminal & Penal Codes to anticipate offenses by preventing acts, it besmeared the Indian Statue Book with a set of repressive laws hardly paralled in any other part of the world'. He tells us that the Indian Press Act of 1910, puts a muzzle on the Press. Few front tank authors of those times described this period of Indian history as pithily as BRA has done.

BRA's reactions to Morley-Minto are noteworthy. Tracing the growth of constitutionalism at different stages, 1853-1861-1892001909, he says in his theses that it was always the intent of the British to make the legislature independent and at the same time muzzle it. He said that it was a Parliamentary system without a Parliamentary executive and in which the Legislature could neither make or unmake the Executive.

After his graduation, BRA took service in Baroda, the state of his benefactor. He was appointed to the post of a lieutenant in the Baroda State Forces. This move was probably a shrewd step fully aware that most offices being manned by orthodox Hindu upper classes it could create an unbearable situation for him. Barely 15 days later BRA had to rush to Bombay to see his ailing father who passed away on 2/2/1913. This was the saddest day of BRA's life. So passes away Ramji Maloji, in debt but with exemplary character and unconscious of his great legacy to his clan, country & humanity. Having infused his son a strength of will to resist worldly temptations & a depth of spirituality unfound in his son's contemporaries, he left him behind the fight the battle of life & to break the world to his way.

THE VISION

Oxford dictionary gives many meanings of the word 'Vision'. However, when one uses this word in association with the word leadership, it is the act of faculty of seeing or power of discerning future conditions, or the foresightedness. Therefore, it is the capacity of the leadership to look forward. It suggests the future orientation and perceiving the possibilities or images of the things to come. Vision gives the sense of direction. It can also be referred to as a conceptual road, mapping from the existing position of the Organisation to its destination in the imagined future. Vision propels one to change for a better future against the maintenance of a status quo. It connotes a standard of excellence, an ideal and implies a choice of values. It has quality of uniqueness. Vision is not for the complacent. Vision articulates a view of a realistic, credible, attractive future for the Organisation, a condition that is better in some ways than what now exists. Renowned authority on Leadership, Kouzes and Posner reports that not every leader they interviewed used the term vision. They used purpose, focus, mission, legacy, dream goal, calling or personal agenda.

THE LEADERS

Based on leader's personal traits, behaviour, functioning style, decision-making process, leader-follower relationship in relation to different situations, a number of models and approaches of leadership have been developed. However, there exists two notions of leadership, which are (1) the traditional and (2) the new notions.

The traditional notions of leadership are based on power and control. Leaders are supposed to detach themselves from mundane routine work, and limit themselves to inventing a grand plan. Magnetize a band of followers with courageous acts. Separate emotions from work and remain lonely at the top. Being on the top makes them automatically leader, and the leadership is reserved for few. Traditional notions are 'based on the assumptions that leadership can't be learnt. Notions of leadership, however, have changed. The changed notions, we refer to them as new notions of leadership, contradict the assumptions of born-leaders. They characterise leadership with challenging the process, changing things, and shaking up the Organisation. It could be a mother, a small model of leadership in her family, a teacher, a principal, and environmentalist, a Chief Executive Officer, or a leader of a community, party or nation.

The new leadership attracts constituents not because it is in a position to command (e.g. Minister) and control them, but because of its unquestionable faith in the human capacity to adapt, grow, and learn. The new leadership believes in long-term strategy. Supernatural powers are not their source of dynamism. Their powers come from strong belief in a purpose, and willingness to express that conviction. Instead of commanding and controlling, this leadership serves and supports. It is involved and in touch with those whom it leads. The credibility of action is the single most determinant of whether the leader being followed or not. Therefore, the new leadership is not about a place or a position. It is an art of mobilising others to strive for shared aspirations. Leadership communicates these shared aspirations - the vision. The new notion of leadership, therefore, emphasises the role of vision in the leadership.

Importance of vision in leadership has been adequately acknowledged. Burns referred to this kind of leadership as 'Transformational Leadership'. Kotter expressed it in terms of three elements, establishing direction i.e. vision, strategies for achieving it and aligning people with the chosen direction and producing change.'

VISION IN LEADERSHIP

Vision provides strength and reflects depth in thinking process of the leader. Vision gives a clear idea of the objectives of the leader. Warren Bennis in his book 'On Becoming A Leader' says that leaders come in every size, shape and disposition, but they seem to share the basic ingredients of a guiding vision. Robert Swiggett, as quoted in 'The Leadership Challenge' says "the leaders job is to create a vision. Without vision the leadership has no meaning because the people won't know where the leader wants to go and what he/she wants to do and how he/ she wants to do it." It is the vision that unites the leader and the followers for achieving common goals, and precisely that is what leadership is about.

Vision brings effectiveness to leadership. It is a bridge between the present and the future constructed by a leader. Vision is the manifestation of a leader's judgment and character and a fresh approach or new option to longstanding problems. Leadership must provide a framework of thought to the people he is leading, as they would not follow without being convinced.

OLD AGE

1. What did BRA achieve - BRA was now 63. His weak constitution could not cope with the rebellious surge in his brains to wrest & wring from the constitution the good he expected for his people who were landless, shirtless, shoeless & hungry. He was aware that his hopes for a better future of his people remain unfulfilled. Opinions may differ on his frequent volcanic attacks, but it would be unrealistic to say that BRA was crying wolf too often.

What had BRA achieved for the untouchables? Their story of their past life was dark. It was for the first time in the history of the past 2500 years that the sun of a better future rose on their horizon. BRA their kith & kin focused world attention on their civic, social and political rights & liberties, made untouchability a burning topic, raised it to international importance. He awakened in them a sense of dignity, self-respect and a burning hatred for untouchability that was worse than slavery. He infused courage in them, which enabled them to voice their grievances and to stand up for justice, equality & liberty. His heroic struggle raised them to political equality with other communities in India. The Untouchables were emerging from the dust, getting government jobs, becoming more politically conscious, organized big conferences and their leaders established institutions of importance. Unfortunately those who progressed tried to become second class Brahmins.

Yet it was an indisputable fact that the SC still suffered social & economic hardships & land & legal impediments in rural areas. Research scholars observed that their housing conditions – small huts mad of tin or coconut leaves had a direct bearing on their moral & health. However, the disease was being cured gradually. The one leader in a liberated India who unceasingly cried for the speedy abolition of untouchability was Veer Savarkar.

2. BRA's Contribution to Hinduism - BRA was a great teacher who taught the common man to have belief in his

potential power, to rouse it up, to develop it and to stand on his own feet. To him nothing was more sacred than learning. No man was born a dullard. He recalled to students the glorious traditions & untiring industry, high aims & sense of public life of Ranade, Tilak & Gokhale. 'You must have a firm belief in the sacredness of your goal'. Blessed are those who are awakened to their duty to those among whom they are born. Glory to those who devote their time, talents & their all to the annihilation of slavery.

BRA did not like that his hungry men should envelop themselves in the coil of Bhakti, the cult of devotion, opium of helplessness. He asked the common man not to resign himself to his fate & accept his position as a divine dispensation. BRA tried to divert the minds of his people from the thought of life after death to their present life of degradation. He wanted them to enjoy material amenities & to bring themselves upto the cultural level of the majority. At the same time to the more advanced man he warned that material comfort is by no means the solvent of all human ills. Man does not live by bread alone, he is a cultural being.

That is why people regard the life of BRA, who was one of the greatest Protestant Hindu leaders of Modern India, as a phase in the renaissance of Hinduism & in the reorganization of Hindu social order. The first renaissance in Hinduism was inaugurated by the Upanishads with their stream of new thoughts when the gods, priests & sacrifices receded into the background. With the resurgence of orthodox priests & idea of sacrifices, decadence set in again with added vigor. At this time Buddha came forward to rejuvenate & reorganize the social & religious system of the Hindus. He attacked priest craft, the institution of sacrifice & stood for the abolition of the ramifications in society.

With the rise of Shankaracharya, Hinduism slowly absorbed Buddhist principles but tightened its hold on the caste system & karmakand. Then came another revival with the spiritual teachings of Ramanuja, Kabir, Nanak, Chaitanya and Namdeo. The fourth phase began with the rise of Raja Ram Mohan Roy, Phule, Ranade, Dayananda & Vivekananda carried forward by Savarkar on a rationalistic basis. Gandhi's contribution was more of a humanitarian nature than of a social one. BRA's movement saw the fifth phase of the renaissance of Hinduism & reorganization of the Hindu social order. He was the first greater leader from the oppressed people during the history of over 2,500 years of their slavery. He started a mental revolution unprecedented in the history of Hinduism, to purify & revolutionize Hinduism, to reorganize & revitalize Hindu society & to save it from decadence / degradation. His contribution, therefore to Hinduism & India would be greater than that of most of the modern Hindu leaders like Dayananda & Vivekananda, for unlike them he has contributed to the constitutional & political thought & development of this country.

BRA demanded liberation of Hindu society from casteism & priest craft. According to his social philosophy, every Hindu must have the liberty to associate in all legitimate ways with his co-religionists. The Hindus must build a common Social Code. BRA was for one national language, the Hindi & one common script, the Nagari. Thus his social philosophy appealed to Hindus to liberate Hinduism & solidify Hindu society, and to revitalize Hindu thought and abolish the caste system & touch me not-ism.

3. BRA the person - By temperament BRA was cyclonic. At the least provocation he flew into anger. The next moment his anger would cool down. It will not be far from the truth if one says that BRA was a not man of the family. He called himself asang, unfit for familiarity. Constant tours, study and public appointments kept him engrossed all the time. There might be none around him who did not suffer rebukes at his hands at some time or the other. Some eminent men described him as a British Bulldog and Sarojini Naidu called Mussolini. His ability, integrity, great learning & untold sacrifice inspired

devotion & confidence. Yet his imperious life was an empire which had lost many cities under the debris of forgetfulness & neglect. BRA did not show enthusiastic familiarity with or admiration for anybody. His truthfulness was shattering.

He had the vision of Buddha but humility was not conspicuous among his merits. His proud self-confidence often verged on boastfulness. In his relaxed mood he talked endlessly. His talks gave his visitors both entertainment & arguments. Besides a strong sense of humor he had an irresistible taste for country jokes & idioms. At times one got more jokes from him in one hour than one got from all other politicians in five years. Though grave & fierce in appearance BRA was a foundation of emotions. When his youngest son died, BRA was so overwhelmed with grief that he would part with the dead body for days. When his first wife passed away his grief knew no bounds.

In his old age BRA found time to hear music for which he had a liking. BRA's house was not a detached villa that gave you an appearance of seclusion. His vast library, rich clothes, his enormous pens, his grand card, the numerous varieties of shoes & boots were the living marks of his conquering personality that marched on removing all obstacles till he felt he had secured all that he was capable of winning in the world in which he lived. Big & varied types of fountain pens had an irresistible fascination for BRA. Rich dress & best cut interested him.

The bookworm in BRA had no time for social life. Once in a while he went to see pictures. Though an expert cook BRA never insisted on any particular dish. When he was angry with family members he remained without words & food. His handwriting had an elegant style, which indicated firmness, clarity & display. He loved fine dogs & would bring one from the farthest corner of the country if his eyes fell on a charming breed. To visit BRA was to visit a speaking museum. His conversation was illuminating, entrancing, vigorous &

communicative. His talk ranged over many subjects, which were stored in his prodigious museum.

The time factor was a legend that revolved round BRA's name. None could encroach upon his time. Two great Indians of our age utilized every moment of their life as life's greatest treasure. They were Gandhi & BRA. To BRA love of books was the greatest means of education & self-development, and the highest type of recreation & enjoyment. Company of books gave BRA supreme joy of life & serious aloofness. The cause of Indian independence drove Tilak into politics, the cause of the Untouchables drove BRA into politics. Goethe said we know accurately when we know little, for with knowledge our doubts increase. He had no flash of a Savarkar or of a Nehru. But when he proved his point, he quoted one after another all the great thinkers on that particular topic to support his point. BRA's thirst for books was ever growing & flowing like the river Ganges. BRA bitterly wept at the thought of loosing his eyesight, for then life would be meaningless. Great was his joy when he wrote a book.

4. BRA the Man - All that is great in men comes through labor, 'You have no idea of my sufferings & labor, you would have been wiped out' said BRA to one journalist. Three personalities influenced the life & actions of BRA. Besides stories from the Mahabharat & Ramayan, which he heard with rapt attention in his childhood, the life of Buddha, the teachings of Kabir and the struggle of Phule contributed tremendously to the building of his personality. These personalities gave him his soul force and Western education gave him his weapons.

But the combination of idealism & practical life, by knowledge & experience, BRA belonged to the race of Ranade, Bhandarkar, Tilak & Telang who unfurled the Indian flag of learning in the world of learning & research. There was Tagore, Bose & Radhakrishnan but that was a different order. BRA was the last link of the batch of scholar politician, the type that was dying out in India and making politics poorer. Yet BRA had one more advantage over the scholar politician save Tilak. BRA led a stormy political life, launched political struggles and passive resistance movements and was in the firing line when it was necessary. He faced cruel attacks & returned merciless blows. In a moment he knew how to begin the fight & thundered / threw thunderbolts into the camps of his opponents. That is why he was rated amongst the best brains, was regarded as one of the dozen most astonishing men & one of the bravest sons of India.

BRA was a powerful speaker both on the platform & in Parliament. Galvanic & embarrassingly brutal to a fault in his speech, he showered a fusillade of pistol shots at these opponents. Like all positive men of character & mission, BRA had his idolaters & detractors. He had a reputation for great personal integrity & fearless intellectual honesty. Yet it was a fact that he paid bills stingily. BRA's hold over his people was unshakeable. One striking feature about BRA was his marvelous combination of obstinacy & resilience & his ability to seize an opportunity by the forelock which quality succeeds in politics. It was resilience & not expediency that made him shed his obstinacy without compromising his stand or conscience. He was shrewd enough to know that dawn does not come twice to awaken a man. He had the gift of catching the ball as it bounced.

BRA did not accept the Geeta at all, to him it was an irresponsible book on ethics, a compromise of all errors. He believed in the necessity of religion. He believed in God in the sense that some unknown power might be influencing human destiny. This faith in God, he, however, unified, since he took an active interest in the revival of Buddhism, with the worship of the image of the Buddha before which he knelt & said prayers morning/evening. As a front rank leader, BRA kept himself away from the controversies over provincialism. But when points came up for discussion, he proudly said that Maharashtrians never acted as traitors to the country, he also said that they would be last people to be scared by the threat of the proposed Pakistan since they had once in their living past routed the Muslim forces in battlefield & battlefield.

BRA was a leader of the masses. Tilak was the first leader of modern India who influenced the middle class and spread his influence over the masses. Gandhi moved the masses while BRA moved the lower strata of society. BRA represented more a cause than an organization. BRA did not try to organize his party on modern lines. There was no regular annual conferences or general meetings. Where & when he sat was the venue of conference & the time for decision. The office bearers had to fall in line with this arrangement. His followers were attracted by his integrity, ability, sacrifice & learning. When he wanted his people to assemble he simply gave them a clarion call and the organization sprang up like the crop in the rainy season.

2

Dr. Ambedkar: Life and Mission

Dr. Babasaheb Ambedkar was a veritable phenomenon of the 20th century. There may scarcely be a parallel indeed in the annals of human history to the saga of struggle that his life represented. Born in the family of 'untouchables', he could nonetheless scale the highest peak of scholarship, leadership and statesmanship. When the Hindu caste system had ordained severe punishment for his community for so much as thirsting for education and knowledge, he had secured the highest academic honours from the most prestigious universities of the world and thus conclusively refuted the basic premise of intrinsic inferiority or superiority based on one's birth proffered by the caste system.

For over two millennia, the Hindu caste system had perfected itself into a self-sustaining mechanism of exploitation that fossilised all the social relationship into a caste cauldron and in process had completely robbed the labouring masses like untouchables of their human identity. He had reclaimed for them this identity, breathed political consciousness and galvanised them into a vibrant movement that changed the course of Indian politics. In the epic battle against the vile and complex caste system, he had single-handedly performed the roles of a researcher, a theoretician, an organiser, a journalist, a politician, a leader etc. against all possible odds and still come out with outstanding results. He was among few who dared the contemporary might of the then Indian National Congress and Mahatma Gandhi and stood his grounds even in the face of threats to his life. At symbolical plane, Manu who was the evil enemy in this epic battle as the code giver for the caste system, had to concede defeat and make place for Ambedkar code in the form of the Constitution of India. Eventually, he enacted the biggest religious conversion in the history that ensconced him with his western attire at the place alongside Buddha as the spiritual deity for his people.

During his lifetime Dr. Ambedkar had consistently faced despise, ignominy and insults at the hand of caste establishment. Even after his death, despite his outstanding statesmanship and sterling contributions like drafting the Constitution of India, Ambedkar continued to be despised and ignored by the ungrateful mainstream till the emerging imperatives of electoral politics needed him. Before that, the mainstream even did not concede him so much as leadership of all the untouchables and preferred to belittle him by projecting as a leader of his own community. It systematically either blacked him out from the recorded history or allowed him place in its margins. It strove to confine him to a small community of Maharashtra in which he was born. So effective was this establishment cunning that barring a few pockets outside Maharashtra, where the movement had penetrated in his lifetime, he remained a stranger for a long time to the very people for whom he lived and died. His published writings were all out of print and were available only in a few reputed libraries.

A vast unpublished material was embroiled in ownership disputes and hence was decomposing in the custody of courts of law. A few biographies of Ambedkar, among them notably one written by Dhanajay Keer in English (first published 1962) and the other written by Mr. B.C. Khairmode in multiple volumes in Marathi (first volume published in April 1952 and the last volume yet to come), that constituted the earliest source material on Ambedkar had significantly contributed to spread awareness and evoke curiosity about him. However, in absence of an easy access to his original writings he was not even known to the well-meaning intellectual community beyond certain heresies and anecdotes. It is only as a result of struggles of his people that claimed increasing space in contemporary politics and partly influenced by the intrinsic need to woo dalits that the State moved to undertake publication of his writings. The Government of Maharashtra undertook to publish his writings and speeches and came out with its first volume in April 1979.

So far 16 volumes have been published which are being translated in Indian languages of some States. Before this project, it needs to be noted that many organisations and individuals claiming allegiance to Ambedkar-thought had brought out reprints of his published writings, compilation of his speeches scattered at many places, and secondary material in his eulogy. It certainly did contribute to spread awareness about the Ambedkar-thought, but due to their meagre resources its reach remained acutely constrained. This constraint was largely overcome when the Government of Maharashtra offered his writings and speeches in well-edited volumes at reasonable prices. Thanks to it, this publication, particularly the ones containing his hitherto unpublished writings, for the first time provided comprehensive introduction to the treatise of his thoughts and expectedly gave impetus to discussions and research work on Ambedkar-thought. The eruption of dalit militancy in the form of Dalit Panthers movement in 70s and the spate of anti-reservation flare ups in 80s, that shook the oppressors as well as oppressed, also significantly motivated the study of Ambedkar-thought.

As the development process picked up momentum in the post-independence period, the contradiction among the ruling classes started growing which in turn manifested into many political parties opening their shops in the electoral market of

India. The heat of competition impelled them to see the importance of the vast market segment constituted by the dalit votes. The latter, being one-fourth of the total market, was significant enough even in any electoral constituency to tilt the scale. The broad strategic response possible was either to fragment this segment, which was easy to do along the existing sub-caste fissures, so as to reduce it to insignificance level or to consolidate it and lure it onto ones side. However, with the passage of time the trend of dalits transcending their sub-caste boundaries and getting emotionally bonded around Ambedkar was increasingly becoming visible. As such the former negative strategy became less attractive and was ostensibly adopted by only the hard-core fascist parties. The large-scale adoption of the latter positive strategy meant competition in claiming Ambedkar's legacy that manifested in hijacking Ambedkar away to the camps of the ruling classes. This cooptation of Ambedkar by the mainstream politics essentially resulted in significant displacement of the genuine Ambedkar by the deformed Ambedkar in the gullible dalit masses. The universal eulogy reflected from the process of cooptation only helped latent tendency towards deification and iconisation of Ambedkar and that virtually made it impossible to review Ambedkar-thought as a living body in the context of changing times and circumstances without incurring the sin of sacrilege.

While the imperatives of electoral politics has changed the attitude of State to the extent of cooptation of Ambedkar, the civil society still reflects the casteist prejudice against him. The process of globalisation driven by the imperialist institutions like IMF and the World Bank since 1980s and which got formally adopted by the Government of India in 1991, in the crisis-ridden economic context unleashed new contradictions that manifested among other, the resurgence of the Hindu fundamentalism. These forces blatantly upheld everything that appeared conclusively condemned by liberal ethos during the post-independence decades. Ambedkar, as a symbol of these ethos naturally became the target for their vicious attack.

Currently these attacks could be seen in the form of defilement of his statues and the pseudo-intellectual cunning represented by some reactionary individuals. Both, the cooptation as well as the vilification of Ambedkar are detrimental to the dalit interests. However, the former is much more injurious than the latter. While the latter represents open opposition to the ideology the former would mean adulteration of the ideology itself to suit the State interests. Unless, one is thorough about the ideological nuances and vigilant about its operative manifestations, it becomes extremely difficult to arrest or contain the damage done through the process of cooptation. The ideological weakness in turn incapacitates the struggle in the realm of the civil society and even its organisational apparatus. The present state of fragmentation of the Dalit movement may be largely attributable to this ideological weakness.

The problems of dalits are far from being resolved. Despite the constitutional provision to the contrary, they are being discriminated against day in and day out. This discrimination ranges from the subtle prejudice exercised against them in the modern sectors of economy in the urban areas to the stark practice of untouchability in the rural areas. Another significant constitutional influence on the dalits has been through the policy of reservation in politics, education and services. While, this policy implemented sincerely in political arena as it basically serves the interests of the establishment and provides legitimacy to the system, its implementation in other two spheres has been utterly pathetic. Even over the five decades of its implementation, the unsatisfactory representation of dalits particularly in the higher echelon of services and consistent denial of their dues by the executive as well as judiciary has amply bared the fangs of the State. The condition of majority of dalits in rural areas is no better than it existed five decades before. Pulverisation of dalit politics under the rollers of electoral allurements has incapacitated the dalit movement. The dalits masses today feel utterly cheated but they do not have wherewithal to see by whom.

The typical responses to the empirical state of the dalit masses and their movement are essentially of two types. The first one tends to externalise the failure by accusing the *savarnas* of cheating or of failing to implement the promises made in the Indian Constitution. The second one tends to internalise it in terms of failure of practice by dalits, particularly the dalit leaders and intellectuals. It accuses the dalit intellectuals and politicians of having snapped themselves off their roots and of betraying the dalit movement. They have come to be a class for itself. Both represent partial truth at some level. These very allegations however tend to submerge the basic question about the efficacy of strategy of the movement and in turn of its ideology that failed to firstly envisage and thereafter arrest the undesired happenings. As for the leaders and the dalit intellectuals (or more correctly the educated dalits), they represent the output of the movement. Insofar as Ambedkar represents a fountainhead of both the strategy as well as the ideology of the dalit movement, his thoughts should constitute essential terrain to search the causes of these failures.

The difficulty in this enterprise is immense despite much of Ambedkar's writings and speeches are available in English language and a plethora of secondary and tertiary literature having been published in recent times.

Ambedkar lived through a turbulent period of the Indian history, creating space for the dalit movement within the interstices between the movements of the contending classes with his meagre resources. His thoughts are therefore heavily contextised by the dynamics of this contention. While simultaneously trying to build the ideological foundation for the movement, they tend to reflect expediency of survival and his anxiety to maximise the short-term gains for dalits. While it may not be difficult to discern the ideological strains in his writings, the task of its precise definition (exaction) poses problematic on two counts. First, many a familiar construct and concept in his usage do not bear their familiar meanings as indicated by him.

For instance, while he adores the dictum of 'liberty, equality and fraternity' propounded by Roussou that blazed the French Revolution, he faults it and finds its perfection in Buddha; while he reflects western liberalism and admires its proponents, he denies being a liberal; while he appears to accept the ideal of socialism in Marxism, he does not seem to talk about the scientific socialism in it and rather finds his dream world in Buddhist Sangha; while he accepts the premise that there are classes in society in contradiction with each other, he rejects the imperative of class struggle and foresees the class conciliation through the constitutional methods.

One could easily go on listing the similar problematic of language. Indeed when eventually, when he embraced Budhhism, it was not to be the Buddhism familiar to the world but the one he interpreted to be propounded by Buddha, the Dhamma of Buddha essentially of his conception. Secondly, while he grants one freedom to test him out on the principles of rationality and on the basis of experience, he appears inaccessible for the purpose, well beyond the impregnable fortification erected by the powerful vested interests.

The collapse of so called socialist regimes and consequent emergence of the unipolar world order is casting its savage shadow on the struggles of the oppressed people all over the world. The ideology of neo-liberalism with the backing of modern media and military might is fast marginalising the resistance and transforming the world into a market where a person is granted a hallowed identity of a customer. His claim to liberty, equality and fraternity is conceded in proportion to his purchasing power in the market where everything is a commodity. The impact of this ideology is already visible in terms of gnawing inequality that is compounding with every passing year. The odds for the oppressed people are indeed mounting on every front. They face an unprecedented ideological crisis today for effectively articulating their emancipatory struggles.

They need to objectively review the weapons in their ideological armoury, to identify the ones that could be regenerated, the ones that could be modified and the ones that need to be altogether replaced. Ambedkar-thought that constituted weaponry of dalits and oppressed people in India, has certain attributes that could be used to recreate the new weapons. It has certain regenerative potential to be of continued relevance provided it is used in the desired manner and not monopolised by the vested and sectarian interests. The time has come to consolidate the ideological armour of the have-nots of the world and the study of Ambedkar-thought here is envisaged from that viewpoint. It is imperative that it is made available to many people in the world. It is necessary that it be subject to review from many viewpoints.

It is vital that it is evaluated on the basis of concrete experience. One respects contributions of great people not in blind allegiance but by serving the cause that he or she lived and died for. As Ambedkar said of great people and demonstrated in relation to Buddha whom he undoubtedly adored most, following him lies in not cold storing his thoughts in a time vault but in constantly using it in the struggle, constantly cleaning and honing it for its usage is bound to dirty it and deform it, constantly review its effectiveness as with the passage of time it might need supplement or replacement. Only the concerted struggle of many committed people can restore true Ambedkar to his people.

Dr. B.R. Ambedkar on Gandhi & the black Untouchables: Gandhi is the greatest enemy the untouchables have ever had in India."

LIFE AND EDUCATION

Bhimrao Ramji Ambedkar was born in the British-founded town and military cantonment of Mhow in the Central Provinces (now in Madhya Pradesh). He was the 14th and last child of Ramji Maloji Sakpal and Bhimabai. His family was of

Marathi background from the town of Ambavade in the Ratnagiri district of modern-day Maharashtra.

They belonged to the Hindu, Mahar caste, who were treated as untouchables and subjected to intense socio-economic discrimination. Ambedkar's ancestors had for long been in the employment of the army of the British East India Company, and his father Ramji Sakpal served in the Indian Army at the Mhow cantonment. He had received a degree of formal education in Marathi and English, and encouraged his children to learn and work hard at school.

Belonging to the Kabir Panth, Ramji Sakpal encouraged his children to read the Hindu classics. He used his position in the army to lobby for his children to study at the government school, as they faced resistance owing to their caste. Although able to attend school, Ambedkar and other untouchable children were segregated and given no attention or assistance by the teachers. They were not allowed to sit inside the class. Even if they needed to drink water somebody from a higher caste would have to pour that water from a height as they were not allowed to touch either the water or the vessel that contained it. This task was usually performed for the young Ambedkar by the school peon, and if the peon was not available then he had to go without water, Ambedkar states this situation as "No peon, No Water".

Ramji Sakpal retired in 1894 and the family moved to Satara two years later. Shortly after their move, Ambedkar's mother died. The children were cared for by their paternal aunt, and lived in difficult circumstances. Only three sons — Balaram, Anandrao and Bhimrao — and two daughters — Manjula and Tulasa — of the Ambedkars would go on to survive them. Of his brothers and sisters, only Ambedkar succeeded in passing his examinations and graduating to a higher school. Bhimrao Sakpal Ambavadekar the surname comes from his native village 'Ambavade' in Ratnagiri District. His Bhramin teacher Mahadev Ambedkar who was so much fond of him, has changed his surname from 'Ambavadekar' to his own surname 'Ambedkar' in school records.

Higher Education

Ramji Sakpal remarried in 1898, and the family moved to Mumbai (then Bombay), where Ambedkar became the first untouchable student at the Government High School near Elphinstone Road. Although excelling in his studies, Ambedkar was increasingly disturbed by the segregation and discrimination that he faced.

In 1907, he passed his matriculation examination and entered the University of Bombay, becoming one of the first persons of untouchable origin to enter a college in India. This success provoked celebrations in his community, and after a public ceremony he was presented with a biography of the Buddha by his teacher Krishnaji Arjun Keluskar also known as Dada Keluskar, a Maratha caste scholar. Ambedkar's marriage had been arranged the previous year as per Hindu custom, to Ramabai, a nine-year old girl from Dapoli.

In 1908, he entered Elphinstone College and obtained a scholarship of twenty five rupees a month from the Gayakwad ruler of Baroda, Sahyaji Rao III. By 1912, he obtained his degree in economics and political science from Bombay University, and prepared to take up employment with the Baroda state government. His wife gave birth to his first son, Yashwant, in the same year. Ambedkar had just moved his young family and started work, when he dashed back to Mumbai to see his ailing father, who died on February 2, 1913.

In 1913 he received Baroda State Scholarship of 11.50 British pounds a month for three years to join the Political Department of the Columbia University as a Post Graduate Student. In New York he stayed at Livingston Hall with his friend Naval Bhathena, a Parsi; the two remained friends for life. He used to sit for hours studying in Low Library. He passed his M.A. exam in June 1913, majoring in Economics, with Sociology,

History, Philosophy, and Anthropology as other subjects of study; he presented a Thesis," Ancient Indian Commerce".

In 1916 he offered another M.A. thesis,

- "National Dividend of India-A Historic and Analytical Study".

On May 9, he read his document Castes in India:

- Their Mechanism, Genesis and Development" before a seminar conducted by the anthropologist.

In October 1916 he was admitted to Gray's Inn for Law, and to the London School of Economics and Political Science for Economics where he started work on a Doctoral thesis. In 1917 June he was obliged to go back to India as the term of his scholarship from Baroda ended, however he was given permission to return and submit his thesis within four years. He sent his precious and much-loved collection of books back on a steamer, but it was torpedoed and sunk by a German submarine.

SELF-DEVELOPMENT

Education in U.S.

BRA's thirst for knowledge & spur for ambition made him restless. He was now in no mood to return to his job, his short stay had been unhappy. In June 1913 the Maharaja of Baroda thought of sending some students to Columbia University for higher studies & advertised. BRA replied to advt, met Maharaja who decided to send BRA & three other students there for higher education. BRA signed an agreement with the Baroda state agreeing to devote his time studying the prescribed subjects & to serve the state for 10 years after completing his studies.

Life in America was a different ball game. He could move freely, read – write -talk-bathe with a status of equality. Life there was a revelation, it enlarged his horizon, and his life gleamed with a new meaning. A letter to one of his fathers friends give us a peep into his mind, 'We must now, entirely give up the idea that parents give birth to the child and not destiny – Karma'. They can mould the destiny of the children and if we follow this principle, be sure that we will see better days ahead – progress will be hastened if male & female education are pursued simultaneously. 'Let your mission' concludes the man of 20, 'thus be to educate & preach the idea of education to those atleast who are near to & close contact with you'.

Imbued with these thoughts & vision BRA knew well that he had to develop his native worth without the backing of name or influence for which tremendous hard work was necessary. Out of his stipend he had to remit some money home every month so expense had to be kept down. His college colleagues related afterwards with pride how BRA seized every possible hour for his study for which he had been given a life's opportunity. He wanted to be a master so took up political science, moral philosophy, anthropology, sociology and economics as the subjects of his study.

Thus started 'Dnyana Yadnya', for 18 hours a day went on the endless digging for knowledge. After two years of hard work, BRA obtained his M.A. degree in 1915 for his thesis 'Ancient Indian Commerce'. He also read a paper on 'Castes in India, Their Mechanism, Genesis & Development' before the Anthropology Seminar of Dr Goldenweiser in May 1916. The second ladder of success was reached not long afterwards. Another thesis of his 'National Dividend of India – A Historic & Analytical Study' was accepted by the Columbia University in June 1916.

8 years later Messrs P.S. King & Son, Ltd, London published an extension of this thesis under the title, Evolution of Provincial Finance in British India. BRA then submitted the required number of copies of the thesis to the University. Columbia awarded him the degree of Doctor of Philosophy for this dissertation. In this thesis BRA traces the growth of the financial arrangements from the Act of 1833 under the imperial system.

From chapters 10 to 12 the book becomes eloquent, interesting & powerful in its appeal. The style of the professor becomes one with the soul of the patriot and BRA bitterly exposes the British bureaucracy, denounces the designs & objects of the imperial system and lashes out at the reactionary forces in the country. While admitting that there was some progress he adds that everybody knows that the whole policy of India was dictated by the interests of the English industries & manufacturers. This book became a companion of the Members of the Indian Legislative Council & Central Assembly at the time of the budget discussions during the British regime, ready reference for students of economics.

Young Americans whose forefathers had struggled for the abolition of slavery of the Negroes were celebrating the success of a young man who had the will & mission of Lincoln & the labor of Booker T Washington. While in America he must have been impressed with two things, one was the Constitution of the U.S. and the 14th amendment, which declared the freedom of Negroes. Two was the life of Booker T Washington who died in 1915. He was a great reformer & the educator of the Negro race in America. From the U.S. he reached London in June 1916. At New York Lala Lajpat Rai tried to convince BRA to join the Indian Revolutionary Party but failed. BRA told Lalaji that he was a student, must complete his studies first without betraying the trust of the Maharaja who had given him an opportunity of his life. Immediately BRA got himself admitted to Grays Inn for Law for the study of Economics to the London School of Economics. While he was studying he was informed that period of scholarship was over and thus had to return to India – Baroda. Wanting to study further but bound by agreement he secured permission from London University to resume his studies within a period not exceeding four years from October 1917.

BRA reached Bombay on 21/8/1917

The British govt faced a deep crisis, depressed by war

reverses, pressed by the Indian Home Rule movement and oppressed by the Indian revolutionary forces. In order to pacify Indians the then Secretary of State declared the policy of gradual development of self-governing institutions with a view to progressive realization of responsible Government in India as part of the British empire. When Montagu visited India all sorts of people met him, for the first time in the political history of India the representatives of the Untouchables met him too.

BRA was felicitated by Sambaji Waghmare & others for his achievements in the academic world but he did not attend the meeting – embarrassed he was. BRA left for Baroda bound as he was to the State for 10 years but no hostel wanted a Mahar to stay so he took shelter in a Parsee inn. The Maharaja wanted to appoint BRA as his Finance Minister eventually but wanted him to gain experience first, made him Military Secretary to the Maharaja first. However he was treated by staff & peons as a leper. One day a group of Parsis armed with lathis asked him to vacate the Parsee hostel that he was living in. No Hindu or Muslim would give him shelter in the city. Neither the Maharaja or the Diwan were able to help. Disgusted he returned to Bombay in the end of 1917.

The Indian National Congress (referred to as INC) was now growing conscious of the existence of the Depressed Classes. But its sudden love emanated from an ulterior motive of winning their support for the Congress-league scheme in which premium was put on the separate identity of the Muslims, but notice was not taken of the Untouchables.

To consider the Congress-League demands the Depressed Classes (referred to as DC) held two conferences in Mumbai. At the first one, a resolution appealed to the Govt to protect the interest of the Untouchables by granting the DC the right to elect their own representatives to legislatures in proportion to their population & by another it asked the Congress to pass a resolution impressing upon the caste Hindus the need for removing all the disabilities imposed upon the DC in the name of custom & religion. Accordingly the Congress passed a resolution at its annual session held in December 1917. The second conference opposed the transfer of power to the caste Hindus and appealed to the govt to grant them the right to choose their own representatives.

Three months after the Congress resolution the DC held it's First All India Depressed Classes Conference on 23-24/3/1918 in Bombay. It was attended by amongst other Maharaja of Baroda, Rabindranath Tagore, M.R. Jaykar, Shankaracharya of Dwarka, Tilak. Everyone asked for abolition of untouchability. At the end of the conference there came out with an All India Anti-Untouchability Manifesto signed by all prominent leaders that they would not observe untouchability in their everyday affairs. Tilak, however did not sign, on account of pressure from his followers.

Early Activism

Reserved & skeptical of the movement of the caste Hindus for the uplift of the Untouchables BRA did not associate himself with this conference. He was waiting for the right time to draw upon his energy & brainpower. First he must have a footing & position for which he had to earn his living. Law was on his mind. Through the help of a Parsi man he became a tutor to two students – started offering advice to dealers in stocks & shares. But soon it became known that its owner was an Untouchable and he had to close it down.

Yet the mind was busy with the ideas of intellectual conquest. BRA reprinted his paper on Castes in India in a book form & contributed a thought provoking paper on 'Small Holdings in India & their Remedies'. In a depressed state of mind he heard of a vacancy in Bombay's Sydenham College of Commerce, applied for the post of professorship. He accepted the post of Professor of Political Economy in November 1918 as his object was to collect money & return to England to complete his education. At first the students were apprehensive on the competence of an Untouchable but as time passed by they respected him, in fact students from other colleges came to attend his lectures.

Some Gujarati professors objected to his drinking water from the pot reserved for the professional staff. Wanton insults & humiliations were goading him to go to the root of the trouble. So gradually he began feeling the pulse of the Untouchables & was silently contacting all the centers of sympathizers with their cause. It was with this intent that he encouraged the felicitation of P Balu on his great achievements in cricket. Another prince Shri Shahu Maharaj, the ruler of Kolhapur did his utmost to promote education among the lower classes, eradicate prejudices and barriers created by the caste system.

Around this time Karamveer Shinde & BRA were called upon to give evidence before the Southborough Committee dealing with the franchise in the light of the Montagu-Chelmsford reforms. BRA demanded separate electorates and reserved seats for the Depressed Classes in proportion to their population. With the help of the Maharaja of Kolhapur he stated a fortnightly paper titled Mook Nayak, Leader of the Dumb in January 1920. In articles therein he wrote it was not enough for India to be an independent country, she must rise as a good state guaranteeing equal status in matters religious, social, economic and political to all classes, offering every man an opportunity to rise in the scales of life & creating conditions favorable to his advancement. He wanted to awaken the DC to their disabilities, take to education & progress. BRA was not prepared for all out attack on Hindu society yet and besides his armory was not yet full with weapons.

At the All India Conference convened by the Untouchables in May 1920 at Nagpur was the first time that during a debate BRA's skills & presence of mind as a debator and his ability as a prospective leader were seen to a remarkable degree. He defeated a proposal by Karamveer Shinde that the representatives of the Untouchables must be elected by the Members of the Legislative Council. It was here that BRA won his first victory in public life. BRA believed that howsoever-hard caste Hindus worked for their upliftment they did not know their mind. That is why he was opposed to any organizations started by caste Hindus for the upliftment of the DC. This Nagpur conference gave him an opportunity of turning the eyes of the Untouchables from the DC Mission. At the end of the conference he called the leaders together with a view to unite them for eg within the Mahar community there were 18 sub-castes.

Back to London

Although BRA drew a good salary as professor he lived a very simple life. He gave a fixed amount to his wife Ramabai for running the household. Dutiful, self-respecting, pious and given to self-denial she spent her early life in struggles yet lived in peace & harmony. Having lost her first two sons in infancy the health of her third son Yashwnt caused her anxiety. Yet she kept herself away from her husband's study, gave him no news of any illness in the family. Like Tilak, Savarkar BRA too had a great wife.

At last he had saved some money plus help from Maharaja of Kolhapur & Naval Bathena he left for London to complete his studies in Law & Economics. Besides his studies he turned his attention to the London Museum where the relics of saintly & scientific thoughts are preserved. Whenever possible he was there from 8 am to 5 pm. He also read several volumes & old reports in the India Office Library, took down notes for his thesis. After a walk and light dinner he would start reading again at night till early morning. BRA lived so sparingly that he survived on a small sum of 8 pounds a month.

Yet he did not forget him main aim in life, he had seen Montagu the then Secretary of State and Vithalbhai Patel and had talks with them on the grievances of the Untouchables in India. He took great interest in his paper Mook Nayak too. The political scene in India was changing with dramatic suddenness. A short while after BRA came to London passed away India's great son, Tilak. In the wake of this misfortune, surged and spread the politics of Gandhi. BRA described these times later as 'the dark age of India'.

Gandhi who while collecting the Tilak Swaraj Fund had made the removal of untouchability one of the planks of the Congress propaganda, now refused to spend on it beyond a meager amount out of the one crore rupees collected. The Congress Working Committee now resolved that the problem of the upliftment of the Untouchables should be left to the Hindu Mahasabha as it was thought that they were alone concerned with the problem. The Act of 1919 recognized for the first time the existence of the DC.

BRA research work was now coming to an end. Thesis 'Provincial Decentralization of Imperial Finance in British India' was completed for which he was awarded the Master of Science in June 1921. In October 1922 he completed his famous thesis 'The Problem of the Rupee and submitted it to the University of London. His studies were now coming to an end. He went to Germany for a while when he was called back to London as his thesis had offended the British who asked him to rewrite the thesis without changing his conclusions. A few days earlier he had read a paper on 'Responsibilities of a Responsible Government in India' before the students union. It created a furor like his earlier writings and he was suspected to be a revolutionary.

Running out of money he returned to India in April 1923. A few days later he resubmitted his thesis 'The Problem of the Rupee' from Bombay. Accepted, he was at last awarded the degree of Doctor of Science. In this work BRA reveals how in the final settlement of the currency problem the relationship of the rupee to the pound was manipulated to the greater profit of the British, and how it inflicted hardships on the Indian people as a whole. BRA was now a Barrister reinforced by a London Doctorate in science, an American Doctorate in Philosophy and studies at Bonn University.

THE LAST JOURNEY

Off to Nepal / Kashi - On 30/11/1956 BRA wrote to D. Valisinha, 'It was a great event and the crowd that came forward was beyond my imagination. We have to consider ways of & means of imparting knowledge of Buddhism to the masses who have accepted His Dhamma and will accept it on my word. I am afraid the Sangha will have to modify its outlook, and instead of becoming recluses, Bhikkus should become like Christian missionaries, social workers & preachers'. BRA now inspite of bad health went to Nepal to attend the fourth conference of the World Fellowship of Buddhists. The Govt of Nepal declared the day of the conference a holiday and banned the exhibition of an Indian film on the life of Shankaracharya, the mighty Hindu leader who liquidated Buddhism in India. (friends this statement is incorrect as said by BRA in earlier chapter, for a more detailed reply please visit section Why on site, there is an article titled 'Why Did Buddhism vanish from India). During this visit the priests in Kathmandu withdrew the recently conceded right to Buddhists to enter the temple of Pashipatinath.

Majority of delegates asked BRA to speak on Buddha & Marx. BRA expressed concern over the fate of Buddhist youngsters in Buddhist countries who looked upon Marx as the only prophet of worship. He stated that the goal of Buddha & Marx was the same. Marx said that private property was the root cause of sorrow. Buddha also wanted to abolish sorrow and its expression was used in Buddhist literature in the sense of property. According to Buddha everything was impermanent and so there was no struggle for property. The Bhikkus were not allowed to own private property. Buddha did not lay the foundations of his religion on God or Soul. So Buddha would not stand in the path of abolition of private property, if the principle of the denial of private property was applied to society. But the two differed. Communism adopted violent methods to abolish private property. Buddhism adopted non-violent means. Marx gave quick results, Buddha's way takes time. Buddhist way was based on a democratic system while the Communist system was based on Dictatorship. According to BRA it is impossible for humanity to live peacefully without the Buddha & His Dhamma.

BRA spoke at the Banaras Hindu University & thought he would achieve for Buddhism what Shankaracharya had done for Hinduism. He spoke on Shankaracharya's philosophy as expounded in the aphorism, 'Brahma Satyam Jagan Mithya'. BRA said that if the Brahman pervaded all, a Brahmin & an Untouchable were equal. But Shankara did not apply the doctrine to social organization & kept the discussion on a vedantic level. Had he applied it on a social level his proposition would have been profound & worth consideration, apart from his erroneous belief that the world was an illusion.

He returned to Delhi. Asked by an admirer why the statues of Buddha from different countries had different features, he replied that till 600 years after the Mahaparinirvana of Buddha there was no picture or statue of Buddha. Someone made a statue from his own imagination & then in all Buddhist countries statues were made in accordance with the standard of beauty prevailing in those lands.

End / Tributes / Thoughts

His health was getting worse. Some Jain leaders came to meet him, presented him with a copy of the book Jain & Buddha. On the morning of 6/12/1956 his wife Savita Ambedkar got up as usual, when she had a look at the bed she saw his leg resting on the cushion as usual. When she touched him she felt that BRA was no more. For eight years she had struggled to save his life and now he had left this world. Long before this in 1946, BRA had said that it was his belief that his life would be prolonged so long as it was necessary for the welfare of the DC. This faith carried him through disappointments & disorders of health.

Nehru, Pant, Jagjivan Ram called on his residence to pay respects to the departed leader. His body was brought to

Bombay. More than half a million people witnessed the last rites at the Dadar Hindu crematorium performed by Buddhist priests. Over a lakh people embraced Buddhism at the crematorium to fulfill the last wish of their departed leader.

The nation mourned his death. Nehru praised him in Parliament, Savarkar said that Indian had lost in BRA a truly great man. Dr Rajendra Prasad, C Rajagopalachari said good words about BRA. Newspapers paid handsome tributes including the New York Times & Times London. Later the Chief Minister of Maharashtra Y B Chavan declared BRA's birthday a public holiday. The govt have away 11 acres of land at Nagpur where the historic Diksha ceremony took place on 14/10/1956 and in 1968 a grand stoopa was erected on the Chaitya Bhoomi at Dadar Chowpatty, Bombay.

BRA's monumental work, The Buddha & his Dhamma was posthumously published. The book is subjective, direct and a good model. The Maha Bodhi, a famous Buddhist journal in India opined that BRA's was a dangerous book, BRA's interpretation of the theory of Karma, Ahimsa & that Buddhism was merely a social system, constituted not the correct interpretation of Buddhism but a new orientation. Indeed the whole book, observed the reviewer, explained the hatred & aggressiveness the neo-Buddhist nourished and displayed. 'BRA's Buddhism' added the reviewer, 'is based on hatred, the Buddha's on compassion. It would seem more important to be careful what we accept in BRA's book as being the word of Buddha'. The Light of the Dhamma, Rangoon, observed that although this was a book by a great men, it was not a great book which the author with all his manifold virtues was not fit to write. Whatever may be the fault BRA's Buddhism would be a reformist plank like the Arya/Brahmo Samaj.

BRA wanted Protestant Buddhism. Hinduism & Buddhism are branches of the same tree, just as the Catholic & Protestant church. So those who worship Buddha in India would do well to remember the world of Dr Rhys Davids who observes: 'We should never forget that Gautama was born & brought up as a Hindu and lived & died as Hindu. His teaching, far-reaching & original as it was, and really subversive of the religion of the day, was Indian throughout. He was the greatest & wisest & the best of the Hindus'.

BRA found a peculiar charm & magnetism in the appellation Bharat. He named one of his weeklies Bhaishkrit Bharat, his printing press was Bharat Bhushan Printing Press. His anxiety to live in Hindu culture, his avowal of embracing a religion that would neither denationalize the DC not harm the ancient culture of this land, all point to the fact that his religion had something to do with the culture, history & tradition of this land. His religion & politics went hand in hand. That is why Buddhist critics say that the Dhamma preached by BRA is not Buddhism but Ambedkarism. And rightly so. His Dhamma preaches the necessity to kill if needed and his message to India is that Indians should be determined to defend the independence of this land to the last drop of their blood.

And so ends the story of one of India's greatest leaders. Friends at 95 word pages this is my longest piece to date. Many a time I felt tired, willing to throw in the towel but the story of his this great son of India inspired me like few others have in the past. He joins the list of my heroes starting Veda Vyassa, Chanakya, Shankaracharya, Shivaji, Guru Govind Singh, Sardar Patel and Veer Savarkar to name a few.

Today we talk of 'Knowledge Economy'. Well BRA realized that nearly 80 years ago. To my mind it is the Power of Knowledge that made him the man he was. There were few within & outside the Congress who could take him on intellectually. I have also read Arun Shourie's book on BRA 'Worshipping False Gods' and tend to agree with a lot that Shourieji has written Yet I would rather overlook them & remember the good things that BRA did.

3

Dr. Ambedkar and Source of His Vision

Dr. B. R. Ambedkar returned to India in 1917 after spending three years at Columbia University in United States of America and one year in London School of Economics. He has earned a degree of Master of Arts in June 1915 and a Ph. D degree in June1916. He came to London in October 1916, and enrolled for the degrees of M. Sc. (Economics) and D.Sc. (Economics) in London School of Economics and Political Science. He also joined Gray's Inn for Law for the degree of Bar- at - Law. He returned to India back in August 1917, as the duration of his scholarship granted to him by the Maharaja of Baroda was over. He was appointed as the Military Secretary to the Maharaja Sayajirao Gaikwad. The Maharaja's intention was to appoint Ambedkar his finance Secretary after some experience. But soon Ambedkar had to leave Baroda in sheer disgust at the harassment and treatment he received as an untouchable. In 1918 he became a professor at Sydenham College, Bombay. He resigned in 1920, and went again to London to complete his studies. He returned to India permanently in April 1923.

Highly educated and articulate, from the very moment of his return in 1917 he was looked to as a leader of the community. In 1919, during a brief period in India between segments of his overseas education, he testified to the Southborough

Committee, which was gathering information to determine the franchise for the Montagu-Chemsford reforms. He also appeared at two major conferences of untouchables during 1920, and launched a Marathi fortnightly MOOKNAYAK (Voice of the Mute or Dumb) in January 1920. Dr. Ambedkar's testimony reveals the difference between the Ambedkar and the other Mahar leaders as well as the leaders of Untouchables in other parts of India. In this testimony before the Southborough Committee he spoke for no group, only as the college graduate among the Untouchables of Bombay province. Eleanor Zelliot in her essay on the Leadership of Baba Saheb Ambedkar says, "His testimony was lengthy, sophisticated, passionate, but never beyond the bound of a lawyer's plea. He fit his proposal into a total plan for the election procedures in the province for all the groups, asking only that "the hardships and disabilities entailed by the social system should not be reproduced and perpetuated in political institutions.' He claimed that the Depressed Classes were entitled to representation because there was no "like-mind ness" and no "endosmosis" between Untouchables and Touchables and hence Touchables could not represent Untouchables. The Depressed Classes were "slaves" "dehumanised", and so "socialised as never to complain" and they must have communal representation "in such numbers as will enable them to claim redress", and under franchise "so low as to educate into political life as many as Untouchables as possible". Terminology used by Dr. Ambedkar in this testimony, indicate formation of his vision.

Vision in the leadership may spring from its original thinking or may be derived from an outside source. Vision, however, is generally expressed as the inner voice, the insight or the intuition in a leader, which helps him in visualising. Kouzes and Posner have defined intuition as the bringing together of knowledge and experience to produce new insights. Vision may not necessarily be a pure conception of the leader, but the leader is the one who chooses the image and articulates it into a vision and focuses attention of the people on it. Where from Dr. Ambedkar's vision sprang? What were the sources of his vision?

Lord Buddha: Dr. Ambedkar choose his three gurus from three era of Indian History - Ancient, Medieval, and Modern - all historical figures, who chose to stand up and challenge the decaying societies of their times. His first Guru is Lord Buddha, who had profound influence on him. Dr. Ambedkar appreciated these beliefs. He learnt from the life of Lord that a man could become great not merely due to his royal birth, but because he was motivated by the dynamics of a social purpose and acted as the scourge and scavenger of the society. Lord Buddha led him to question the infallibility of the Vedas; the faith in the elevation of the soul; the efficacy of rites, ceremonies, and sacrifices as means of obtaining salvation; the theory that god created man or that he came out of the body of Brahma; and the doctrine of Karma, which is the determination of man's position in present life by deeds done by him in his past life. The impact of Lord Buddha's teaching can be seen in his writings. Saint Kabir: He was the second guru of Dr. Ambedkar. Again a historical figure St. Kabir was a weaver cum poet of medieval time. In fact he was the leader of the band of Untouchable poets. Saint Kabir opposed Varnashram system vehemently and challenged the superiority of Brahmans. He opposed fundamentalism of Hindus and Muslims both, and unified himself with the suffering of the downtrodden, lower castes, and untouchables. Kabir's liberalism and opposition to fundamentalism of Hindus and Muslim can be seen in Dr. Ambedkar's book on Pakistan, where he has criticised both the communities in unequivocal terms.

Jyotiba Phule: His third guru died in November 1890, merely five months before Dr. Ambedkar was born. Jotiba Phule was the Mahatma of the poor and Untouchables. Jotiba Phule educated Shudras and ati-Shudras and women and worked for their upliftment. He was the first modern Indian who questioned the hegemony of Brahmins and exposed the priest-craft through his speeches, ballads, writings and programmes. Phule's stress on education and knowledge showed a striking contrast with the upper-caste efforts to acquire technology while maintaining 'traditional' values of many cultures; he made it clear that education was a weapon to change 'eastern morals' and to bring about a kind of Cultural Revolution as well as technological one. He and his wife, Savitribai Phule founded Satya Shodhak Samaj, which launched a strong movement for the rights of the downtrodden. Dr. Ambedkar considered him the greatest Shudra of Modem India who made the lower classes of Hindus conscious of their slavery to the higher classes and who preached the gospel of that for India, social democracy was vital than independence from foreign rule. He dedicated his book, Who were the Shudras? to this greatest Shudra of Modern times. Following his third Guru Jotiba Phule, Dr. Ambedkar also considered struggle against social bondage more important than the foreign bondage.

Apart from these three personalities, John Dewey, famous American intellectual and his mentor at Colombia University in New York, Karl Marx, and Booker T. Washington, Justice Ranade also had profound influence on Dr. Ambedkar. History of Roman Empire, Irish Struggle and Slavery in United States also shaped his actions and vision.

DR. B. R. AMBEDKAR AND HIS VISION OF UPLIFTMENT OF DALITS

As mentioned above that the leaders job is to create a vision. Without vision the leadership has no meaning because the people won't know where the leader wants to go and what he/she wants to do and how he/she wants to do it. In fact it was the vision that differentiates Dr. Ambedkar from his contemporary leaders. His contemporary Dalit Leaders were though educating the Dalits, but have hardly analysed the socio-economic causes of their degrading and inferior position in the society. Dr. Ambedkar was fully equipped to go into the depth of the socio-economic problems and fix the problem. In contrast to other leaders, who were supporting the British Government for the upliftment of the Dalits, Dr. Ambedkar emphasised on the concept of self-help or Atta Deepo Bhava. He realised the lack of ideological hollowness of the Dalit Movement and provided necessary ideology to it.

Not improvement in caste status, but Annihilation of Caste: In contrast to earlier efforts of Dalit leadership claiming higher status of Khastriyas, Dr. Ambedkar never claimed high caste status for Untouchables,since such claim implied an acceptance of upper caste superiority. He did not claim that the Untouchables were pre-Aryan, the original settlers of the land. Dr. Ambedkar argued that the Untouchables' position in the Indian Society was of social, not racial origin and therefore subject to change. By 1935, Dr. Ambedkar had concluded that unless caste is totally annihilated, degrading position of Dalits in Indian society wouldn't improve. For him, caste embodied Brahmanical superiority.

Alternative to Brahamanical Social Order (BSO): For Dr. Ambedkar eradication of Caste required a repudiation of 'Hinduism' as a religion and adoption of an alternative to this religion. He considered Buddha Dhamma and alternative to Brahmanical Social Order or alternative to Hinduism. His choice of Buddhism was essentially linked to his strong dedication to the reality of India, its rich historical heritage, which he sought to wrest from the imposition of a 'Hindu' identity.

Rationalism: He stood for rationalism. His 22 commandments are reflecting his rationalism.

State Socialism: He stood for a responsible state, taking due care of the despised, downtrodden and socially and economically weaker sections.

Autonomous Dalit Movement: Dr. Ambedkar firmly believed in an Autonomous Dalit Movement with a constantly attempted alliance of the socially and economically exploited. If we analyse these corner stones, we find that he stood for an alternative form of society, economy, polity, religion and culture. His programmes were intended to integrate the Untouchables into Indian Society in modern, not traditional ways, and on as high a level as possible. This was in contrast with Gandhi's 'Ideal Bhangi' who would continue to do sanitation work even though his status would equal that of a Brahman. Dr. Ambedkar wanted depressed classes "to raise their educational standard so that they may know their own conditions, have aspirations to rise to the level of highest Hindu and be in a position to use political power as a means to an end."

Dr. Ambedkar vociferously advocated equality. He meant not equal status of Varna, but equality in social, economic and political opportunity for all. He said "Equality may be a fiction but nonetheless one must accept it as the governing principle."

AMBEDKAR'S MISSIONS

While practicing law in the Bombay High Court he ran head long in to uplift the untouchable to educate them. To achieve these goals his first organisational attempt was the Bahishkrit Hitakarini Sabha. An organisation to promote education, socio-economic uplifting and for welfare of "outcastes" or the depressed classes. By 1927 Dr. Ambedkar decided to launch active movements against untouchability. He began with public movements and marches to open up and share public drinking water resources, also he began a struggle for the right to enter Hindu temples.

He led a satyagraha in Mahad to fight for the right of the untouchable community to draw water from the main water tank of the town. He was appointed to the Bombay Presidency Committee to work with the all-European Simon Commission in 1925. This commission had sparked great protests across

India, and while its report was ignored by most Indians, Ambedkar himself wrote a separate set of recommendations for future constitutional.

AMBEDKAR: COLONIALISM AND NATIONALISM

Ambedkar's critique of colonialism ranges across a whole spectrum from the economy to the nature of the colonial discourse. In terms of the later, Ambedkar demanded that the terms of the discourse be altered. He had no defence to offer in favour of colonialism but he did not want power to go to those who would not promote partisan ends in the name of the people.

Ambedkar's considered judgment was that colonialism benefited the untouchables least, except for the rule of law which it inaugurated, allowing some space for them. He insisted on a responsible and accountable government based upon adult franchise, and was one of the first top rung leaders in India to demand universal adult franchise early on in his submission before the Simon Commission, in the strongest possible terms.

However, Ambedkar remained wary of nationalism, particularly given the experience of the Second World War. He was primarily concerned with a regime of rights, based on justice and upholding democracy. In a way, he was forced to engage with nationalism seriously when the Muslim League made the demand for a separate Pakistan in 1940.

With respect to nationalism Ambedkar placed a great deal of emphasis on the volitional factor. He felt that once large masses of people begin to believe that they are a nationality, then, their identity as a separate nation had to be faced. He blamed both the Congress and the Muslim League for precipitating this tendency.

He, however, felt that different nationalities had often remained within a single state and have negotiated terms of associated living. National self-determination is not something inevitable, but the pros and cons of whether nationalities decide to live together in a single state or wish to go their own ways, have to be assessed. He felt that under certain conditions it might be better to be separated than to live in a united state.

Ambedkar did not take an active interest in international relations except in its broader ideological implications. But, where there were some issues that he felt were significant for the future of India. He located India's place firmly in Asia and in the cultural traditions infused with Buddhism. He saw a threat to India from the Communist bloc, particularly given the age-old strategic interests.

He was deeply concerned with the occupation of Tibet by Communist China and the response of the Nehru government to this issue. His view regarding Jammu and Kashmir was that it comprised three regions: Kashmir, Jammu and Ladakh. He considered it appropriate to hand over Kashmir to Pakistan and to integrate the other two regions with India.

AMBEDKAR AND CONSTITUTIONAL DEMOCRACY

The major area of Ambedkar's work was on constitutional democracy. He was adept at interpreting different constitutions of the world, particularly those that mattered insofar as they were committed to democracy, along with their constitutional developments. This becomes obvious if we note the references that he adduces to the different constitutions, in the debates of the Constituent Assembly.

He was a key player in the constitutional developments of India from the mid-1920s and on certain issues such as Uniform Civil Code he was to anticipate some of the major issues that have been the topics of debate in India. Ambedkar evolved certain basic principles of constitutionalism for a complex polity like India but argued that ultimately their resilience would depend on constitutional ethics.

Ambedkar also dwelt on several substantive issues of law. In fact, we can understand the significance that law had in his scheme of things by recourse to his larger social and ideological understanding. He was deeply sensitive to the interface between the law on one hand, and customs and popular beliefs, on the other.

He felt that law was definitely influenced by customs and popular beliefs but stressed that customs may defend parochial interests, but may not uphold fairness, and may be based on their usefulness for the dominant classes. They may not be in tune with the demands of time or in consonance with morality and reason.

Ambedkar also admitted the possibility of customs having the upper hand over law when they begin to defend vested interests, but that with its emphasis on freedom and democracy, law could be placed in the service of the common good. On the other hand, customs, while promoting healthy pluralism, may give rise to a highly inegalitarian order. At the same time, he defers to pluralism, if it can uphold rights.

In all these qualifications, Ambedkar's contention is that the legal domain is an autonomous sphere. He also deployed a complex understanding of rights to situate the domain of law. He distinguished the realm of constitutional law from the acts of legislature, but acknowledged that popular aspirations and the democratic mandate was the common ground for both.

At the same time, it is law which determines what are popular and democratic aspirations and what constitute the relevant categories, given the existence of domain of rights. The constructionist role of the state, confronted with long-drawn and irreconcilable disputes, is so prominent in Ambedkar's writing that quite often he avoids substantive definitions and resorts to the legal fiction that "so and so is that was specified by law". He did not reconcile the tension between democracy and law and in his exposition, the domain of reason and morals are often in contention with that of law. Ideally, of course, he envisaged a democracy informed by law and a law characterized by sensitivity to democracy.

At the same time, he looked to a system of law which upheld reason and morality, though he saw reason and morality as far too feeble to ensure social bonds without the authoritative dictates expressed in law. Religion, according to him, could play a major role in lightening the task of law. Ambedkar's views on constitutional democracy were reflected in his relations with Gandhi and Nehru on the issues of untouchability and the Hindu Code Bill respectively.

DR. AMBEDKAR AS A SOCIAL REFORMER

Dr. Ambedkar believed in peaceful methods of social change. He was supported to constitutional lines in the evolutionary process of social transformation. He thought the factors like law and order which are indispensable for social life. It also strives to sustain institutions that will make better "social order?. He was opposite to the aggressive method in communal change for it obstruction the composure and create chaos. He had no faith in anarchy methods. A welfare state of all cannot be developed on the grounds of terror, force and brutal methods. According to him violent method to a peaceable culture is not only inappropriate but too irrational and immoral.

He was a true Renaissance man, a person who excelled in many different areas of inquiry. Though he was hated by conventional Hindus and labelled as a demolisher of Hinduism, historians now realize the crucial role Dr. Ambedkar played in recognizing Hindu society. Far from being a traitor, he played an important role in revitalizing Hinduism, reviving it by challenging everything that was unjust and unfair within it. In fact, he brought about a renaissance of Hinduism by provoking the Hindus to rethink some of the basic tenets of their religion.

Dr. Ambedkar had a great faith in social reformers to create public opinion for against of the gross inequalities in the society. He urged them to found organizations to deal with urgent cases of discrimination.

The organizations should deal the powerful section of society to give a chance to the oppressed and depressed classes to work in different sectors. The Hindu society should give a space to depressed sections by employing them in their various sectors suited to the capacities of applicants. According to him, social change and social justice are indeed critical to the egalitarianism that any democracy must aspire it.

As a social democrat Dr. Ambedkar worried on a much broader view of steady rebuilding of country with comprehensive expansion and cultural integration in the Nation without caste discrimination. As the major architect of the Indian constitution, Dr. Ambedkar constructed the safeguards for establishing a more equitable society to millions of oppressed and depressed classes. He was strongly believed that political institutions were responsible for reforming the existing social institutions by using legislative force to yield the results. Political institutions will survive only when they actively work for social reformation. Dr. Ambedkar was a freedom fighter of the truest kind, not merely dreaming of setting India force from British rule, but of transforming India into a country where freedom holds meaning for everyone.

While Mahatma Gandhi led fellow Indians in a struggle against discrimination in South Africa, Dr. Ambedkar led a battle, too, against prejudice within his own country. By securing equality for his community, he was creating a more equal world for us all.

DR. AMBEDKAR AS AN EDUCATIONIST

Dr. Ambedkar considered education as a powerful instrument for raising the overall status of the depressed and deprived classes. He thought, It is education that furnishes moral arsenal for any social movement, the more education the more the chances for progress. In his struggle for the liberation of the Dalits from the Hindu social slavery, Ambedkar had the right cognizance of the role that education has to play.

He desired the elevation of the depressed classes to be the responsibility of the enlightened people in the country. Thus he established a chain of schools colleges and hostels under the shield of the People's Education Society which he had founded in 1945. His emphasis, however, does not rest merely on academic education.

He had realised the importance of mass education. Accordingly he conceived education as a means to make the Dalits aware of their social realities and to develop in them courage and commitment to fight casteism. He published four periodicals namely 'Mooknayak' (1920), 'Bahishkrit Bharat' (1927), 'Samatha' (1929) and 'Janata' (1930). He exhorted his followers that 'it is disgraceful to live at the cost of one's self respect and it is out of hard and 4 ceaseless struggle alone one derives strength, confidence and recognition.

His career as teacher, principal and member of legislative enabled him to get insight into the academic and administrative problems of higher education, it also provided him rich experience and knowledge of the complexities of educational concerns. He urged the teachers and the educated parents to meet the requirements and challenges of the modern world and called on them to work for inculcation of rational thinking and scientific temper among the masses in general and the young generation in particular.

To him, education is the only right weapon to cut down social slavery. It will enlighten the dalits to achieve elevated social status, economic betterment and human and political rights. It would enhance adjournment of the age old values and would inculcate the values required for a pluralist society. It is out of this conviction that he made 'educate' the first word of his slogan "Educate, Agitate, Organise".

VISIONS AND ICONS OF GREAT PERSON

Every great person has a vision that impels all her/his works. Its discernibility may vary from case to case, generally being the function of the degree of turbulence around her/him, her/his relative position within the power structure in the given environment, her/his own equipment and conception of self-role. Marx, for instance, offers an articulate vision in clearest terms as he assumed the primary role of a philosopher to bring about revolutionary change, whereas Ambedkar had donned the mantle of mass-leadership in his primary role to spearhead the change; the degree of turbulence in the work domain of Marx had been minimal as he basically struggled in the realm of thought spanning complete human history whereas Ambedkar situated himself in the political turbulence that obtained in India as his strategy; Ambedkar's position in the power structure that bounded his work domain was certainly weak relative to Marx's.

This is neither to undermine the role of Marx as the activist constantly trying out his philosophy in the realm of practice nor to belittle the problems he suffered in life. With regard to personal equipment, both Ambedkar as well as Marx, could be taken to be equally equipped to undertake their respective tasks that they had undertaken. Marx had started off with philosophy and adopted the class-consciousness of the proletariat quite unlike Ambedkar, in whose case it was his own consciousness - the consciousness of an untouchable built up through concrete experience that had propelled his philosophical search.

Marx was well aware of his role in the revolutionary project, that he had to provide requisite tools and tackles for the working class for bringing about a change in the overall interest of humanity. But, Ambedkar was always loaded with anxiety as he had to strategize his way through the political maze around him, winning for dalits the maximum he could in a short span of time.

In process, his role also underwent transformation with the expanse of the battleground. Inevitably, his thoughts and action always remained context-laden, polemical and pragmatically purposeful. It is therefore a relatively difficult task to discern a coherent vision underscoring the life work of Babsaheb Ambedkar.

It is a moot point as to what extent a great person, who is essentially anchored in her/his space and time, could transcend these barriers and be equally effective in a different situation. A great person basically is the product of prevailing social relations. It is a particular moment in history that reflects an acute demand for such a person.

Depending upon her/his location in the social setting, s/he imparts her/his individual feature to the historical moments and movements in terms of working out specific means for resolving contradictions that engender them and releasing the forces of history in a specific direction. The masses whose cause she / he espouses throng around her/him in this process, depending upon the level of their collective consciousness. The longevity of the ideas a great person propounds in a historical setting depends upon the nature of contradictions, the size and expanse of problems and the time domain in which they are situated. Generally, the classes that share the vision and ideology of such persons tend to iconise them with specific attributes of their class choice, in an attempt to institutionalise the latter. In this process, they would de-contextise some of the ideas and proffer them as universal theorems, if they perceive a pay-off for themselves in the sphere hegemonised by them. This phenomenon becomes clear only over a long time horizon. For instance, the religious principles that were sprouted in the soil of certain specific social relations have basically blossomed in an alien soil with the help of the nutrients of class interests. Very broadly speaking, the trend of iconisation of great persons and the attempt of institutionalising their ideas is a gauge to assess the forces of status quo in the society.

AMBEDKAR: COMMITMENT AND CONSTRAINT

In the case of Babasaheb Ambedkar, iconisation was inevitable. The combination of factors like his high stature, his devotion to the cause of his people; the historical setting in which he lived, the low level of literacy and political consciousness in masses; and the vested interests of internal as well as external people have been its cause. The problem is not with iconisation as it is with its multiplicity. A question may be pertinently asked can Ambedkar be uniquely represented by a single icon? As Prof. Upendra Bakshi had outlined in one of his articles during the centenary year of his birth anniversary that there were many Ambedkars and had questioned as to which Ambedkar do we commemorate? When he said so, Prof. Bakshi was referring to different facets of Ambedkar's personality that could be virtually segregated. One can even periodise some of them. For example, the pre-1942 Ambedkar as a young, untouchable man endowed with highest scholastic distinctions, struggling within and without for the emancipation of his people is a grossly different personality than the Ambedkar as a member of the viceroy's Executive Council or the Ambedkar as the law minister in the Nehru cabinet in the post-independence India or the Ambedkar as the chairman of the drafting committee for the Indian Constitution or even the Ambedkar of still later years who had completely identified himself with Buddhism and in a way completely spiritualised himself.

What comes clearly however, from this review is that the changes in his outlook and role were essentially driven by his unstilted commitment to the cause of emancipation of oppressed humanity in general and dalits in particular. He might not have had appropriate methodological tools to deal with the problem at hand. With the equipment that basically belonged to a school of social engineers, he tried to dissect history. Paradoxically, he attempted to demolish the establishment with the very tools that were forged to serve the ruling classes. By training he did not have the facility to look at history as the continuum of human struggle with a certain inherent logic. He did use history as a repertoire of human episodes and attributed even logic to it but its source was externalised.

Non-Dialectical Solution: State and Religion

It appears that Babasaheb Ambedkar had really internalised the doctrine of momentariness (*Anityatawad* and later *Kshanikwad*) of Buddha and therefore even refused to care for consistency in his views and opinions. This doctrine states that every thing changes every moment, that things are constantly becoming.

It follows that in this situation of flux not even mental processes could be static, they had essentially to match the dynamicity of the material world. He thus never hesitated in changing his thoughts or strategy as per the unfolding situation. Viewed another way, these changes can be understood in relation to foci of control. The degree of consistency in thought and action is generally inversely proportional to the distance of the subject from the foci of control of its surrounding.

Ambedkar had nil or little control over his situation. He had to consistently create space for himself and strategize to influence the situation to his advantage. (The dynamics of the situation was propelled by the forces that were variously placed in the adversary camps.) The framework within which he conceived his struggle had exposed him to his lot to respond to this dynamics. The hallmark of Ambedkar's thoughts is the dynamic rationale, which he has consistently employed to comprehend situations and to strategize his response thereto. 'Ambedkar' therefore cannot be captured in static terms. His icon will have to represent the dynamism that he lived. Since, this is an infeasible proposition; we will have to discern the underscoring vision behind his works, the intransient essence of his entire mission to create a suitable icon. This icon, even if it does not resemble the familiar Ambedkar, alone could be the beacon of the dalit movement.

The concept of *Anityawad* in Buddhism essentially belongs to dialectics that has made Buddha an early dialectician philosopher. The dichotomy that creeps in can only be resolved by dialectical method. It may be questioned whether Ambedkar's method was dialectical. It appears that while he accepts constant becoming of things as the principle underscoring the universe, he faces a dilemma with respect to the conception of order in this State. It could be resolved dialectically in terms of systemic attribute of self-regulation - a characteristic of internal control. But the conventional conception of order, essentially a non-dialectical conception, leads to externalisation of control. Ambedkar, having experienced the brutal aspects of history and unbridled exploitation of man by man, appears in need of a control mechanism operating at two levels, viz., internal and external, so as to maintain the societal order in the desired State.

His internal control mechanism is the moral code provided by the religion and the one for external control is the State. If this moral code is internalised by all individuals and in turn by society as the summation of the latter (as the liberal tradition held), society is expected to have an internal order. If however the baser instincts of some people or group of people defy this order, either as a result of conflicting codes they follow or for any other reason, then in such case the State will step in and restore the order. The will of the collective is supposed to be embodied in the State by the Constitution.

It is therefore that Ambedkar has reservation in agreeing with Marx that 'religion was the opium of masses' or the 'State shall eventually wither away'. Ambedkar certainly did not know that the order could be the attribute of the system itself. It is only in the sixties that Cybernetics principles came to lime light that the complex probabilistic systems, which the social systems certainly are, do have the inherent capability of self-regulating and self-organising control.

Liberalism and Reformism

By upbringing and training Ambedkar was influenced by western liberalism. The openness and liberal values of the western society had struck him with pleasant surprise by his own admission. There is a reason to believe that he had studied Marxism. His first essay on caste reflects some amount of analytical orientation of Marxism. One of the subjects in his curriculum also happened to be related to Marxian socialism and his guide Prof. Seligman was well versed with the economic interpretation of history. However, as his later work reveals, Ambedkar reflected more closeness with the liberal tradition than Marxism.

However, consciously he never identified himself with the Liberalism. Being aware of its pitfalls, he needed to declare that he was not a liberal reformist, although while having reservations with the postulations of Marxism he could never hide his attraction towards it.

The pitfall of his thinking emanates from his conception of the moral force of religion divorced from the material reality. He therefore hopes that without any bloodshed, the society based on liberty, equality and fraternity could be created. Of course as hypothesized above, he conceptualizes the constitutional State based on these principles. With this wishful thinking, he tends to ignore the fact that regardless of the pretensions of ruling classes, the impact of liberal governance in the multi-centric iniquitous society is bound to result in sustaining multi-centricity and inequality.

This liberalism rather promotes politics of casteism and communalism, schism among dalits, their use in political power games, subversion of their real problems and protects the interests of the few rich. It was a kind of contradiction in terms to assume that liberal democracy, which is actually the manifestation of the political power of the bourgeois, will do justice to the paupers. It might appear to extend certain concessions to the weaker sections, but its real motive is to maintain the existing rule of the ruling classes. Liberal democracy might appear better than the decadent Hindu caste system but it is incapable of bringing any real change in favor of dalits. It muffles the tension of the exploitative system and kills the revolutionary motivation of its victims.

Redefinition Project

Many of the constructs employed by Babasaheb Ambedkar in his working have a qualified meaning. Firstly, they are not absolute as they appear. They are the derivatives of his thought process, the source of which could be traced to his basic objective of annihilation of castes and creating a society based on equality, liberty and fraternity. Even these three principles that he held so dear to his heart, bear very different meaning from the familiar ones associated with the French Revolution. He said he had them from Buddha. What Buddha said also is to be understood from his interpretation, which could be as different from the accepted version as to be disproved by the Buddhist church.

His Buddha and His Dhamma, for instance, had faced this kind of disapproval initially from many Buddhists. Understanding Ambedkar thus essentially demands extra consideration and care about the specific meanings of the constructs and concepts he uses. The lack of it has already caused much misunderstanding among many people. It is one thing to have a clear understanding of what he said or meant but quite another to extrapolate it to something congruent to his basic objective or vision that may be useable in shaping the future movement. Quite like Marx had said of philosophy, it could be said that the issue is not to understand Ambedkar as he is but to possibly think of him as a weapon in the struggle to which he devoted his life. The redefinition referred to here will have to essentially address both these issues. From the viewpoint of one seeking a revolutionary change, there are indeed many dimensions on which Ambedkar calls for critical interpretation. Many of the concepts that seem to act as the props for his formulations are rooted in the reactionary camp. Paradoxically, he brings them to work for his emancipatory project, which potentially is no less than a revolution. Predominant among these concepts are identified as State, religion, liberal democracy, constitutionalism, revolution, socialism, violence and Marxism, that some way or the other have been the cause of misunderstandings about him.

It is important to appreciate that Ambedkar employed the search process that is essentially rational and the underlying objective undoubtedly radical. There could be flaws in the specific design or the application of the search process, depending upon the State of his knowledge and complexity of the situation to which it is applied. Besides this, the end result depends upon the repertoire of alternatives used for the search. What it means is that the specific method, thought or action of Ambedkar may constitute the historical facts but they cannot be taken in their face value if one wants to comprehend the ideological aspects of Ambedkar. In his usage of the above concepts for instance he does not always exercise the academic rigour. Besides the reason that much of his usage was addressed to the un-academic lot, most of the times he tended to impart his own meanings to the terms he used. With the changed contexts or with the change in information, he readily changed his opinions. For, hypothetically speaking, if Ambedkar had lived longer he would have certainly changed his views, looking at more information available or experiencing the undesired aftermath of some of his own beliefs and opinions. Had he not disowned the Constitution, which he had so laboriously written and so forcefully defended, saying that he was used as the hack to write it? Whatever he had done had several limitations. He never hesitated to change his opinion or stand if he was convinced that it was right. The redefinition project proposed here, in a way, is something, which he has done himself, all his life and would have continued doing if he had been alive. It is essentially something in the nature of continuing his unfinished task.

The methodological aspects of this exercise consists in the process of conceptualisation of the core vision and ideological proclivities of Ambedkar through the analytical study of his life within its contextual parameters, oriented towards capturing its intransient content. It should reflect the basic purpose, that is, to see whether and how he could catalyse the emancipatory movement of dalits and in turn democratise the Indian society.

This process may not be free from bias. The bias could be in favour of the change craved for by the have-nots, not of the ruling classes that has necessarily been colouring the history so far. It cannot escape the viewpoint of the latter.

The viewpoint is rather embodied in the basic intention to forge Ambedkar as the weapon for the future struggles of dalits. The process of conceptualisation may be formalised by drawing out multiple ideological patterns based upon the constituent parameters of the hypothesised vision and testing them with the facts in their macro and micro settings.

The test results could be used to refine the definition of the parameters and repeating the exercise until they can no more be improved. The iterative process will eliminate the tactic-based episodes and increasingly highlight the intransient dimensions. The radicalisation consists in derivation of the programme from these dimensions with any scientific methodology.

It is not possible to demonstrate adoption of this methodology within the space of this paper. The following discussion therefore directly deals with the salient dimensions of Ambedkar's life in order to capture its intransient essence.

AMBEDKAR AND FUTURE OF INDIAN SOCIETY

Ambedkar's writings, exhortations, untiring efforts and his inputs in the Indian constitution have undoubtedly had tremendous effect in raising the self-pride, aspirations, status and desire to unshackle themselves from the age-old bondages of the depressed classes.

They have also helped in material advancement of some of them, who are proving to be role models for others to follow. Reservations for Scheduled Caste/ Schedule Tribes in recruitment and promotions in government services have ensured their easy entry into the bureaucracy.

Many literary, social and political groups have been formed among Dalits to further the cause espoused by Ambedkar and to capture political power. Special provisions for S. Cs./S. Ts. in education have vastly helped in increasing their enrolment at primary level as well as in providing higher education to them.

Among various government services S.C./S.T. groups and unions have also come up which are very active in furthering the interests of schedule caste/schedule tribe employees: Bamsafe and DS-4 are noteworthy among them. Propelled by the government officials covertly and overtly, the conversion of S. Cs. to Buddhism is gaining momentum day by day. Lately, Ambedkar's ideas are reported to be influencing some disadvantaged groups in western countries also. For example, the Romas Of Hungary, who are stereotyped as thieves and criminals by other Europeans, are reportedly organizing themselves under the influence of Ambedkarites.

Therefore, it can be confidently concluded today that Dr. Ambedkar has succeeded greatly in his mission 'to uplift his community.' However, a fair critique of the effect of Dr. Ambedkar's labors on the future of the nation as a whole requires consideration of many other factors and circumstances.

Dr. B. R. Ambedkar had proclaimed, 'Attempts to uplift my community rather than win Swaraj for the nation is my goal.' There is no doubt that the then Hindu society provided enough grounds for an angry Dalit to prefer liberation from the shackles of caste over attainment of Swaraj for the nation, yet one cannot overlook the truth that without Swaraj the condition of neither the Dalits nor others would have improved substantially. Even if British conceded to pass laws granting social equality and reservation in legislature and government services to Dalits, the country would not have progressed enough economically to bring any substantial change in the education, occupation and status of Dalits.

Moreover the bondage of foreign yoke would have kept them- along with others- servile and lacking in self-pride. The truth is that Swaraj for which the nation's heroes fought and democracy which Gandhi and Nehru cherished have been almost exclusively responsible for bringing the sea change in the life, thinking and status of Dalits. Any effort, howsoever mighty, would not have produced even a fraction of that result.

Dr. Ambedkar wanted implementation of communal award and separate electorate for Dalits as he had his reasons for not trusting upper caste voters to send such representatives to the legislature as would speak for the welfare of Dalits.

Although, in order to save fasting Mahatma's life, he had relented on this issue, but later he criticized Mahatma's 'dubious' ways of pressurizing him. His followers term Mahatma's tactics as 'Kshadyantra against the Dalits'.

However, today the efficacy- or the absence thereof- of separate electorate can be seen in Pakistan, where Hindus have a separate electorate. The truth is that Hindus there have little or no voice in governance, which has resulted in their systematic dwindling in number as well as social status. A separate electorate necessarily generates a feeling of being a separate nation; and Mahatma Gandhi rightly apprehended such a consequence, if separate electorates on caste/communal lines were granted.

Dr. Ambedkar was all for annihilation of castes, which is certainly necessary to bring social equality and unity. Yet, he made provisions in the Constitution for reservations in legislature and government services on the basis of caste alone.

How can caste be abolished so long as this remains the sole basis for grabbing power and jobs? The truth is that such caste-based reservations have divided the entire society and the bureaucracy in competing caste groups, which care more for their castes than for public good.

Further, more and more castes are competing fiercely for inclusion in the most beneficial reservation-list irrespective of any ground reality with respect to their eligibility for the same. Fight between Minas and Gujars in Rajasthan, inclusion of Jats among O. B. Cs. in U. P. and recommendation of previous U. P. Government to include many more castes in the Scheduled Caste List are some of the glaring examples.

Unfortunately, these caste divisions have sprung some of the most corrupt self-seeking politicians and bureaucrats to prominence. Thus, it is obvious that Dr. Ambedkar's labors have resulted in just the opposite of what he cherished, i. e., annihilation of castes and bringing social unity.

Dr. Ambedkar had rightly apprehended,

'This urge for self- realization in the down-trodden classes must not be allowed to develop into a class struggle or class war. It would lead to a division of the House. That would indeed be a day of disaster. For, as has been well said by Abraham Lincoln, a house divided against itself cannot stand very long.'

And in order to fulfill that urge of self-realization and to bring liberty, equality and fraternity among the depressed classes, he exhorted them to convert to Buddhism. He himself also changed his religion to became a Boddh.

However, any serious reader of history of nations and any observer of present day communal conditions in various nations would readily agree that mass conversion of nearly one fourth S. Cs./ S. Ts. to Buddhism would sooner or later make a recipe for this nation to become a house divided, which is ultimately a recipe for disaster according to Dr. Ambedkar himself. After all is said and done, there is no doubt that the most powerful element in a nation's unity has been religion. When conversion of S.Cs./S.Ts. to Buddhism is completed, the composition of Indian society will be about 25% Buddhists, about 20 % Muslims, about 10% others and about 45 % Hindus.

Which nation in the world with such a religious composition has existed peacefully? Iraq, Ireland, Sri Lanka, many African nations, erstwhile Spain, etc. are glaring examples of unrest caused by religious disunity in their population. India itself got divided in 1947 only because Muslims had become a very substantial minority here. So, given the momentum with which conversions are taking place, we shall not only be a house divided but may also become a country divided within this century.

The genius and genuineness of Dr. B. R. Ambedkar is beyond question and beyond compare and so are his success in his mission to uplift the Dalits; the consequences of his more noteworthy actions, although unintended, will most likely prove to be divisive and disastrous for this nation in the long run.

Conclusion

Dr. B.R.Ambedkar was a multifaceted personality. His public service started during the second decade of twentieth century. He belonged to the category of politician putting their service to humanity before themselves. Dr. Ambedkar's was a short life and yet a most extraordinary one.

He rose up from dust, from being treated worse than an animal to becoming the father of the Indian Constitution. A genuine emancipator of Dalits, a great National leader and patriot, a great author, a great educationalist, a great political philosopher, a great religious guide and above all a great humanist without any parallel among his contemporary.

All these facets of Ambedkar's personality had strong humanist underpinnings. Dr B.R.Ambedkar was in fact a designer of a nation and a universal leader instead of just a

Dalit leader or leader of the backward classes. It's just because efforts of Dr. B.R. Ambedkar we are pleased with the principles of social justice.

Babasaheb is the individual, who with his efforts had build India in her early years. They fought for the independence of India and then strived to build India of their dreams. It is only regrettable that the press in the past as well as the contemporary has projected Ambedkar mainly as a great social rebel and a bitter critic of the Hindu religion. Critics of Dr. Ambedkar have ignored his basic humanistic instincts and strong humanitarian convictions behind his every act or speech throughout his life. Thus we conclude Dr. Ambedkar was one of the foremost makers of Modern India.

4

Man of the Hour

BRA now decided to practice law that would provide him with opportunities, means & leisure to devote himself to the aim of his life, the uplift of the Untouchables. With the help of Naval Bathena he started his life as a Barrister in June 1923. The thorns of untouchability, the color of his skin, the inexperienced legal mind & unhelpful surroundings in courts turned his path into an uphill task. But BRA knew that excellence in pursuit is achieved by laborious application.

BRA joined the Appellate side of the Bombay Bar as success in practice on the Original side depended more upon one's influence with the solicitors than upon one's ability. The Solicitors would not have anything to do with him on account of his untouchability and thus he had to be happy with whatever work came his way. Whats new, all famous legal luminaries had to start their early career cooling their heels.

By now outer influences and inner forces had brought about a visible change in the mental & moral outlook of the DC. The spread of education, development of communications, mode of traveling & spirit of nationalism had gradually begun to act as an effective correctness to the prejudicial ideas of untouchability. The rise of the textile industry during World War I helped the DC too since they had to work with other classes & stimulated them to better their own condition. On the top of it was the impetus to democratic ideals generated by the inevitable forces of World War I that gave an impetus to social reformation the world over.

About this time D Gholap, the first nominated member of the DC in the Bombay Legislative Council, moved a resolution in order to make primary education compulsory in order to bring it within the reach of the DC. But the most important resolution was one moved by S K Bole which the Bombay Legislative Council adopted on 4/8/1923. Moving the resolution he said that untouchability was a stigma on the good name of India: 'It is in the interests of the country that the DC should be given better treatment. The Council recommends that that the Untouchable Classes be allowed to use all public watering places, wells & dharamshalas which are built & maintained out of public funds'. Bole's work was widely appreciated by the DC of Bombay.

Another notable proclamation was made concerning the DC at the end of 1923. Stimulated by Gandhi's support to the Indian Muslims on the issue of Khilafat, presiding at a meeting called to present an address to Gandhi at Madras, Yakub Hussein once openly enjoined upon the Muslims the duty of converting all the Untouchables of India to Islam.

1924, Savarkar, Gandhi, BRA – this was one of most eventful years in Indian history. After undergoing a hellish life for 12 years in Andaman Savarkar was released & interned in Ratnagiri. Gandhi too was released on health grounds after suffering for nearly two years consequent to the debacle of his Khilafat-Swaraj Movement. Savarkar worked for the consolidation of Hindu society & for the upliftment of the DC. Gandhi too did the same. BRA prepared himself for the same. He convened a meeting in March 1924 to consider establishing a central institution for removing difficulties of the untouchables & placing their grievances before the Government. So in July was formed 'Bahishkrit Hitakarini Sabha, activities confined to Bombay. Its aim was to promote the spread of education – culture among DC, advance &

improve their economic condition, to represent their grievances. Why was BRA chartering a different path? BRA was looking at social reforms in the sense of the reorganization & reconstruction of Hindu society on the basis of equality and not at issues like widow remarriage, education of women etc. Despite the good work by the Prarthana / Brahmo Samaj / princes none could stir in the heart of these suppressed people an emotion of confidence, hope & aspiration for their own salvation. Self-help is the best help. The conservative feeling in the country at this juncture was unmoved as a rock. Only the conscience of the more political minded Hindus was tweaked when they were reminded by the rival Muslim politicians that more than one-third of the Hindu population was not accepted by the Hindus as part & parcel of the community. That is why the Hindu Mahasabha & the Arya Samajists could not succeed much in their work of consolidation of Hindu society.

To be fair to the Hindu Mahasabha it must be said that they undertook a mission, which the conservative minds looked upon disfavor. Now when they were fighting foreign rule by raising the issue of social reform they ran the risk of alienating the conservative Hindu whose support they needed. But more than that the reason for their failure was that some of their first rate leaders were orthodox at heart, resolutions / intent were good but execution bad. Their apathy & indifference was so much that even Swami Shraddhananda had to resign from their camp. No wonder the Mahasabha was described by the World Press as reactionary instead of having great leaders like Shraddhananda & Savarkar. Congress leaders were concerned only with Muslim sentiments, did not care about the disabilities of the DC or note their conversion to Islam & Christianity. They did follow Gandhi's movement for uplift of the Untouchables.

Gandhi believed in the caste system & the four varnas. He wanted to raise the DC to the status of the fifth class, improve their lot but cared not to hurt the sentiments of his orthodox capitalist admirers who were the prop of his movement. His was more propaganda than effective change while Savarkar / BRA were social revolutionaries. Savarkar stand was nationalistic, realistic & revolutionary in outlook & action in as much at molding different castes into a casteless society in which all Hindus would be socially, economically & political equal. But as he was interned in Ratnagiri district the impact could not be seen outside that district.

BRA was one amongst the DC. He knew what it meant to be born & live the life of an untouchable. He gave vent to their passions, mind & stifled self. A man of great knowledge & boundless energy he was a man who regarded the woes & miseries of those classes as a personal humiliation, and thus had taken a vow to make self-respecting citizens out of those virtual slaves. He urged the Untouchables to fight for self-elevation. He cried out excerpts 'You have been groaning from time immemorial & yet you are not ashamed to hug your helplessness as an inevitability'. The spate of his burning speeches began to have a telling effect upon their minds & to rouse them against their slavery.

BRA did not join the movement for the political independence of India. Those who were deprived of their political rights by foreign rulers were busy fighting them since they would rule India once the foreigners left. BRA's aim was liberation of the DC for which he knew he would have to fight with caste Hindus & to deal with the British govt in respect of political rights. He however realized that hatred of British rule would be inviting double enmity of his people. So he thought it prudent to cooperate with the British so far as that cooperation would be able to secure rights for the DC.

With the birth of the Bahishkrit Hitkarini Sabha dawned a new age of self-respect. It started in 1925 a hostel at Sholpaur, a monthly magazine named Saraswati Vilas. The DC were now being attracted to BRA's personality. He provided over the first conference of Untouchables at Malwan in Ratnagiri district in April 1925. But the most o/s event of the year was the satyagraha sponsored by Ramaswami Naicker, a non-Brahmin leader at Vaikam in the Travancore State for vindicating the rights of Untouchables to use a certain road to which they were forbidden entry. Another important incident took place when an untouchable by name Murgesan entered a Hindu temple in Madras despite a ban on Untouchables.

BRA was watching these events closely, his message of self-elevation was gathering force in its appeals. He was also gaining foothold as a lawyer. The spasms of social resolution were stirring the society. Inspite of the Bole resolution a number of Local Boards & Municipalities had not granted DC their civic rights. Bole moved another resolution on 5/8/1926 recommending to the govt not to give grant to those Municipalities etc which refused to give effect to the resolution passed by the Council three years ago.

BRA continued to live in these B.I.T Chawls; three storied buildings each containing about 80 one-room tenements, common baths. Men of authority came to see him at home. At times he was without his full dress when people came to see him without appointments. Although he was best qualified to fill the position of the Principal of Sydenham College he was not appointed inspite of the best efforts of Dr R P Paranjpye, then the Member for Education. He accepted a part time post of a lecturer in the Batliboy's Accounting Training institute where he taught Mercantile Law.

It was during this time that his wife gave birth to a son Rajratna. Before that his wife gave birth to a daughter who passed away in infancy. However BRA lost Rajratna in July 1926. He was very grieved & depressed because of the death. He had acquired strength of mind, knowledge of all most all the scriptures. Like a yogin he was now spending his days in penance & austerities, immersed in silent contemplation. Men of DC came to him for help, legal advice, he fought their cases free, treated them with care & love. BRA was an expert at cooking.

The most important attribute of a great leader, next to spotless sincerity, is the possession of an ever flowing heard towards his men who are ready to do or die at his command.

BEFORE THE BAR OF WORLD OPINION

Temple Entry Nasik - 1930 was a year of action & reaction. It was in this year that Gandhi inaugurated his great movement for the liberation of the country on 12/3/1930 & transformed the whole country into a theatre of passive resistance. Ten days before the Dandi March of Gandhi, BRA launched his temple entry movement at Nasik ie at the Kalaram Temple. A clarion call was issued to the DC to come to Nasik & assert their right of worshipping Shree Rama in the said temple. In response 15,000 volunteers came. On 2/3/1930 a conference was held there under the presidentship of BRA to consider the situation & adopt ways/means for launching the satyagraha. At 3 in the afternoon, the congregation divided itself into batches of four extending itself over a mile long procession, the biggest in the history of Nasik. As soon as the procession came to the eastern gate of the temple, the D Magistrate/other officials greeted them. Since all the temple gates were closed they proceeded to the Godavari Ghat.

It was decided to launch a non-violent struggle before the gates of the temple. The satyagraha continued for about a month. April 9 dawned, the day the chariot procession of the image of Rama. A compromise was patched up whereby the chariot would be drawn by the touchables & untouchables. On d day before BRA & his choicest gymnasts stood near the gate. But before they could touch the chariot, they were engaged in broils by the riotous elements of the caste Hindus, who ran away with the chariot. A daring Bhandari youth broke through the police cordon and in moment's crowds of untouchables pursued the chariot amidst showers of stones. BRA though protected received minor injuries, there was fierce fighting between groups of Untouchables & caste Hindus all over the city. This satyagraha provoked considerable ill feeling towards the DC, their children were thrown out of schools, maltreated etc. But so great was the resolve of the DC that the caste Hindus had to keep the famous temple closed for a whole year and agitation continued right up to the end of October 1935.

Attitude Brit govt - DC Nagpur Conference

At long last the Simon Commission came out with its report in May 1930. It deliberately ignored the Indian view, recommended a continuation of separate electorates for want of agreement between Indian political parties. It allocated 150 seats to the Hindus including the DC out of a total of 250, proposed DC joint electorates with reservation of seats but no DC candidate was allowed to stand for election unless his fitness was certified by the Governor of the Province opposed subsequently by BRA.

The first session of the DC Congress held at Nagpur on 8/8/1930 under the presidentship of BRA. He declared that it was possible for the people of India to become one united self-governing community. If Yugoslavia, Russia with all their differences in race, creed could function as self-governing communities why not India. But he affirmed that the diversity of conditions & peoples prevalent in India must be taken into account while framing the constitution for a self-governing India. BRA demanded adequate safeguards for the downtrodden untouchables in the Constitution & pleaded for direct representation in the Councils commensurate with the strength of the DC. He said 'the ideal of Dominion Status seems to be superior, for it has in it the substance of independence without the attendant risks involved in complete independence'. He was opposed to Gandhi's Civil Disobedience Movement because it was extremely inopportune.

Attitude towards British govt. Like Ranade, he regarded the advent of the British as providential, and responsible for the intellectual awakening & the concept of liberty, equality & fraternity. Yet he described the British govt as the costliest govt in the world and he asked his people whether there was parallel to the poverty of the Indian people in any part of the world. 'In the first quarter of the 19th century when the British ruled India, there were five famines with an estimated loss of 10 lakh lives. During the second quarter there were six famines with a recorded loss of 50 lakh lives. And during the last quarter what do you find? 18 famines with an estimated mortality which reached an awful total between 150 to 260 lakhs'. The Brits were the cause of this chronic poverty.

He told his people 'It is only in a Swaraj Constitution that you stand any chance of getting political power in your hands without which you cannot bring any salvation to our people'. BRA said that the Congress did not prescribe the removal of untouchability as a franchise for its membership nor did Gandhi set out on a crusade against untouchability. The safety of the DC lay in being independent of the Govt & the Congress. Although BRA insisted upon the necessity of securing political power he said their salvation lies in their social education.

This declaration of Political Independence was a definite departure from the old policy, a landmark in the history of the movement carried on by the Untouchables. Another memorable statement by BRA at this Congress was that he told his audience that he would not abjure Hindu religion whatever might be the hardships afflicted upon him by the caste Hindus. Seeing his criticism of the Govt some of the papers appreciated his change in attitude like the Kesari.

DEPARTURE FOR 1ST ROUND TABLE CONFERENCE (RTC)

As declared the British convened the first RTC consisting of reps of India, British govt & political parties to frame the constitution for India. It consisted of 89 members, 53 representing various interests except the non-cooperating Congress and 20 of the Indian states. BRA's invitation was epoch-making in the history of the Untouchables for it was at this conference that they were being vested along with other Indians with the right to be consulted in framing the constitution of India. Felicitated by his people he said on eve of departure, 'I will demand what is right for my people, and I will certainly uphold the demand for Swaraj'. He also promised that he would meet the leaders of Germany, Russia, America and acquaint them with the problems of the suppressed Indians. Congress hated, abused & cursed those leaders who cooperated with the British.

Indeed the times were unfavorable to any leader who was opposed to the ways of the INC. The left wing of the Congress was impatient of the Liberal leaders who believed in maturity/ patience. Patriotism was for some to be the exclusive domain of the Congress organization. BRA was criticized by Bose. It was typical of Congress leaders that they acted upon the principle of non-violence where the British & Muslims were concerned and behaved with hatred & violence where other parties were concerned.

On reaching BRA found the political climate sympathetic to the cause of DC, began to contact Britain's important political bosses in connection with the problems of the DC. Yet he was keen to know about the Court judgment on the Chowdar Tank case, Mahad.

4. The RTC evinced interest because never before had British & Indian statesmen, rulers of Indian states met to discuss the future system of the govt of India. Said Sir Tej Bahadur Sapru, 'India wants & is determined to achieve a status of equality – equality with all members of the British Commonwealth – an equality that will give it a govt that is responsible to popular voice'. The Maharaja of Bikaner declared that the Princes were prepared to federate of their own free will with self-governing Federal British India. This was a surprise to all but endorsed by the Nawab of Bhopal & Maharaja of Patiala. Muslim members welcomed an All India Federation but with great vigor pressed for a status of N.W.F.P. equal to other provincial units & creation of a separate Sind province.

At the outset BRA declared that he was placing the viewpoint of 20% of the total population of British India. He then asked for a govt elected of – for – by the people. He said that inspite of 150 years of British rule the condition of the DC had not improved as compared to pre-British days for e.g. 'Before the British we could not draw water from the well, has the British secured us the right to the well. Before the British we were denied entry into the Police Force, does the govt admit us into the force now? Of what good is such a govt to anybody? It was a govt, which did realize that the capitalists were denying the workers a living wage & landlords were squeezing the masses dry, and yet it did not remove social evils that blighted the lives of the downtrodden classes for years'.

BRA upheld the demand for Dominion Status but expressed doubts whether the DC would be heir to it unless the political machinery for the new constitution was of a special make. The fearless tone & bold criticism in the speech had a wonderful effect upon the Conference. One man was esp. proud, Maharaja of Baroda, who had sponsored his education earlier, invited him to a special dinner in London. BRA won praise from all.

Muslim issue – liberal leaders like Sapru, Setalvad tried to reach an agreement with the Muslim delegates on the communal question. But talks broke down over the Muslim demand for the separation of Sind and their refusal to grant the same proportion of reserved seats to the Hindus & Sikhs in the Muslim majority provinces as they asked for themselves in other provinces.

After the general discussion the Conference appointed nine sub-committees, BRA found himself on most of these committees. BRA pleaded before the Defence committee that recruitment to the Army should be open to all Indians consistently. The most important work BRA did to achieve his goal was the preparation of the Declaration of Fundamental Rights safeguarding the cultural, religious and economic rights of the DC. He prepared it with great labor & submitted it to the Minorities Sub-Committee for being included in the future constitution of India. BRA dispatched copies of this declaration to his followers in India and asked them to hold meetings in support of the demand presented to the Minorities Sub-Committee.

One point not sufficiently known about the deliberations of the RTC was the compromise arrived at between Dr Moonje & BRA in regard to the rights of the DC. It was announced by them jointly that there was no cause for the DC's to quarrel with caste Hindus. Muslims were not favoring the untouchables for they feared that caste Hindus & the untouchables would any day become a united force & oppose their demands jointly.

5. Results RTC - Such was the devotion of BRA to the cause of the DC problem that he availed every opportunity to meet/ communicate with Members of the British parliament/foreign journals. The result was that the world came to know for the first time that the fate of the Untouchables in India was worse than that of the Negroes in America. BRA's profound study, great industry & conquering intellect created a tremendous impression upon the delegates & British statesmen. He inspired awe & hatred.

During his visit he snatched some time to enter some second hand stalls to purchase rare books. Three boxes of books were sent to India thru V M Pawar. It was in London that BRA received the news of the victory of his people over the orthodox in the Mahad Tank case at the Mahad's sub-judge's Court and that of his nomination to the Bombay Legislative Council. Another thing that pleased him then was that as directed by him, his trusted lieutenants, Deorao Naik & Kadrekar started a new fortnightly paper called Janata.

After recording the reports of the various Sub-Committees, the RTC adjourned on 9/1/1931. It was followed by a debate on India in the House of Commons where one Issac Foot spoke about establishing safeguards for the DC's. This was a tribute to BRA's ceaseless work in London.

The most notable contribution of this session of the RTC to Indian political thought was the evolution of the conception of a united India. Another solid outcome was the definite emergence of the DC in the political picture of India and more important was the brilliant & moving exposition of their insufferable conditions by BRA before the bar of world opinion. Owing to disagreement amongst different communities on the question of seats and on the system of election whether joint / separate electorates with reserved seats should be employed, the Conference was adjourned. Without the Congress too no major decision concerning India could be taken.

BRA on his return said that grant of political power depended upon the solution of the minority problem and concluded by expressing his satisfaction that in the future constitution of India the place of the DC was secure & their disabilities would be non-existent. Meanwhile the political situation in India was changing. Within a week of the termination of the RTC, Gandhi after protracted negotiations with the Viceroy Irwin made a pact abandoning the Civil Disobedience Movement and promising to attend the second RTC.

It was decided by leaders of the DC to revive the agitation for temple entry at Nasik, which was suspended in 1930 on the assurance of Dr Moonje. BRA went to Nasik, made a great speech, aroused his people's feelings, laid stress on discipline & non-violence. The procession of untouchables passed off except for some stones thrown by orthodox groups. A notable point, at its Karachi session, the Congress made a declaration that it would be strictly neutral in matters religious. A little before this session, Gandhi declared in Mumbai that we would fight for temple entry after freedom was won.

In April 1931 BRA convened a Leader's Conference where prominent DC leaders from Bengal, C.P., Maharashtra & Madras came. BRA submitted a report on what he had done at the RTC. The Conference appealed to the Govt to nominate the reps of DC on the Federal Structure Committee, to grant adequate representation at the next RTC and demanded that reps of DC be provided with cabinet responsibilities in future cabinets of the Provinces. It expressed gratitude to people who fought for the DC cause at the RTC liked Sir Tej Bahadur Sapru, Issac Foot amongst others.

SIGNAL CONTRIBUTION OF AMBEDKAR

Dr. Ambedkar's signal contribution was the enactment of the article in the Constitution (Article 32) which guarantees a citizen the fundamental right to move the Supreme Court directly for enforcement of his or her fundamental rights instead of first approaching the High Court before a single judge and thereafter in appeal before a division bench. The rationale was to secure speedy and inexpensive justice. Dr. Ambedkar regarded this provision as "the very soul of the Constitution and the very heart of it".

The tendency of some judges of the Supreme Court to relegate citizens to the High Court even in cases where there is a clear violation of their fundamental rights is certainly not in keeping with the heart and soul of the Constitution. Hero worship is endemic in our country and the personality cult flourishes. In the process, the tendency is to entrust heroes and heroines with vast powers and uncritically accept their authority without insisting on accountability. Dr. Ambedkar was aware of these lurking dangers. In the Constituent Assembly, he emphasised John Stuart Mill's caution, namely, not "to lay liberties at the feet of even a great man, or to trust him with powers which enable him to subvert their institutions". Baba Saheb was aware that hero worship in our country plays a part in politics unequalled in magnitude to the part it plays in any other country. He warned: "Bhakti in religion may be a road to the salvation of the soul. But in politics, Bhakti or hero-worship is a sure road to degradation and to eventual dictatorship." We did not heed this prophetic warning and had to suffer the spurious June 1975 Emergency. The slogan "India is Indira and Indira is India" was repeatedly chanted in the sycophantic hero worship of the charismatic leader.

Recently, we witnessed nauseating sycophancy when Congress leaders and politicians vied with one another in their heartrending attempts to persuade Sonia Gandhi to revoke her sensible decision to decline the Prime Ministerial office. Dr. Ambedkar attached great importance to constitutional morality in the working of the Constitution.

He endorsed the view of the Greek historian Grote, that constitutional morality required "a paramount reverence for the forms of the Constitution, enforcing obedience to authority acting under and within these forms". He stressed that diffusion of constitutional morality should be "not merely among the majority of any community but throughout the whole-since even any powerful and obstinate minority may render the working of a free institution impracticable without being strong enough to conquer ascendancy". Dr. Ambedkar then posed the question: "Can we presume such a diffusion of constitutional morality?" His frank answer was, "Constitutional morality is not a natural sentiment. It has to be cultivated. We must realise that our people have yet to learn it." Surveying the present scene it is apparent that we have not yet learnt it. Indeed constitutional morality seems to be alien to our legislators and people at the centre of power.

Participation in Drafting the Constitution

In 1947, India achieved independence and Ambedkar, who had already been elected a member of the Constituent Assembly, was invited by J. Nehru, the first prime minister of the country, to join the Cabinet as Minister for Law. A few weeks later the Assembly entrusted the task of framing the Constitution to a Draft Committee, and this committee elected Ambedkar as its chairman. For the next two years, he worked on the Draft Constitution, writing it almost single-handed. Despite ill health, Ambedkar completed the Draft Constitution by the beginning of 1948 and later that year introduced it in the Constituent Assembly. Thereafter he steered it through the legislative process and in November of 1949 it was adopted by the Assembly with very few amendments. Ambedkar's resignation from the Cabinet in 1951 marked the virtual end of his political career. In the general elections of January 1952 he failed to win a seat in the Lok Sabha or House of Representatives, and was equally unsuccessful when he contested a by-election the following year. In March 1952 he was, however, elected to the Rajya Sabha, the less influential upper house of parliament, as one of the seventeen representatives of the State of Bombay. He was soon vigorously attacking the government from his new position.

Architect of Indian Constitution

Dr. Ambedkar was the main architect of the Indian Constitution. He was born in a very poor low caste family of Madhya Pradesh. In U.S.A., he did his M.A. in 1915 and Ph.D. in 1916. From 1918 to 1920, he worked as a Professor of Law. Dr. Ambedkar set up his legal practice at the Mumbai High Court. Ambedkar was the main inspiration behind the inclusion of special provision in the Constitution of India for the development of Schedule Caste people. Dr. Ambedkar was the Law Minister of India from 1947 to 1951. He took part in the Satyagraha of untouchables at Nasik in 1930 for opening the Hindu temples to them. Dr. Ambedkar was emancipator of the 'untouchables' and crusader for social justice. This liberator of the down trodden was affectionately called "Baba Saheb". He was posthumously awarded 'Bharat Ratna' in the year 1990.

Ambedkar's Movement

While coming back to India in 1923, Ambedkar again experienced humiliation. The upper caste lawyers would not even have tea at his desk. But his greatest consolation was his clients, whom he treated with liberal mind. His reputation and fame among the Depressed Classes began to grow. He visualised and struggled for a casteless and equal India. By the time he returned to India, Bhimrao had equipped himself fully to wage war against the practice of untouchability. In 1924 he started the organisation 'Bahiskrit Hitakarini Sabha' (Outcastes Welfare Association), for the upliftment of the untouchables. Ambedkar adopted a two-pronged strategy. First, the eradication of illiteracy and economic uplift of the downtrodden and second, initiating nonviolent struggle against visible symbols of casteism, like denial of entry into temples and drawing water from public wells and tanks. The problems of the downtrodden were centuries old and difficult to overcome. Their entry into temples was forbidden. They could not draw water from public wells and ponds. Their admission in schools was prohibited. Ambedkar won two major victories when the High Court of Bombay gave a verdict in favour of the untouchables.

On 25th December 1927, he led the Mahad March at the Chowdar Tank at Colaba, near Bombay, to ensure the untouchables right to draw water from the public tank. The marchers were met with the brutality of caste Hindus. He then burnt copies of the 'Manusmriti' publicly terming it a document of discrimination with a number of his supporters. It was an act of great courage to do so in the den of violent Chitpawan Brahmins in Maharashtra. The two struggles shook the religious foundation on which the caste system is built. This marked the beginning of the anti-caste and ant-priest movement in Maharashtra. The temple entry movement launched by Dr. Ambedkar in 1930 at Kalaram temple, Nasik is another landmark in the struggle for human rights and social justice. He was fully convinced that nothing could emancipate the Dalits except through a complete destruction of the caste system. He continued his movement to attack the base of caste system in every possible way.

In the meantime, the Simon Commission visited India and Dr. Ambedkar met the commission in Pune in which Ambedkar presented his position on depressed classes. He then followed it up during the round table conference after which Ramsay McDonald announced 'Communal Award' as a result of which several communities including the 'depressed classes' were given the right to have separate electorates. Gandhiji wanted to defeat this design and went on a fast unto death to oppose it. On 24th September 1932, Ambedkar and Gandhiji reached an understanding, which became the famous Poona Pact. According to this Pact, in addition to the agreement on electoral constituencies, reservations were provided for untouchables in Government jobs and legislative assemblies. The Pact carved out a clear and definite position for the downtrodden on the political scene of the country. For the first time in Indian history it opened up opportunities of education and government service for them and also gave them a right to vote. Dr. Ambedkar attended all the three Round Table Conferences in London and each time, forcefully projected his views in the interest of the 'untouchable'.

He exhorted the downtrodden sections to raise their living standards and to acquire as much political power as possible. He was of the view that there was no future for untouchables in the Hindu religion and they should change their religion if need be. In 1935, he publicly proclaimed," I was born a Hindu because I had no control over this but I shall not die a Hindu".

Ambedkar-The Socialist

It is also interesting to note and which not many Ambedarkites have ventured, that Dr. Ambedkar was a socialist to the core of his heart. The disappointing relation with the communist movement stands as the single most unfortunate paradox of contemporary Indian history. It didn't come out of much of ideological differences, which certainly existed in the form of certain unclear theoretical constructs in the mind of Ambedkar-as from the attitudes of the communist leaders towards the Dalit movement. These leaders in the Trade Unions of Bombay dogmatically regarded the caste question as an unimportant super-structural issue, which would automatically disappear when the revolution takes place. Their orthodox outlook regarding untouchability, caste disparity, discrimination was the basics on which Ambedkar's entire thesis on Communism was formed. For historical reasons the leadership of this communist movement however came from the middle class educated youth who had to come from upper castes communities, the majority being the Brahmin itself. Ambedkar's writing on Marxism is heavily reflects his frustration with the Bombay-Communists. This legacy to identify Marxism with its self-appointed practitioners still appears to be followed by Dalits. They cite examples of the parliamentary communist parties to show the lacuna or inapplicability of Marxism. It is necessary for them to understand that Marxism intrinsically solicits criticism but it presupposes its careful study.

As Anand Teltumde puts it, although Ambedkar could not discuss the philosophy of communism in the manner it deserved, he was never antagonistically disposed towards it. Rather, he acknowledged the beauty of communist philosophy and said that it was closer to his own. Preoccupied with the mission of liberating the Dalits, he insisted, quite like Marx, that the test of the philosophy was in practice, and opined that if communists worked from that perspective, to win success in India would be far easier than in Russia (Janata, 15 January, 1938). He always regarded communism as the ultimate benchmark to assess his highest ideal-Buddhism. With unpleasant experience with communist dogma and vulgarity of his times, he did sound polemically against Communism and appeared at times even professing its doom but it all underscored his wrath against the dogma that occupied the communist practice. Despite all these aspects of Ambedkar's disagreements with Communism it is cannot be ruled out that Ambedkar was not a Socialist.

He was a socialist of a different kind. One of his prime conflicts with Marx was 'dictatorship of the proletariats', which he condemned saying that dictatorship of any kind is unethical. His stood for greater democracy of, by, for and among the oppressed ones in every field. At one stage he was clearly of the opinion that the historical conflict is between the exploited and exploiters and that all. It is with this idea that Dr. Ambedkar, formed the Independent Labour Party, participated in the provincial elections and was elected to the Bombay Legislative Assembly. During these days he stressed the need for abolition of the 'Jagirdari' system, pleaded for workers' Fight to strike and addressed a large number of meetings and conferences in Bombay Presidency. In 1939, during the Second World War, he called upon Indians to join the Army in large numbers to defeat Nazism, which he said, was another name for Fascism.

He stood for the nationalisation of property like land, banks etc. Ambedkar was also an advocate of women's rights. He struggled for women's liberation from the caste-entrenched patriarchal system. At the conference of the Depressed Classes Women in Nagpur in 1942, he stated: 'let every girl who marries stand by her husband, claim to be her husband's friend and equal, and refuse to be his slave'. He resigned from the Nehru's cabinet as Law Minister only when the cabinet refused to pass the Women's Rights Bill. This strongly proves that his idea of Socialism was embedded in his core agenda of freedom for all from all forms of bondage.

Ambedkar and After

The post Ambedkar Dalit movement had witnessed several ups and downs. On one side a categorical awakening among the Dalits had grown beyond all levels of history and on the other it has somewhere stagnant after Ambedkar mainly due to ideological disposition of stagnation. It would be opportune to look at the post Ambedkar Dalit movement and do a stock taking of the changes within the Dalit politics to understand the phenomenon. Subash Gatade says that the ups and downs through which the Dalit politics passed through after the death of Dr. Baba Saheb Ambedkar can be broadly divided into three phases-Rise and Fall of the Republican Party, emergence of the Dalit Panthers and thirdly the growing assertion of Dalits for political power and their consequent refusal to remain satisfied merely with education and job opportunities arising out of the policy of reservation. At this stage there is another factor that developed among Dalit castes too. These are organising themselves under the banners of their respective caste and sub-caste for achieving their rights. Consequently their guns are trained besides the Varna system also on the so-called rich Dalit castes or the creamy layer in them, which they feel, have monopolised a large part of the reserved posts. The Mahar/ neo-Buddhists vs. Matang and Charmakar debate in Maharashtra, Mala vs. Madiga in Andhra Pradesh are symptomatic of this rising trend. This propensity is similar in most states where the marginalized Dalits are organising themselves into a movement for castewise categorisation of reserved seats in educational institutions and jobs etc., which could not avail of the quota for historical reasons, could avail of it.

It is indeed ironical that at a time when the issue of Dalit assertion has got acceptance even in the mainstream polity in the 90s a counter tendency has emerged which seem to fracture the new found identity. One could also perceive the whole process as an explosion of identities hitherto suppressed by the hegemonic caste and class structure. In the beginning of the 70s the term Dalit denoted a broad, homogenous fraternity. This is no more the case. If you just say Dalit you are making an incomplete statement. It would be necessary to also specify whether he is a Mala or a Madiga or a Matang or a Charmakar. This process has thrown up new 'icons' from among the different castes and the sub-castes as well. This clearly gives a broader picture of the fact that how much the individual caste identity had become more important than the collective one of the 70s.

Another aspect that the Dalit movement in the post-Ambedkar era failed to address is that of the direct challenges of communal fascism. Communal-fascism is exploring its way to elaborate its base, activities and action. It appears that building of philanthropic and religious institutions like Saraswati Sishu Mandir, Vanvasi Kalyan Ashram, Sanghs, Deen Dayal Shodh Sansthan, Sanskriti Bihar, Vikas Bharit, Gayatri Pariwar, Brahmakumari Samaj, etc. are some of the strategies adopted to create inroads among the Dalits & Adivasis. Another strategy applied is the steady and systematic capturing of the community panchayats and organisations. The best example of this is Gujarat where the communal fascists have got their stranglehold and successfully executed the carnage against the Muslims by communalising Dalits and Adivasis. Resultant is the perpetual assurance of control over these communities plus a bonus of sustaining casteism. Expansion of caste fascism has so far and is disintegrating the Dalit ideology, theology, and identity and intimidated their very existence. Apparently this ruptures the community, deteriorates the noble notions of sharing, caring and cooperation, expansion of patriarchy and battered the inkling of community ownership over resources. Let us not forget Ambedkar was the greatest fighter against religious fascism and historical caste fascism.

Thirdly Dalit movement neither understand the politics of imperialist globalisation not address it in any form. Rather than entering the debate in a critical way from the subaltern perspective, it remained passive to the process of globalisation, and many times joined the sustaining party. Globalisation in India marked through Economic Reforms launched in July 1991 in India were in nature of a crisis management response to the economic and political crises that erupted in early 90s. The blue print for the Reforms was provided by the combination of macroeconomic stabilisation and structural adjustment programme of International Monetary Fund (IMF) and World Bank respectively, which had been adopted by many countries before in similar situations. This had quantitative and qualitative adversities on food security, employment, inflation, poverty alleviation schemes as well as social security. For example reservation in the educational institutions and the financial assistance in the form of scholarships and freeships had gone out of context, with the advent of education as an industry. Without education, all constitutional safeguards including the reservation in services would be futile. The Reforms have already resulted in freezing the grants to many institutions and in stagnating, if not lowering, the expenditure on education. The free market ethos has entered the educational sphere in a big way. Commercialisation of education is no more a mere rhetoric; it is now the established fact. Commercial institutions offering specialised education signifying the essential input from utilitarian viewpoint have come up in a big way from cities to small towns.

It is the same way that the employment sector had its impact due to the thus called 'economic reforms'. Howsoever, unsatisfactory the results of the implementation of reservation in employment may be, its importance from the Dalit viewpoint cannot be under emphasised. As could be evidenced by the organised private sector, where it would be difficult to find a Dalit employee (save of course in scavenging and lowliest jobs), without reservations Dalits would have been totally doomed. The importance of reservations thus could only be assessed in relation to situations where they do not exist. Whatever be their defects and deficiencies, they have given certain economic means of livelihood and some social prestige to the sons and daughters of over 1.5 million landless labourers. Whether they get real power or not, over 50,000 Dalits could enter the sphere of bureaucratic authority with the help of reservations. Besides these tangible benefits promised by the policy, it has instilled a hope in Dalit community. This hope predominantly manifests in the form of spread of education among them. Their emotional bond with the nation and its Constitution despite heaps of injustice and ignominy they bear every moment of their life may also be significantly attributable to the Reservation Policy. The selling out the PSU, the disinvestments of PSUs, promotion of privatisation, the letting off of land to the corporates, etc. had crafted formulae of neo-colonisation. This is high time that Dalit leadership across the country enters this debate in a big way, which it had until now failed to do. Coming back to Ambedkar, he was not dogmatic but pragmatic. He had rightly confronted the forces of fascism, communalism and capitalism. He believed that any system that promotes unequal human relationships should not thrive. Unfortunately, his socio-economical writings were kept aside while his writings on religion and caste system of 30s were used more by the representatives of the movement, thus clearly alienating a vast masses of the unorganised labour away from the mainstream Ambedkarite movement. That is why today, despite globalisation resulting in wars and multiple conflicts, yet Dalits simply remain as silent spectators, just waiting for their turn of reservation. Dalits are confined to use the Dalit card for just reservation in education and employment, nothing else. The forth barrier of the post Ambedkar Dalit movement is the emergence of a new sect of Dalit elite.

This Dalit elite whom Baba Saheb had opposed tooth and nail in his lifetime had become the Sarkari Babu Sahab clan, who not only take the benefits of reservations but also conveniently forget the community once they get there. It is also observed that while this sect functions throughout with the brand 'Dalit', also engage in all the corrupt practices that was once the cornerstone of Brahministic culture and ethics. It is interesting that Ambedkar fought for the rights of Dalits and had a broader vision, which couldn't be inculcated by post-Ambedkar Ambedkarites. He wanted to give his people an identity so that they get out of Varna System, but here what we see is the stimulation of the culture of varna and caste within the Dalit communities.

Despite the leaps and bounds, the Dalit movement made in Indian context, the failure of Ambedkarite movement to address the questions of fascism, communalism, globalisation, imperialism and the most importantly patriarchy in relation with casteism has altogether dragged the Dalit movement to the crossroad in the present context. Any pragmatic and progressive movement cannot stand on the selective criticism of a few religious texts or political ideologies and conveniently keeping quiet on other questions. A movement cannot be built on superfluous philosophy of negativism. It has to provide its own alternative to the people. To quote V.B. Rawat, Dalits have their own distinct identity and culture and those claiming to provide them an alternative God really misquote Ambedkar and kill their revolutionary spirit as suggested by many Dalit activists. Ambedkar's popularity among the Dalits is not due to the corrupt Dalits who use all tactics to grab money and power but the poor Dalits who consider him as the liberator.

A LION AMONG MEN

Ambedkar was born in a cast which was considered as the lowest of the low. People said that it was a sin if they offered him water to drink, and that if he sat in a cart it would become unclean. But this very man framed the Constitution for the country. His entire life was one of struggles. And his personal life was too misirable; he had lost his first wife and sons. But even though he did not lost hid dareness. It is no wonder that everyone called him 'Baba Saheb', out of love and admiration. Bhimrao Ambedkar was the lion-hearted man who fought for equality, justice and humanity.

"Inequality is the soul of Hinduism," wrote Ambedkar. He characterized the oppressive caste system as the tyranny of Hinduism. After spending a lifetime in a crusade against the oppressive Hinduism, Ambedkar finally renounced Hinduism, and converted to Buddhism and exhorted his followers to do the same. It is an irony that BJP and other Sangh Parivar outfits are trying to appropriate such a historic personality as Dr. B.R. Ambedkar.

They have started unveiling Ambedkar photos and statues. Some Sangh ideologies have torn some quotations of B.R. Ambedkar on Islamic invasions out of context and misinterpreted them to fit Ambedkar in their own anti-Islamic framework. Vinay Katiyar took out an Ambedkar Yatra in UP. Mayawati unveiled a statue of Ambedkar's wife even though her party, the BSP, shamelessly betrayed the Ambedkar tradition by aligning with his arch ideological-political foes, the Hindutva brigade, in a coalition for the sake of power.

To attract dalits to its fold, the BJP made Bangaru Laxman its ornamental chief but he had to ignominiously bow down from office for accepting Tehelka cash bundles. But before his resignation he made a speech in the Nagpur session of the BJP National Council almost equating Ambedkar with Hedgewar. In fact, the actual history convincingly refutes the dirty tricks of the Sangh Parivar.

During the freedom movement, because of the failures and neglect of the Congress a few political streams arose independent of it. Because of the Congress neglect of Muslims and the influence of Hindu conservatism and Hindu dominance in Congress leadership, Muslims rallied independently under the Muslim League. For similar reasons, Sikhs also rallied under the Akali Dal. Brahminical upper caste forces dominated the Congress leadership and the party turned a blind eye to the aspirations of nationalities. In Tamil Nadu, Periyar E.V. Ramasamy fought against this, first through the anti-Brahmin movement and then went on to represent the nationality aspirations of Tamils.

It was Ambedkar who squarely put social reform on the agenda during the freedom struggle and launched a simultaneous movement against untouchability and the caste order that were the hallmarks of Hinduism, and championed the interests of dalits. In this he was far to the left of Gandhi. On the other hand, far to the right of Gandhian leadership there was first Hindu Mahasabha and later RSS streams, which often collaborated with the British and considered, with open hostility, even Gandhi too liberal. This hostility finally culminated in the assassination of Gandhi by an RSS man

Nathuram Godse. Ambedkar was lifelong at loggerheads with the Hindu fundamentalists. Even in his Thoughts on Pakistan, (on which Katiyar's portrayal of him as an anti-Muslim Hindutva figure rests), he ruthlessly critiques the Hindu Mahasabha and Savarkar. He writes: "The Hindu nationalist who hopes that Britain will coerce the Muslims into abandoning Pakistan, forgets that the right of nationalism to freedom from an aggressive foreign imperialism and the right of a minority to freedom from an aggressive majority's nationalism are not two different things, nor does the former stand on a more sacred footing than the latter."

This clearly illustrates his criticism of aggressive majorotarian nationalism. He further criticizes Savarkar, commenting that "strange as it may seem, Mr. Savarkar and Mr. Jinnah instead of being opposed to each other on the two nations issue, are in complete agreement about it". But Ambedkar exposes Savarkar's authoritarian intent: "Mr. Savarkar wants the Hindu nation to be the dominant nation and the Muslim nation to be the subservient nation under it." Such being the historical evolution of different political streams in India, it is clear that the legacy of Ambedkar and Hindu fundamentalism are irreconcilably hostile to each other. Hindutva forces today are trying to delink Ambedkar from his entire legacy, cover up their hostility towards him and try to appropriate him for electoral use.

The fundamental hostility of the Sangh Parivar against Ambedkar was clearly brought to the fore by the vile campaign unleashed against him by RSS ideologue and a BJP minister in Vajpayee's cabinet Arun Shourie through his book Worshipping False Gods. Shiv Sainiks, the soul mates of Hindutva forces, also launched a struggle against Ambedkar's book The Riddles of Hinduism. This is the actual record of Hindutava forces vis-a-vis the heritage of Ambedkar, which they are trying to hide now in order to appropriate his glorious image for their own vested interests.

Ambedkar was the architect of the constitution of India. Sangh Parivar is even opposed to the marginal secular and liberal features of this Constitution and that is why they have formed a committee to tinker with it. While Ambedkar had total enmity towards Hindu Mahasabha and RSS and other Hindu fundamentalists, he was generally pro-left and, befitting a true democrat in a semi-feudal society, he had a positive attitude towards Marxism though it was unfortunate that the communists in those days failed in their united front tactics and failed to develop a proper relationship with Ambedkar. This was part of their general weakness and shortcomings in India.

The Contrast between Ambedkar and Savarkar

Savarkar's strategy of dissolving more than 3,000 castes into one pan-Hindu identity involves pan-Hindu temples, pan-Hindu dinners, inter-caste marriages, anti-untouchability programmes and the removal of injunctions on caste-ridden vocations and sea-voyage. Thus, Savarkar seems to have admonished Hindus to break off the seven shackles that according to him hindered the progress of the Hindu society. Did this programme really denounce Hinduism? The answer to this question has to be in the negative because the anti-caste programme particularly relating to injunctions against inter-caste marriage and advocating vedic rights for the sudras and ati-sudras given by Savarkar did not have vigour and genuine thrust to attack the Hindu shastras and caste system.

Savarkar's contention regarding inter-caste marriages looked to be so casual that he offered only a qualified support to such marriages, thus replacing the need for creating any conscious motivation necessary for the radical mobilisation of the people towards reaching the desired end. Similarly, Savarkar's attempt to grant the study of vedas and vedic rituals to non-Brahmins though apparently liberal may effectively lead to the Brahminisation of the non-Brahmin castes thus according legitimacy to Hindu shastras.

On the contrary, Ambedkar considers inter-caste marriages as the effective means for abolishing caste system. But Ambedkar is also aware that inter-caste dining or even inter-caste marriages are not enough to eliminate casteism. He was of the opinion that for realising the desired goal of casteless society through inter-caste marriages it is necessary to destroy the belief in the sanctity of Hindu shastras.

And for destroying this belief, Ambedkar suggests that people should not only discard the shastras, but they should deny their authority as Buddha and Nanak did. Thus; it can be argued here that socially radical Ambedkar was very unlikely to be attracted by Savarkar whose proposal, according to one of the sincere Savarkarites, contained reformative zeal aimed at revival of Hinduism rather than its denunciation.

Ambedkar was never a Marxist. He could not carry forward his struggle for thorough going abolition of semi-feudalism and against imperialism through a democratic revolution like Mao did in China. He focused mainly on the petty bourgeois and bourgeois intelligentsia from the oppressed communities and worked largely within the system representing their interests in the form of reservation etc. Nevertheless, despite this limitation, he remained an outstanding bourgeois revolutionary democrat who was head and shoulders above many in the Congress leadership and was clearly far more radical than Gandhi.

In the course of his differences against the Congress, he never made any concession to the Hindu Right and always remained hostile to them.

Against Brahminical Hinduism During his boyhood Ambedkar had to suffer lots of personal humiliation due to untouchability. In Chowder Tank satyagraha led by Ambedkar in 1927, the upper caste Hindus attacked him and physically injured him. During the freedom movement Ambedkar emerged as the tallest leader of social reform in India.

Ambedkar asserted: "I was born a Hindu, but never will die a Hindu. What is required is to get rid of the doctrine of

'Chatuvarna'. That is the root cause of all inequality and is also the parent of the case system and untouchability, which are merely other forms of inequality". It is relevant to note here that while both Hedgewar and Golwalkar upheld Manu and thus rationalised the caste system inherent to the Hindu religion, Ambedkar even burnt copies of Manusmruti through a campaign. On December 25, 1927 Ambedkar observed a "Manu Smruti Dahan Din", and publicly burnt Manusmruti. The struggle was known as the "Maha-Sangharsha" of Mahad Satyagraha, and it is an important milestone in Dalit struggle against Brahmanism and Brahminical Hinduism.

Manuvadis had conspired so that Ambedkar did not get a ground for the meeting, but a Muslim gentleman, Mr. Fattekhan, gave his private land to observe this protest. There was a strong reaction in the Brahmanical press, Baba Saheb was called "Bheemaasura" by one paper. Dr. Ambedkar justified the burning of Manusmruti in various articles. Ambedkar made a scathing attack on Hinduism: "I tell you, religion is for man and not man for religion. If you want to organise, consolidate and be successful in this world, change this religion. The religion that does not recognise you as a human being, or give you water to drink, or allow you to enter temples is not worthy to be called a religion. The religion that forbids you to receive education and comes in the way of your material advancement is not worthy of the appellation 'religion'.

The religion that does not teach its followers to show humanity in dealing with its co-religionists is nothing but a display of a force. The religion that teaches its followers to suffer the touch of animals but not the touch of human beings is not a religion but a mockery. The religion that compels the ignorant to be ignorant and the poor to be poor is not a religion but a visitation!"

He added this on the upper castes: "It is your claim to equality which hurts them. They want to maintain the status quo. If you continue to accept your lowly status ungrudgingly, continue to remain dirty, filthy, backward, ignorant, poor and disunited, they will allow you to live in peace. The moment you start to raise your level, the conflict starts. Untouchability is not a transitory or temporary feature; it is eternal, it is lasting. Frankly it can be said that the struggle between the Hindus and the Untouchables is a never-ending conflict. It is eternal because the religion which assigns you the lowest status in society is itself divine and eternal according to the belief of the so-called high caste Hindus. No change warranted by change of time and circumstances is possible." Such being the views of Ambedkar, those who offer political patronage to outfits like Ranvir Sena can have no claim over Ambedkar. The ideologies of Hindutva are trying to rationalise caste system saying that it is a division of labour. Ambedkar refuted this saying, "Caste System is not merely a division of labour.

It is also a division of labourers. It is an hierarchy in which the divisions of labourers are graded one above the other." While the Hindutva brigade is known for defending Manu and the caste system, Ambedkar made a trenchant criticism of the caste system associated with Hinduism: "There cannot be a more degrading system of social organisation than the Chaturvarna. It is the system which deadens, paralyses and cripples the people from helpful activity." He further added, "Caste in the hands of the orthodox has been a powerful weapon for persecuting the reforms and for killing all reform." Relating the inseparable relation between caste system and Hinduism, Ambedkar wrote, "Hinduism is a veritable chamber of horrors. The sanctity and infallibility of the Vedas, Smritis and Shastras, the iron law of caste, the heartless law of karma and the senseless law of status by birth are to the untouchables veritable instruments of torture which Hinduism has forged against untouchables."

In Buddha and His Dhamma, Ambedkar has enumerated the evils of Hinduism in the following manner:

1. It has deprived moral life of freedom;

2. It has only emphasized conformity to commands; and
3. The laws are unjust because they are not the same for one class as of another.

Besides, the code is treated as final. According to Ambedkar, "what is called religion by Hindus is nothing but a multitude of commands and prohibitions." The Sangh Parivar is out to make this code the official code in India under their scheme of authoritarian Hindu rashtra. Sensing the alienation of dalits, many people, from Savarkar to Gandhi, made token gestures against casteism. The RSS was also forced to come out with some tokenist pronouncements. But Ambedkar put things in the right perspective by saying, "Caste cannot be abolished by inter-caste dinners or stray instances of inter caste marriages. Caste is a state of mind. It is a disease of mind. The teachings of the Hindu religion are the root cause of this disease. We practice casteism and we observe untouchability because we are enjoined to do so by the Hindu religion. A bitter thing cannot be made sweet. The taste of anything can be changed. But poison cannot be changed into nectar."

Ambedkar even made a sarcastic comment against Gandhi: "There have been many mahatmas in India whose sole object was to remove untouchability and to elevate and absorb the depressed classes, but everyone has failed in their mission. Mahatmas have come, mahatmas have gone but the untouchables have remained as untouchables." Ambedkar told dalits that, "You must abolish your slavery yourselves. Do not depend for its abolition upon god or a superman. Remember that it is not enough that a people are numerically in the majority.

They must be always watchful, strong and self-respecting to attain and maintain success. We must shape our course ourselves and by ourselves." He further stressed that, "What you have lost others have gained. Your humiliations are a matter of pride with others. You are made to suffer wants, privations and humiliations not because it was preordained by the sins committed in your previous birth, but because of the overpowering tyranny and treachery of those who are above you. You have no lands because others have usurped them; you have no posts because others have monopolised them. Do not believe in fate; believe in your strength."

It may be recalled that Advani recently raised a controversy over a Buddhist symbol like Ashoka chakra figuring in the national flag and a Buddhist symbol being the national emblem. Regarding their origin Ambedkar explained, "Even though Buddhism is almost extinct in India, yet it has given birth to a culture, which is far better and richer than the Brahminic culture. When the question of the national flag and the national emblem was being considered by the Constituent Assembly we could not find any suitable symbol from the Brahminic culture. Ultimately, the Buddhist culture came to our rescue and we accepted the Wheel of Law (Dhamma-Chakra) as the national symbol." No wonder, a Brahminical high-priest of Hindutva like Advani wanted to do away with these symbols introduced by Ambedkar and his colleagues.

In his slanderous campaign against Ambedkar, the RSS ideologue Arun Shourie questioned the patriotism of Ambedkar. Ambedkar, however, defined patriotism thus, "I do not want that our loyalty as Indians should be in the slightest way affected by any competitive loyalty whether that loyalty arises out of our religion, out of our culture or out of our language. I want all people to be Indians first, Indian last and nothing else but Indians." And despite all his differences with the Congress, Ambedkar remained a staunch nationalist.

For Ambedkar, the conception of a secular state is derived from the liberal democratic tradition of the West. In contrast to the Gandhian misinterpretation of secularism as 'sarva dharma samabhava', Ambedkar said, "No institution, which is maintained wholly out of state funds, shall be used for the purpose of religious instruction irrespective of the question whether the religious instruction is given by the state or by any other body". He further explained the corruption of the concept of secularism in India, "This country has seen the conflict between ecclesiastical law and secular law long before Europeans sought to challenge the authority of the Pope. Kautilya's Arthshastra lays down the foundation of secular law. In India unfortunately ecclesiastical law triumphed over secular law. In my opinion this was the one of the greatest disasters in the country."

Ambedkar effectively punctured the false supremacy of the narrow Brahminical elite: "In every country the intellectual class is the most influential class. This is the class which can foresee, advise and lead. In no country does the mass of the people live the life for intelligent thought and action. It is largely imitative and follows the intellectual class. There is no exaggeration in saying that the entire destination of the country depends upon its intellectual class. If the intellectual class is honest and independent, it can be trusted to take the initiative and give a proper lead when a crisis arises. It is true that the intellect by itself is no virtue. It is only a means and the use of a means depends upon the ends which an intellectual person pursues. An intellectual man can be a good man but he may easily be a rogue. Similarly an intellectual class may be a band of high-souled persons, ready to help, ready to emancipate erring humanity or it may easily be a gang of crooks or a body of advocates of narrow clique from which it draws its support."

Though changing one's religion through conversion is not going to abolish the semi-feudal inequalities, Ambedkar's decision to convert to Buddhism in the evening of his life—just a couple of months before his demise on 6 December 1956—only underlined his disgust and bitterness with the highly iniquitous Hinduism. About 2 lakh dalits converted to Buddhism along with him in October 1956. Since then neo-Buddhism has remained a trend. This clearly rattled the Hindutva bosses who are clamouring for anti-conversion legislation in every state.

5

Ambedkar and Dalit

DALIT MOVEMENT AND POLITICS OF IDENTITY

The initial concern of the Dalit movement for securing dignity and justice was expressed as the Dalit assertion for human rights. Dalits sought to enter Hindu temples in order to assert that as human being they too had equal rights to temple-entry, which was denied to them by the system of Untouchability. The Mahad Temple Entry Satyagraha, the Nasik Kalaram Mandir Satrygraha, and Parwati Temple Entry in Poona were some examples of these struggles.

Another expression came in the form of assertion for Dalit identity, which was to be constructed defiantly outside the framework of Brahmanism, through a rediscovery of Dalit history and culture located in an egalitarian order, real or imaginary, as opposed to the iniquitous brahminical social order. This ideological assertion reflected in various 'adi' movements in India, namely, 'adi-Dharam' movement in Punjab, and 'adi-Dravida', 'adi-Andhra', 'adi-Kannada' movements in South India advanced an ideological claim that Dalits were the original inhabitants of this country—*a la* sons of the soil—and belonged to a superior egalitarian cultural tradition. In Uttar Pradesh, for instance, Dalit groups such as

Mehtars, Bhangis, Chamars, Doms, and Jatvavs claimed that they were Buddhists, questioned caste discrimination against them and asserted that they were the original inhabitants of India who were conquered by deceit and manipulations by the Brahmins coming from outside. In the south the ideological assertion was seen in Iyoti Thass' attempts of conversion to Buddhism. From 1870s he had initiated movement of Buddhist conversion among the untouchables.

Of course, apart from this assertion of human identity in the traditional and religious framework, rediscovery of traditions and religiosity, the Dalit movement in later years approached the question of justice in the modern secular context. During the Ambedkarian struggle the ideological basis for Dalit assertion came from ideals of justice, liberty, equality and fraternity based these ideals. He engaged with the colonial state in the ideological framework of modernity and advanced the untouchables' claims for dignity in the language of rights. This was seen in Ambedkar's continuous critique of Brahmanism, its philosophical foundations, its ideal of Chaturvanya, in the language of denial of Untouchables and women into the membership of community of humanity. Even Ambedkar's articulation and reconstruction of Buddhism, to which he converted with his five lakhs followers in 1956, exhibits both critique of Brahmanism and socially embedded character of Buddhism. Buddha's Dhamma for instance was fundamentally social and that Buddha advocated reconstruction of society on the principles of justice, equality and reason as guiding principles of social organization. The democratic values that Dr. Ambedkar adhered to and the parliamentary form of governance that he advocated had roots in Buddha's Sangha. Further during 1930s Ambedkar was working towards a broader unity of the oppressed based on their social and economic experiences of marginalization. While speaking before the G.P.I railway workers he had pointed out that the oppressed in this country have to struggle against two enemies: Brahmanism and Capitalism. Through the

Independent Labour Party he had advanced a broad category of the oppressed--Dalits, marginalized peasantry and unorganised sector working classes.

This ideological legacy was later reinvented during the radical assertion of Dalit youth during early 1970s. Following the Black Panthers of America, these creative writers named themselves as Dalit Panthers. The panthers who experienced alienation from the ruling class oriented post-Ambedkarite Dalit politics, were disturbed on the issue of growing atrocities on Dalits in rural areas and sought to radicalised culture and politics as tools of resistance. It is they who gave currency to the term Dalit and also posited it with the new broad content—the referring to untouchables, landless agricultural labours and urban working classes and women. The panthers stormed the sites of atrocities and sought to reinvent self-respect and struggle as means of addressing faced by Dalits. Despite the fact that Panthers were to later split on egoistic expressions of right interpretation of Ambedkarism, Dhasal going the Marxist way and Dhale sticking to Buddhism seen as opposed to Marx, the movement gave rise to new literature that brought with it expressions of altogether different world unknown to the middle class Brahmanical taste, and one that depicted pain, oppression and resistance. This literary movement inspired political and literary movements in other parts of the country. This was very briefly in seen Gujarat and later in Karnataka in the form of Dalit Sangharsha Samiti. During the last two decades Dalit Panther is once again being reinvented in Tamilnadu as aggressive stance towards Dalits atrocities by the dominant land owning backward classes.

THE FORMATION OF A DALIT IDENTITY

Social and Political Background of the Dalit Movement

Jotirao Phule's first activities were completely based on education of the lower class masses. He was for sure aware of the reason of the backwardness of his people, which have been held away from any form of education for thousands of years. Modern teaching was first established in the Mesopotamian area 4 millenniums before Christ. But the lower castes of Hindu society were intentionally kept illiterate with the help of peoples' religious beliefs.

Being aware of this fact Jotirao Phule knew that to overcome the millenniums long Brahman superiority the only way was to create a literate society and also Dalit intellectuals. Phule had begun his social service activity with schools for Untouchables and women; had founded the Satyashodhak Samaj with backing from the well-to-do non-Brahmans, primarily contractors and a few professionals; and had moved fairly quickly to establish a peasant base."

When it is considered that the low castes had always been the majority of the over populated India (Shudras 58%, untouchables 24% apprx.) , we have to assume that those movements were a drop in the ocean. Because of the completely ignorance of the low castes against any intellectual human ideology whether coming from West or India, the organizational and institutional besides cultural development of the low caste society was too slow, when compared to the literate Brahman society. Following the struggle put forward by Phule, there were still only two or three newspapers were being published by the Dalit society. This is an indication of the poor environment for the ideas to flourish and the low number of people who were really capable of intellectual communication. But for the Brahmans the situation was different. Phule mentions this situation in his famous book "Slavery: (Under the Cloak of Brahmanism)".

- All the editors of the Marathi papers in Poona are Brahmins and they naturally do not want to write anything against their own caste-men. The Chairman of the Municipality was an Englishman and he would not allow the trickery of the Bhat. All the Bhats then raised a chorus of criticism (a hue and cry) against him to the effect that his policies were harmful to the interests of the riots, which were totally untrue; they ganged up against him and troubled him a lot. Finally he was so disgusted with the shabby situation that he resigned his chairmanship in sheer exasperation and washed his hands of the Municipal Committee thenceforth.

What we learn from Phule is the strength of Brahman bureaucracy inside the British administration and also the intellectual environment where all of the editors of the papers are Brahmins. The harsh reality, which is the illiteracy of the non-Brahman people, made the whole Dalit movement mostly a peasant movement rather than an urban and intellectual movement from the very beginning. It was not easy to produce thousands of intellectual in one day, but it was possible to talk to crowds and tell them what situation they were in. Because of this fact the political Dalit movement had easily found ground over the non- Brahman masses.

- The work of Phule and his colleagues has to be understood in this context. Phule's own writings reflect its sporadic nature of non- Brahman organizational development: they are unsystematic, sporadic, pictorial rather than discursive, hard-hitting but designed more to shock people into an awareness of the situation than to provide an extensive analysis. And he notes in the introduction to Sarvajanak Satya Dharma he had wanted to write a more thorough book but felt it was more important for the book to be useful to the daily life of the people. Non-Brahman leaders it was more important to speak to the masses than to engage in finely spun analysis.

Satyashodhak Samaj and Identity

Identity had been defined within caste context in India for the last two and a half millenniums. But within the intellectual environment of enlightement, new definitions had to be accepted. The lower castes and especially untouchables began feeling the need for an escape from the cruel realities created by the Brahmanic social system. They were also trapped in the new situation created by the West where an Indian and Hindu identity was forming against the British imperia. The Aryan theory was not first established in India and it was not for the Indians. It was a tool for some of the new powerfull nations of Europe to legalize their existence and power historically. This need will later give the birth to the fascist and national socialistic ideologies all over the continent. With the Aryan theory it was possible to for the Europeans to claim that their rule over the world was natural and this happened to be a historical fact which was also in close connection to the idea of superiority.

Especially Friedrich Max Muller, a man who spend his whole career for the search of Eastern studies, was one of the most important figure who proved the link between the Sanskrit and modern European languages. Suddenly Europens and Indians realised that the two societies were cousins. The superiority of the Europeans or the British in our case was a fact during the 19th century. And as we have seen most of the Brahmans find their ways into the British imperial society by getting Western education. This feeling was improved with the glamouring Aryan theory linking them directly to the rulers of the country.

- But we have to say that, British Government was not on the side of caste disrcrimination, at least officially. British Government had laid down a policy of imparting education to low castes, one sharply at variance with earlier Peshwa rule. Section 591 of the Education Commissioner's Report said "that the principle has been laid down by the Court of Directors in their letter of 5th May, 1854, and in a subsequent reply to Government's letter dated 20.5.1857.". According to these letters, "nobody should be refused admission to a Government college or school merely on the ground of caste". This principle was reaffirmed in 1863. It was applicable to all institutions which were maintained at the cost of public funds, provincial or local.

Ironically this attitude of British Government should be one of the reasons for the rise of religionist nationalism within upper caste Hindus, where they always strongly opposed the abolishment of the castes. It is interesting to find that all of the Hindu press, excepting only a few non-Brahman newspapers, was critical of the government's action permitting low-caste boys into the public schools.

Reformation of the Dalit Movement at the beginning of the 20th century

Although Satyashodhak Samaj was still an effective power in the Maharashastra, the province where it all began, it is hard to say that the newly emerging leader of the untouchables, Dr. Ambedkar was effected or get into connection with it. Satyashodhak Samaj was slowly disintegrating when Dr. Ambedkar first appeared. So the intelligent environment from which Dr. Ambedkar had been benefiting was completely different from the environment of Jotirao Phule's one. Being represented in a national congress was not even considered by the Dalits. Phule defined the first Poona political organization Sarvajanik Sabha, as a bath (Brahmin) sabha.

He saw little difference in the Indian National Congress:

- These cunning Aryabhat Brahmans regard all the world's people as insignificant and hold scorn and envy of them in their minds... Even if these Aryans people establish hundreds of national congresses in counterfeit imititation of the religiously united Americans or French, still I can say with assurance that Shudras and Atishudras will never be members of their National Congress.

And it happened as he said when the first Indian National Congress was established in 1885. In its first session 80% of the Madras delegates and 100% of the Poona delegates were

Brahmans, and this dominance continued to be maintained. At that time the Indian Congress was being accepted by the non-Brahman community as the represantative of the upper castes. And they had good reasons to believe this.

Legal Ebolishment of the Caste System

The borders of this study is not enough to define the social politics within the Indian society during the 19th and 20th centuries. But in order to draw a picture of the last century, a method had to be chosen, and in this case we choose to build the subject over the great figures or let's say the corner stones of the lower caste movements who were Ram Mohan Roy, Jotirao Phule and Dr. Ambedkar.

In previous stages we tried to give a brief story of the social changes of the 19th century considering the upper and lower caste relations and also the effects of the colonializm over the country. With the help of the photograhps which we have taken from the antiquity and later 19th and 20th century, we hope that an image of India should be formed within the readers mind. But it must be mentioned that the complexity of the subject causes a need for further reading.

Dr. Ambedkar

The last figure that must be mentioned to complete the greater and historical picture of the position and movements of the lower castes is Dr. Ambedkar. To start the subject wefound it more helpfull to tell the beginning of the story of Ambedkar from an Indian writer, Dhananjay Keer. The manner of the writing will also help us to understand what Ambedkar meant for some Indians.

- The Ambedkars come from Konkar, a region which provided India with great brains and great fighters, men like Tilak, Karve and Paranjpye. Ambedkar's ancestral village is Ambavade, five miles off Mandangad, a small town in the Rantnagiri District. The family was of some consequence in that village. It

> enjoyed the honour of keeping the palanquin of the village goddess and naturally the yearly festival was a great occasion for the family to attract the attention of the whole village. Ambadkar's grandfather Maloji Sakpal came of a good Mahar family. Of all the untouchable communities in the fold of Hindu society the Mahars are the most robust, adaptable, intelligent, fighting, brave, virile and leading community.

From the beginning the writer readies us for an epic story. A story which he believes in the heart. It's reflection of how the caste system has entered the Indian mind. The writer tells us that Dr. Ambedkar comes from a good family and even a good caste which is called Mahar. Now we learn that there are more brave, adaptable, intelligent, fighting, virile and leading communities within the untouchables as well.

And this small text also reminds us of a man who was born a leader within his own community with the help of being a member of a good family. Keer continues:

- The family belonged to the devotional Kabir school of thought. This Bhakti school of thought found consolation in the human attributes like compassion, benevolance and resignation to God. These devotees sought and found moral and spiritual broadening effect upon their mind was that the followers of this Bhakti school had abolished the rigidity of the caste system, as Kabir, the founder of the school, had roundly condemned it. This was one of the reasons why some Untouchable families turned to the Kabir cult. To the followers of the Kabir anybody who worshipped God belonged to God irrespective of caste and birth.

The Second Dalit Generation

It looks like that the soul of resistence which Ambedkar had within was a hereditary from his family. The interesting point about Ambedkar is the job of his father, where he was a member of the British military force. We know that most of the military personnel of the British colonial army was not British at all, but members of the lower castes.

The higher castes preferred to work withing the civil bureocracy rather than the military one. And this must be another clue of the British effect over the Indian society. Because Ambedkar's father was a literate person despite his caste. He usually read the national epics, the Ramayana and the Mahabbarata to his children. He was also able to speak and read in English where he was able to teach his children the language. And within this environment Ambedkar was enrolled to school when he was only five years old.

- There is an interesting case of a similiar battle, though with one important difference. In this event, the persons who carried through the war were Mahars themselves. They were retired British Army personnel. Ratnagiri District was the chief recruiting ground of the British Bombay Army, and a large portion of men enlisting there for service in infantry regiments were from the Untouchable Mahar and Chambar castes. After completion of their service, or retirement, they settled in some central of favourite village or town with some piece of land, cultivating their crops and bringing up their children, leading a peaceful quiet life. Of such men, a few commissioned and noncommissioned officers settled at Dapoli. This is the place where Dr. Ambedkar, the emancipator of the Untouchables, spent his early childhood and received his primary education.
- Subhedar Major Gagnak and nine other military pensioner, including Ambedkar's father, sent a petition on 1 July 1892 to the president of Dapoli Municipiality asking that their sons be admitted into the Municipial school and taught along with other boys. They stated that this arrangement would induce their boys to study hard and to emulate the example of the boys of other castes in the hope of attaining a high rank in their class.

The environment where Bhim (Dr. Ambedkar) grew shows us the great change within the life of the lower castes thanks to the improvements achieved by the leaders of the 19th century such as Jotirao Phule and also the British rule, although they did not ask for this conclusion. Ambedkar was born in 1891 when the efficiency of the untouchable and non-Brahman movement was on the rise.

- Ideas and behaviour patterns, very different from those to which the people were accustomed, were thus presented as isolated from religion. The policy of comparative non-interference naturally gave scope for the revolt of the castes that were not quite comfortable under the Brahmin supremacy. Later on, with the incoming of industrial cities, large numbers of peoples congregated in cities of mixed populations, away from the influence of their homes and unobserved by their caste or village people. This is the background of the picture of the contemporary caste.

So we can observe the rise of the second generation of literate Untouchables, where the first generation saw education as a tool to break the unfortunate destiny of their kids. And Dr. Ambedkar was of that second generation who find the chance to get a better education what ever the conditions were. But we have to say that there are no physical links between the schools or other institutions of the non-Brahman movement lead by Phule and the new born Ambedkar. But later Ambedkar would call Phule as his teacher.

Childhood and Education of Ambedkar

Bhim as a child who were genius and full of desire to learn soon realised the fact that he was not an ordinary student. Because he did not belong to the upper castes. He was just an untouchable, nobody desired to touch, speak or even see. He felt the harsh reality of discrimination in every level of his education. Not only by his school fellows, but also from his Brahmin teacher.

- Bhim and his brother were usually made to squart in a corner of the class on a piece of gunny cloth which they carried to school. The teachers would not touch their note books, nor did some of them even ask them to recite poems or put questions to them for fear of being polluted! When these two boys felt thirsty in the school they turned their mouths upwards and then somebody would kindly pour drinking water into their mouths as if through a funnel.

These examples shows us although most of the upper classes were well educated within the British education system, they felt no pitty to behave the lower classes as if they were beasts. And it is for sure that this behaviours must have sharpened Bhim for his later struggle against the upper classes. The only teacher who treated Bhim well was also a Brahmin teacher.

A teacher who Bhim decided to carry his surname and become famous as Ambedkar. Ambedkar, after finishing his primary education, found support from the non-Brahman Maharaja of Baroda to continue his education in the U.S.A and with this scholarship he left India in 1913.

Ambedkar turned to India in 1923 after nearly ten years of study in the United States and England. He was a highly educated man; his degrees B.A., M.A., Ph.D., M.Sc., D.Sc., Barrister-at-Law are sung in a sort of incantation in one of the Mahar songs about him. He was a highly political person, practical and pragmatic. Still, for personal as well as public reasons, he had to come to terms with the Mahar myths. At the end Ambedkar became an important figure not only for the Untouchables but also for the whole India as a modern country.

- By 1930 the British authorities had recognized the right of the Depressed Classes to representation through special electorates which their associations and spokesmen had been demanding since 1917. While the

Statuory Commission had already recommended for them reservation of seats in joint electorates, the British Government nominated two of their spokesmen, namely B.R. Ambedkar and R. Srinivasan, to the Indian Round Table Conference which commenced its work in London on 21 November 1930 so as to enunciate their status in the future constitutional set-up of India.

Ambedkar's Ideological Stand

Ambedkar became a respectful person in the eyes of other castes, who became to be a member of the council, which prepared the Indian constitution after the independence of the country. And he was the man who managed to abolish the term of untouchable at least in front of the Law. He was also a reformist who led his community to point of rejection of the Hinduism as a religion and acceptance of Buddhism. After the long struggles with the masters of the Hindu religion the Brahmans, he decided to completely throw away a religion, which simply turned out to be ignoring them as humans.

- Naturally no account of Buddhism in the Sub-Continent would be complete without mentioning the still extremely controversial figure of Dr. Ambedkar and the Neo-Buddhist Movement which he started with his mass conversion of Dalits or the exuntouchables. Today, more than 90% of all Buddhists in India (only 6.5 millions according to the 1991 census) are the so-called neo-Buddhists converted by Ambedkar, a lawyer by profession, who was one of the founders by modern Indian constitution. This is quite remarkable, considering that from the 11th-12th centuries until the mass conversion (including Ambedkar who officially renounced Hinduism and embraced Buddhism) which took place in October 1956 in Nagpur, Maharashtra, Buddhism had almost completely disappeared in India, its land of birth.86

To understand what was the Dalits were demanding we have to look what Ambedkar says. We believe that there are no clearer examples than Ambedkar's own words to draw the picture of Dalit problem in India.

What Path Freedom

D. B. R. Ambedkar... There are two aspects of conversion. Social as well as religious; material as well as spiritual. Whatever may be the aspect, or line of thinking, it is necessary to understand the beginning, the nature of untouchability and how it is practiced. Without this understanding, you will not be able to realise the real meaning underlying my declaration of conversion. In order to have a clear understanding of untouchability and its practice in real life, I want you to recall the stories of the atrocities perpetrated against you.

The instances of beating by caste Hindus for the simple reason that you have claimed the right to enroll your children in government schools, or the right to draw water from public well, or the right to take a marriage procession with the groom on horseback, are very common. You all know such instances, as they happen before your eyes. But there are several other causes for which atrocities are committed on the Untouchables by the caste Hindus that, if revealed, surprise foreigners.

The Untouchables are beaten for putting on clothes of good quality. They have been whipped because they used utensils made of metal like copper, etc. Their houses are burnt because they have brought land under cultivation. They are beaten for putting on the sacred thread. They are beaten for refusing to carry dead animals and eat carrion, or for walking through the village with socks and shoes on, or for not bowing down before the caste Hindus, for taking water in a copper pot while going out to the fields to ease themselves.

Recently an instance has been noted where the Untouchables were beaten for serving chapattis at a dinner party. You must have heard and some of you must have experienced such atrocities. Where beating is not possible, you are aware of how the weapon of boycott is used against us. You all know how the caste Hindus has made daily life unbearable by prohibiting your men from entering the village. But very few of you have realised why all this happens. What is the root of their tyranny? To me, it is very necessary that we understand it.

The instances have nothing to do with the virtues and vices of an individual. This is not a feud between two rival men. The problem of untouchability is a matter of class struggle. It is a struggle between caste Hindus and the Untouchables. This is not a matter of doing injustice against one man. This is a matter of injustice being done by one class against another. This struggle is related to social status. This struggle indicates how one class should keep its relationship with another class of people.

The struggle starts as soon as you start claiming equal treatment with others. Had it not been so, there would have been no struggle over simple reasons like serving chapatis, wearing good quality clothes, putting on the sacred thread, fetching water in a metal pot, sitting the bridegroom on the back of a horse, etc. In these cases you spend your own money. Why then do the high-caste Hindus get irritated? The reason for their anger is very simple. Your behaving on par with them insults them. Your status in their eyes is low; you are impure, you must remain at the lowest rung.

Then along will they allow you to live happily? The moment you cross your level the struggle starts. The instances given also prove one more fact. Untouchability is not a short or temporary feature; it is a permanent one. To put it straight, it can be said that the struggle between the Hindus and the Untouchables is a permanent phenomenon. It is eternal, because the high-caste people believe that the religion, which has placed you at the lowest level of the society, is itself eternal. No change according to time and circumstances is possible. You are at the lowest rung of the ladder today. You shall remain lowest forever.

This means the struggle between Hindus and Untouchables shall continue forever. How you will survive through this struggle is the main question. And unless you think it over, there is no way out. Those who desire to live in obedience to the dictates of the Hindus, those who wish to remain their slaves, they do not need to think over the problem. But those who wish to live a life of selfrespect and equality will have to think over this.

DALIT HISTORIOGRAPHY

There is a significant scholarship coming up from Dalits in writing their own history. Their intervention is crucial in many ways. The history writing came along with the dalit struggles. In search of their identity, they dig the past in all possible ways. In writing of dalit history or interrogating dominant history from Dalit point of view, Dalit scholars/ activists/ writers may not be systematic, argumentative but are striking in their attack and provide an alternative forcefully. One may find many missing links in the construction of the dalit history or questioning the dominance from Dalit point of view.

They are in vernacular languages. These writings are often reproduction of oral narratives. Some of them are in the form of autobiographies. In this connection this document presents historical claims of dalits of Telugu society as a case study. The word 'Dalit' in telugu society become familiar with Dalit Mahasabha, which came into existence with Karamchedu massacre of 1985. Dalit movement had taken roots at popular level and oppressed Dalit masses started questioning the dominance and hegemony of the upper caste people. The newly emerged dalit middle class, however small, played a role in production of knowledge systems in the fields of literature, culture, politics, philosophy and history. Dalit movement provided the spectacle through which they could uphold the culture, history and politics of the lower caste. Dalit intelligentsia is making serious attempt to construct their cultured past and history as against the upper caste Brahminical hegemony. The literature coming in the name of Dalit, shattered the existing canons of Telugu society.

As a Telugu Dalit writer G. Kalyana Rao (2000) felt, 'We have to dig a lot and simultaneously bury a lot.' The Dalit intelligentsia is active in this mission to strengthen the on going Dalit struggles. Of course, within Dalit movement, there exists a variety of political positions. However, caste becomes a reference point in understanding history, philosophy, culture and politics, with active Dalit struggles. From the trained historians, though negligible, there exists significant number of historical writings. Kancha Ilaih's Why I'm Not a Hindu (Nenu Hindunetlaitha in telugu) is a prominent intervention from Dalit-Bahujan perspective against Brahmanism. It is a critique on hindutva, culture, politics and economics from a sudra perspective. He reflected on these issues from his social experience. He argues that dalit-bahujans have different food habits, culture, customs, and religious practices, which are unique, democratic and different from brahminical Hinduism.

Dalit bahujans culture emerged from their involvement in labour. They are productive classes and so their culture is real, natural and authentic. The Dalitbahujan Understanding of Telugu culturtal and Literary History, he argues that construction of history taking place from two opposite and conflicting views: the Brahminical and dalit bahujan. He questions us to whether the brahminical writings (based on Sanskrit language, Sanskrit texts, and Sanskrit lipi, etc.) should really be called history at all? 'For brahminical people, history is a march of god on earth; where as for dalit bahujans, history is the march of people (that is, the dalit bahujan majority) on the earth.' Further, the dalit bahujans history mostly lies in folklore/oral tradition. The language of this folklore is far richer, humanitarian and democratic-perhaps that is the reason why it has been relegated to the margins by the brahminical historians. On the other hand, productive castes had their own Telugu language, but it never figured in the brahminical writings. Though it is in autobiographical form, the arguments directly go against the dominant forms of knowledge systems. A. Sayanarayana, Professor in History made an attempt to write history from dalit bahujan perspective in his book Dalits and Upper Caste, Essays in Social History.

He tried to construct dalit history by using the alternative literary discourses of dalits which are marginalized in the mainstream literary discourses. Y. Chinna Rao's doctoral dissertation Dalit Movement in Andhra, 1900-1950 captures the dalit struggles of colonial times. This tried to establish that alternative struggles of dalits in colonial times rarely found mention in both colonialism and nationalism. To focus on the specific nature of resistance and struggles of dalits against the dominance, he uses the framework of James Scott's 'Weapons of the Weak.' The major argument is that contemporary dalit struggles are in continuation of these struggles. In other words, charging the mainstream historians for not documenting the dalit struggles.

'Dalit movements have not become a part of Indian historiography yet, even though their study is of immense importance in view of their inherent radical democratic identity and their interrelation with contemporary movements. The available studies on dalit movement in India suffer from lack of historical and written documentation, leaving scope for ambiguity.' Moreover, there are attempts from the conscious Dalit activists also. From late nineties, there are considerable numbers of books on history. Katti Padma Rao, Sanskrit teacher and activist in rationalist movement turned to a leader of Dalit Mahasabha. In the process of his active involvement in dalit struggles reflected on many issues in relation to the liberation of dalit community. His Dalitula Charitaconstructs the history of the dalits based on the sources of Sanskrit texts. His Caste and Alternative Culture makes an attempt to construct history and struggles of the untouchable and sudra castes against Aryan –Brahmin-Hindu culture. He explores this theme from ancient times to contemporary times. He is even critical of the communist movement of contemporary times led by the upper castes like Reddy and Kamma communities and their silence on the issue of annihilation of caste. He explains the philosophical background of dalit movement. The matriarchal culture, Carvakas materialism, Budhist sangha philosophy and humanism are the foundation of dalit movement. He argues that in the Indian sub- continent, the makers of history are the dalit people.

Ancient Indian culture was matriarchal in character, founded on the principle of equality. The Aryans after arriving in India established Hindu kingdom and tried the culture of the ancient indigenous Indians. They introduced casteism, patriarchal culture and politico-economic dictatorship. Suppressing all the indigenous castes, they propagated their own Hindu culture in Indian society, and forcefully implemented Hindu way of life. Dr. Vijaya Bharathicame out with three books on Puranalu-Kulavyavastha. She has critically evaluates the puranas and their role in protection of caste system.

Though the puranas are not considered as history, but are intend to cultivate ideal society to control the different social groups. On analysing the story of Satya Harischandra, though this story seems to uphold the truth, but its purpose is essentially to consolidate the varna system and controlling the women in the name of pativratyam. She made her analysis based on Markandeya puranam, skandha puranam and Harischandropakyanam. 'If we observe the stories and the constructed ideology around the avataramurthi's of different yugas, the whole effort is to implement and introduce the sanctions of the varna systems in the lives of ordinary people.

Dharmasamsthapanam means varna dharma samsthapanam. The stories of the shatchakravarties (Pururudu, Purukutsudu, Harischandrudu, Sagarudu, Naludu, Karyaveeryarjunudu) are made popular because they stand as the symbols in protection of varnadharma. In a similar fashion the mythological god Rama represents the dominant brahminical system. Bonigala Rama Rao made an attempt to trace out history of untouchables. In his Antarani Jathula Charitra, he tried to establish that untouchable communities are not only the sons of the soil but also earlier ruling communities. Though weakened economically, they are protecting their culture and social ideology.

He proposes an arugument that the names of the untouchable communities are nothing but the relics of the vanished kingdoms. To construct the history of untouchable communities he relied mostly on historical texts, books of linguistics and inscription rather puranas and epics. He further wrote Mala Kannamaneedu and Adiguruvu Acharya Chandala. The writings of Kathi padma rao and Bonigala Ramarao have influenced the later writings on the history of dalits – this includes Dr. K. Lakshmi Narayana who tried to explore history of dalits in the Aadibharatteyula Charitra (from 2500 BC to 2500 AD) and Pilli Rambabu's Adi Baratheeyulu.

Apart from these, Dalit literature as a creative intervention of dalit intelligentsia played a significant role in constructing dalit history. The historical consciousness is very much internalized in the structure of their literary narratives. The importance of dalit writings lies in authentic representation of the community by questioning the existing brahminical and progressive writings. The protest against the caste and class dominance is central to the dalit writings. Mostly, Dalit literary writings are autobiographical reflections of the community.

Dalit writings are conscious effort of bridging the oral and written cultures. Dalit writings often invoke social memory as the source of their knowledge system. This also helps in maintaining the historical continuity. Dalit literature enriched with content and description of dalit struggles for human dignity. There has been constant effort from dalit writers in translating the condemned life styles and practices of marginalized people into symbols of protest and pride. In the process of writing their own history, they thoroughly interrogated the existing histories of dominant caste/class groups in their literary writings. As Dalit writer, Sivasagar marking the assertion of dalits in writing their own history against the brahminical history centred around advaita of Sankara. With a smile on his face/Shambhuka is slaying rama/ with his axe/Ekalavya is cutting drona's thumb away/with his small feet/ Bali is sending Vamana down to pathala/ With needles in his eyes/ and lead in is ears/Manu, having cut his tongue is seen rolling on the graveyard/standing on the merciless sword of time/and roaring with rage/The chandala is seen hissing four hounds on Sankaracharya/ Oh..!/ The history that is occurring today/Is the most Chandala history.

DEMYSTIFYING THE CONCEPT OF DALIT

Origin and Definition

The concept is believed to be originated in the 1930s in journalistic writings according to Michael, and as a Hindi and Marathi translation of 'Depressed Castes', the term the British used according to Webster. The term, however, was chosen, according to Zelliot, by the group itself and is used proudly. In her view, 'Dalits' implies those who have been broken, ground down by those above them in a deliberate and active way. There is in the word itself an inherent denial of pollution, karma and justified caste hierarchy. However, according to Massey, 'dalit' more as a concept and in its present use has its seed in the writings of two great Indian personalities, Phule and Ambedkar. He believes that Phule in his writings used the title Shudra-Ati-Shudra for Dalits and he knew it was a Brahmin conspiracy against Shudra-Ati-Shudra (both being Indigenous people) to divide them into two castes or classes in order to make them their slaves.

Similarly, he says that for the 'Dalit', Ambedkar used the title 'untouchable' (achuta) in his writings. Guru also explains that the category dalit was first used by Ambedkar himself in his fortnightly Bahishkruit Bharat. He (Ambedkar) defined it comprehensively: Dalithood is a kind of life condition which characterises the exploitation, suppression and marginalisation of dalits by the social, economic, cultural and political domination of the upper caste brahminical order.

But Massey makes one point clear that is many Dalits today prefer to be called Dalits (name self-given) as it is not merely a name or title but has become an expression of hope for them in recovering their past self-identity.

Shah however argues that with the change in market structure in the post-independence and the rise in education among small sections of Harijans, small entrepreneurs and a white-collar middle class have emerged among the Scheduled Castes. These have become militant and call the Scheduled Castes the 'Dalits' that is a poor and exploited class.

Oommen, on the other hand, argues that the Dalits suffer from cumulative domination (socio-cultural, economic and political) and multiple deprivation. He has however excluded the section of the 'Harijan bourgeoisie' among the SCs from this category since they are economically well-off and politically privileged (even though not entirely emancipated from socio-cultural oppression). Thus, in his view, only those Scheduled Castes who have low ritual status, appalling poverty and powerlessness fit into the definition of Dalits.

Contradiction, Multiple Terms and Heterogeneity

According to Guru, the term 'dalit' is not accepted by all those who belong to this category. It has faced criticism, particularly by the urban, educated middle class dalits, as socially regressive, derogatory and hence undesirable. Thus, they look at the term with disdain. Guru also states that a small section of neo-Buddhists rejects the concept of dalit which includes all the oppressed classes and prefers to be called Buddhists and tries to restrict it to those who suffer from untouchability and other social handicaps. Some even prefer to confine the term Dalit only to Ambedkarite Buddhists, but for many others, Dalit is not necessarily only Buddhist but also all socially oppressed persons in general and untouchables in particular.

There is also a section of the community, according to Guru, who prefer bahujan over both the Buddhist as well as dalit categories. However, the problem with such a formulation is that it neglects the dialectical relationship between 'dalit' and 'bahujan' which has a bearing on the formation of the dalit category and its marriage with bahujan. Similarly, speaking on the notion of harijan vis-à-vis dalit, Guru argues that the category harijan is artificially imposed on the untouchables and is an ascribed one as it does not flow from the untouchables' own experiences. Given its divine association, it is inadequate for capturing the specific realities since it also replaces the need for internal critique. On the other hand, the category dalit derives its epistemic and political strength from the material social experience of the community which renders it authentic and dynamic rather than passive and rigid. Ambedkar also said that even though Gandhiji wanted assimilation of the untouchables with the mainstream, he made it impossible by his euphemism, Harijan. In his own words, '... such assimilation was not possible from the new name, Harijan given to the untouchables... his new name counteracted assimilation and made it impossible'. However, in Sharma's view, historically dalits imply not a structure, but a processual phenomenon emanating from a politico-legal entity known as 'Scheduled Castes' and the latter being an outcome of the preceding moral-political entity which Gandhiji referred as Harijan. What I believe is that the concept of 'Harijan' has to be seen in its proper historical context.

In the context of various dehumanizing terms such as Achhuta, Dhedh, Chandal being used for the Dalits, Gandhiji's euphemism did provide some respectability even though only in name. What is important to understand is the evolutionary framework and the specific context and time in which 'Harijan' appeared. Today almost all conscious and educated Dalits are scornful of this notion and reject it out rightly. So, now it is imperative to discard this notion in the context of contemporary discussion on dalit issues though it will be unavoidable in the context of a historical account of such issues. However, Dalits in general do not have any problem with the constitutional concept of SCs. They are relatively comfortable with it even though the notion, they believe, reminds themselves and others about who they really are and where their social space is.

However, it must be borne in mind that the category 'Dalit' is not a homogeneous category. It involves a number of castes. According to Shah, they have internal hierarchy. Neo-Buddhist Mahars look down upon with contempt on the other Scheduled Castes who have not converted to Buddhism. There is also conflict between the Mahars and the Mangs. In this connection, Michael Moffatt argues that the cultural system of Indian untouchables does not distinctively question or revalue the dominant social order.

Rather it continuously recreates among untouchables a microcosm of the larger system. Even Ambedkar realized that 'graded inequality' within the untouchables was a hurdle in their emancipation from their controls of the caste Hindus. Similarly Shah argues that there are middle class Dalits and the poor Dalits whose problems and interests are of different kinds. While for the former, the problem of identity and reservation is important, the latter is grappled with the problem of poverty and exploitation.

Webster's Critical Analysis

Webster's critical analysis of two of the prevailing ways to define 'Dalits'-class analysis and communal analysis-holds much significance here to simplify the understanding of the concept. Those using a class analysis of Indian society subsume Dalits within such class or occupational categories as peasants, agricultural labour, factory workers, students and the like. This can be seen in most Marxist historical writings, the sub-altern studies volumes and to a lesser degree, in the Dalit Panther Manifesto. In fact, the concept was made popular by the Dalit Panthers in the 1970s. This class analysis is fraught with serious problems, according to Webster, since it not only fails to take account of the basic contradiction and oppression of the Dalits but also hides these by using categories which diverts attention away from them. By their own admission, Webster argues, Ambedkar as well as Jagjivan Ram indicated the existence of such contradictions.

Similarly, those using a communal analysis of caste tend to view only those untouchables as Dalits who remain Hindus by religion. If they convert to another religion, then they cease to be Dalits. Webster argues that this view is at serious odds with the realities uncovered by studies of castes among Christians and Muslims. Thus, he says that at least for Dalits, the stigma of untouchability and its accompanying disabilities based on caste are an Indian rather than Hindu phenomenon. And '... these were and still are the defining characteristics of a Dalit even if a Dalit moves up in a social class or changes religion.

AFFIRMATIVE ACTION TO HELP THE DALIT IN INDIA

Dalit is a Sanskrit word meaning that which like a grain of peas or lentils has been ground into coarse pieces, or that which has been stamped under foot. For me it best describes the condition of utter degradation, poverty and servitude to which upper caste Hindu society has over centuries reduced an entire community or, better still, a whole conglomeration of jatis, through an astute use of the notions of pollution and karma.

Besides, it is the word preferred by members of these jatis to denote them. To call them untouchables is to suggest that other than the stigma of untouchability these people suffer no other disadvantages.

For similar reasons leaders of dalits have never quite liked the name Harijan given to them by Gandhi. Expressions like scheduled castes or depressed classes, being neutral bureaucratic nomenclatures, bespeak a prudishness which is out of place when discussing a social phenomenon which must be faced frontally and removed completely, if Indian society is to become truly democratic and egalitarian..

Discrimination against the lowest castes—in fact castes lying beyond the pale of traditional Hindu *varna* system—engaged the attention of Hindu social reformers and Dalit leaders since around the middle of the 19th century. To a limited extent the colonial administration, which took a first tentative step in 1850 in the form of the Removal of Caste Disabilities Act, also took interest in helping the lowest castes. The need to help the dalits and scheduled tribes pull themselves out of their economic and social backwardness thus came to be recognized by Indian political and intellectual leadership years before the republican constitution of India outlawed all forms of discrimination based on caste.

The constitution provided for the reservation of 15 % of the seats in all representative bodies in states and at the federal level for what were called scheduled castes for a period of fifteen years and enabled the adoption of a similar reservation policy for fifteen years in the case of employment by government. A law banishing untouchability was enacted and took its final shape in the Protection of Civil Rights Act of 1976. The reservations policy, both in the matter of representation in the federal parliament and state legislative bodies and of government employment, has been renewed every ten years since 1965.

Parliament appointed a body, the Gokur Committee, to make recommendations about the revision of the list of castes that would benefit from the reservations policy. The Committee's report submitted in 1965 never received parliamentary approval, a constitutional requirement, and lapsed due to the dissolution of the lower house of parliament in 1967. The 1997 'Report of the Expert Committee for Specifying Criteria for the Identification of Socially Advanced

Persons Among the Socially and Educationally Backward Classes' was not acted upon. There have been no other significant moves to consider modifying the extent of reservations for dalits in any manner, with the exception perhaps of a conference organized by the Congress Party led Government of Madhya Pradesh in early 2002 which produced the Bhopal Document. I shall return to it by and by.

Over the years governments in the states and at the federal level have designed a whole range of preferential policies covering many sectors ranging from education, health care, drinking water to housing. Marc Galanter whose 1984 book, 'Competing Equalities: Law and the Backward Classes' is probably the most detailed and thorough examination yet of India's affirmative action programmes, makes a quick listing of a large number, though not all, of such programmes. Since 1984, many other programmes have been added. With the exception of the reservation policy, these diverse measures do not attract much attention beyond the time of their adoption by governments. Also lacking is a systematic evaluation of the quality of implementation and the impact of all these programmes: the annual reports of the Commissioner for Scheduled Castes and Tribes are little more than compilations of statistics about budgetary allocations and numbers covered by different programmes, but mainly about reservations..

As Marc Galanter says in his book, 'If only one policy area is to be developed at length, government employment has to be an obvious choice, for in a number of ways, it is the paradigm case of compensatory discrimination. It relies on the reservation device as the core of the programme; it is promoted by both state and central governments; policy in this area is made with due deliberation by informed agencies; the various groups of interested participants are attentive and responsive; the actors have recurrently sought judicial intervention. It is an area that in the eyes of proponents and opponents occupies a central symbolic position in envisioning the compensatory discrimination policy…'As a consequence, more than any other device of compensatory discrimination it is the policy of reserving government jobs for disadvantaged classes—the definition of disadvantaged classes has become wider over the years—which gets discussed the most. The scheme of reserving a proportion of seats in legislative bodies for members of scheduled castes and tribes in contrast attracts attention only at the time of the now decennial renewals and then recedes from public attention. It has also proved to be a more potent device for the empowerment of the scheduled castes and tribes as a body than any other by ensuring the presence of their representatives in legislative bodies and in governments who occasionally speak for the social group they represent. At the minimum, their presence in legislative bodies and governments acts as a brake on excesses against their communities in a society which has yet to fully embrace the need to eradicate discrimination against and oppression of dalits and tribal groups.

Even though in the beginning there was resistence to the policy of reservations for the scheduled castes and tribes—and there was resistence, for it required constant prodding from the concerned departments of Government of India and from the law courts to ensure the minimum required reservation of places in government departments—over time it came to be accepted by liberal opinion and at least acquiesced in by others in Indian society at large.

Indian society had also by and large come to accept that even though meant initially to be a temporary measure, job reservation for dalits was going to continue indefinitely. The debate over the reservation of government jobs reopened when Government of India decided in 1990 to implement the 1980 recommendations of the Mandal Commission concerning 'other backward classes' (OBC's, in the jargon used in the discourse on this subject). There were bloody clashes in 1990 in different parts of the country as there had been earlier in some states when the Mandal recommendations were sought to be implemented.

The Mandal dispensation was not only contested but never acquired the same legitimacy in the eyes of liberal Indian intelligentsia as compensatory discrimination for dalits had, for three reasons. The first was the not unfounded belief that the decision to implement the Mandal recommendations was born out of political expediency rather than conviction. Secondly, there was the perception that most of the intended beneficiaries were not the economically most deprived groups but prosperous intermediate caste farmers and traders, sometimes more prosperous than the poorer among the higher castes. Thirdly, the Commission's own rationale for recommending reservations for other backward castes looked ersatz. It said: 'It is not our contention that by offering a few thousand jobs to OBC candidates we shall be able to make 52 per cent of India's population as forward. But we must recognise that an essential part of the battle against social backwardness is to be fought in the minds of the people. In India government service has always been looked upon as a symbol of prestige and power. By increasing the representation of OBC's in government services, we give them an immediate feeling of participation in governance(sic) of this country. When backward caste(sic) candidate becomes a collector or superintendent of police, the material benefits accruing from his position are limited to the members of his family only. But the psychological spin off of this phenomenon is tremendous, the entire community of that backward class candidate feels socially elevated. Even when no tangible benefits flow to the community at large, the feeling that it has its 'own man' in the corridors of power acts as a morale booster.

'The additional reservations brought in by the Mandal recommendations were seen as an attempt by politicians at creating a base of electoral support among intermediate castes. Even those political parties which had initially been lukewarm towards the Mandal recommendations or opposed to them came in course of time to accept and support them. Since the implementation of the Mandal recommendations politicians and political parties have periodically made ever more bizarre, opportunistic, even risible suggestions for reservations for members of upper castes, Muslims or Dalit Christians, forgetting the original rationale for reservations for dalits and tribal groups.

There is no evidence to suggest that anyone in the political class is tormented by the thought that for as many as 49.5 % of the population—this proportion would have been higher if the Supreme Court of India had not placed a ceiling of 50% on all reservations—there should be a departure from the fundamental democratic principle of equality of opportunity for all.

Since, as has been pointed out above, there has been no systematic evaluation of the impact of the various affirmative action programmes including the reservations policy, it is not known whether fortyfive years of job reservations for dalits have created a significant Dalit middle class capable of and interested in speaking for and helping other dalits or whether on the contrary those dalits who have benefited from reservations have been content to integrate themselves into the rest of the middle class, happy to be able to enjoy and preserve what must be privileged existence in the eyes of other poorer dalits, happy also to ensure that their children also enjoy the advantages of reservation and other affirmative action programmes. To take the former or the latter to be the case is most often a matter of one's *parti pris.*

Criticism of the reservations policy, never entirely absent, has become generally sharper since the adoption of the Mandal recommendations. Most of the criticism has come from intellectuals arguing from theoretical perspectives or from members of upper castes. It is difficult to deny the force of all of the critics' arguments Some have argued that the indefinite continuation of reservations, accentuating existing divisions in society, have had a largely deleterious effect. Others say that the benefits of reservations have tended to be appropriated by a relatively advaced but small section among the dalits. Yet others have commented on the inadequacy of reservations of government jobs as an instrument of affirmative action.

André Beteille in a 1991 essay says:' I take it for granted that policies for the redress of severe social and economic disadvantages are in themselves desirable. Such policies have to aim at different sectors of society and at the widest possible base.

An obvious field for the application of preferential policies is that of education where the maximum attention should be devoted to primary and secondary education which develop the base on which the success of higher education depends. Other fields for which preferential policies may be designed include those of child care, health and housing.' The attention that the policy of reservations in government employment receives has led to the relative neglect of these other areas in which effective action, preferential or otherwise, is likely to produce greater, wider and more substantial welfare.

In the Bhopal Document it is said that the reservation policy in government and government corporations can at best benefit six or seven million, leaving some 175 million Dalit individuals untouched by it. The authors of the document call for more effective action for the upliftment of the Dalit and propose a five point programme for the country to consider and adopt:

> *"(1) Diversity or SC/ST's due representation in all public institutions of India, whether universities or academic or autonomous or registered bodies. Those institutions which do not abide by the principle of Affirmative Action, must lose recognition and state funding.*
>
> *(2) All private industry/corporate houses must accept Diversity in workforce immediately.*
>
> *(3) Every government and private organization must implement Supplier Diversity from socially disadvantaged businesses and Dealership Diversity in all goods and services.*

(4) Every SC/ST child must be given quality[and] free education at State's expense. And every English medium school must implement Diversity in Admissions.

(5) In cases of atrocities against SC/ST's, a system of collective punishment has to be evolved as oppressors enjoy community support and protection and escape the law."

Without attempting to engage in an examination of this agenda, I shall note in passing that not only some of the vocabulary but also some of the ideas(points 2&3) from the discourse about affirmative action programmes in the USA have been included without due examination of their practicability, particularly if the authors have legislation in mind.

Another novel idea(point 5) amounts to the derogation of a basic principle of law that only the person committing a crime must be punished, in all cases where upper caste groups are suspected of having committed atrocities against dalits so that another group may enjoy to the full its right to equality. Other than recent talk about compelling private businesses to reserve jobs for dalits, nothing has so far been done to adopt the recommendations contained in the Bhopal document.

But the Bhopal document is remarkable in the sense that it is an indirect pointer to the very considerable disadvantages and oppression still faced by dalits, half a century after the adoption of an official affirmative action agenda to help them. Numerous episodic or impressionistic accounts suggest that affirmative action programmes for dalits have been no more than partial successes in alleviating the Dalit's condition. The limited success may be due to apathy or even resistence among upper caste bureaucrats who administer these programmes or it may be due to the general inefficiency and incompetence of the machinery of the state, but it certainly explains why the Dalit has by and large remained where he has always been.

IMPACT OF THE REFORMS ON DALITS AS A DISADVANTAGED SOCIAL GROUP

The social disadvantage suffered by the dalits in India was taken note of in the Constitution of India, which was drafted under the chairmanship of Dr. Ambedkar-a person who had spearheaded the most momentous anti-caste movement of the depressed classes. It provided the dalits with many safeguards, *viz,*

- Social, educational, cultural and religious safeguards,
- Economic safeguards,
- Political safeguards,
- Safeguards for employment.

The free market ethos unleashed by the Reforms, conceptually can neither confirm to the democratic spirit of the Indian Constitution of 'one vote, one value', nor can it coexist with the system of positive discrimination embodied in these safeguards.

For, the market grants moneyed person more value, and overtly believes in the jungle law of 'might is right'. To a large extent, the primary motivation behind these Constitutional provisions was liberal democratic aspirations that characterised the freedom movement. However, these aspirations and the initial ideological zeal of the founding fathers withered away in no time and what survived was its utilitarian dimension for the electoral politics. The sorry state of the executive compliance with these Constitutional provisions amply bears out the fangs of the intrinsically iniquitous Indian society.

The Reforms will bring a kind of legitimacy to this attitudinal resistance of the upper castes and classes to the movements for change by the downtrodden. These safeguards will stand eroded as the Reforms gain in momentum. Influence of the Reforms is bound to be all pervasive. However, only a few issues of importance to the dalit masses have been picked up for discussion here.

Reservation and Financial Assistance in Education Institutions

Reservation in the educational institutions and the financial assistance in the form of scholarships and freeships constitute perhaps the most important factor in the development scheme for dalits. For, it is primarily responsible to make the basic input of education available and affordable to them.

Without education, all the constitutional safeguards including the reservation in services would be infructuous. Under this scheme the dalit students whose parental income is below a specified level, get freeship, reservation in admissions to all the colleges getting grants-in-aid from the government, and scholarships.

Without this assistance, even today, it would be difficult even for the second-generation educated dalits to send their children to school. The Reforms have already resulted in freezing the grants to many institutions and in stagnating, if not lowering, the expenditure on education. The free market has entered the educational sphere in a big way.

Commercialisation of education is no more a mere rhetoric; it is now the established fact. Commercial institutions offering specialised education that signify essential input from utilitarian viewpoint, have come up in a big way from cities to small towns.

Their product-prices are not only based on the demand-supply consideration in their market segment but also are manipulated by their promotional strategies. In a true spirit of globalisation, many foreign universities are invading the educational spheres through hitherto unfamiliar strategic alliances with non-descript commercial agencies, of course at hefty dollar equivalent prices.

Many elite institutions like IIMs and IITs, suddenly facing fund crunch had to resort to raising their fee structure and other prices many fold. They were already beyond the reach of the dalits. When they eventually turn self-financing, their prices would be benchmarked against their international counterparts, which any way would be affordable to the same top market segment that constitutes the focus of all the Reform-talk. As the job markets become acutely competitive, owing to a sharp decline in job opportunities, the polarisation between the elite and commoner would also sharpen.

Various kinds of price barriers would be erected to thwart the entry of downtrodden to the portals of development. Even the sphere of primary education the coverage of which has been so miserably inadequate as to leave out multitude of children in villages as illiterate, could not remain unaffected, notwithstanding its already existing divide between the vernacular and English schools.

Corporatisation has entered this arena, transforming the education into an enterprise for profits. The quality of input these expensive schools will provide will benchmark the products in the contracting job markets. Even today, because of preponderance of the English language in business circles, the divide between village and towns is almost complete in the field of education.

It is so difficult for a village student, educated in vernacular medium to compete with his convent educated (now an understatement!) counterpart in cities and towns. If this is the situation of general village population, the plight of the dalits who besides being the poorest of the village population carry additional burden of social discrimination, is indeed a worrisome matter.

Despite several kinds of State assistance, the dalits are plagued with alarming rate of school dropouts. This may be explained out as much by the need for dalit children to supplement their meagre family incomes for making the two ends meet as also by the erosion of their faith that education could be the instrument to change the pathetic course of their lives. This sense of alienation is going to grow with the progress of the Reforms, giving rise to increasing lumpenisation and criminalisation of the dalit youth.

Atrocities

The caste atrocities are an integral feature of the dalit life. The government machinery keeps on collecting their statistics year after year and issues it in a report of its Commissioner for the SCs and the STs (now the National Commission for the SCs and the STs). There are at least three Articles (15,17 and 23) in the Constitution of India, which seek to mitigate the evil.

To give effect to these Constitutional provisions the following acts also have been in operation:

- The Untouchability (Offences) Act, 1955, later amended and retitled as the Protection of Civil Rights Act, 1955
- The Scheduled Castes and Scheduled Tribes (Prevention of Atrocities Act) 1989 and The Bonded Labour System (Abolition) Act, 1976

Despite this, the statistics of the registered atrocities read like a balance sheet of a blue chip company with consistent rise every successive year. It is pertinent to remember that owing to the dependency relationship of the dalits with the perpetrators of atrocities, not every occurrence of the atrocity gets registered.

Rather, it can be safely assumed that behind each registered atrocity over ten atrocity cases go unreported. As per the latest statistics, every day nearly 50 cases of atrocities are registered all over the country. Over three dalit women are raped and six are disabled on each day round the year. The National Commission analysed the causes of each of the atrocities in a sample of 45 cases.

The analysis shows that out of 45 cases 13 are clearly attributable to the economic reasons. The balance can also be explained out by some kind of weakness of the dalits. Coupled with the weakness of the dalits, their growing assertiveness and the refusal to submit to the casteist dictates of the village lords, rebellion assimilated through the Ambedkarian struggle and the process of general awareness, also cause atrocities to increase.

Atrocities are basically a rude reassertion of power over the powerless by the powerful in the wake of threat.

It is thus an expression of insecurity by the powerful who perceive power slipping their hand. In the pre-colonial closed loop production system of a typical village since, everyone followed his or her calling under the divine authority of religion, there were no atrocities of the kind we experience in the saner age of globalisation today. If any one questioned or defied this system, the religious code provided for the punishment. In this scheme, it was more important to fortify the religious control on populace than physically taming them to comply. Although the emphasis was on enslavement of mind, physical punishment did exist as a contingency measure. Atrocities on the dalits today are in essence a physical punishment for their act of forsaking the bondage. The physical punishments or atrocities presuppose material power in the hands of perpetrators of atrocities.

Not only that the dalits lit the fire of anger in materially powerful upper castes by defying their notion of caste authority but also they added fuel to it by coming in competition for partaking scarce resources. The emergence of the land owning middle castes during the post-independence development process who at the one end replaced the traditional upper castes and wore their mantle of superiority but who at the other end found itself in competition with the dalits for resources like education and employment moreover led to accentuation of atrocities.

These middle castes lacked the cunning and sophistication of the upper castes and enraged themselves into physical response on slightest provocation. They could not stomach the dalits who were utterly dependent on them in the village setting asserting their human rights or competing with them on equal platform for scarce resources and eventually winning them away in some cases with the help of reservations. This commonplace experience is amplified by the vested interests of the ruling classes to make out all the dalits as robbers of the share of these middle castes. Thus, the essential ingredients for atrocities on the dalits can be identified as the existence of material power in the hands of perpetrators of atrocities, enduring sense of social superiority, increasing scarcity of resources, and growing popularization of the masses.

The directional impact of the Reforms on the atrocities on the dalits therefore can be inferred from the effect it would have on the existing dependency relationship in the villages that the dalits are engaged in with the powerful middle castes; on the caste system itself; on the availability of certain critical resources like jobs; health care, education etc.; and on the income distribution to the people. Atrocities are seen to occur where the dependency relationships are more pronounced. Villages, where the dalits as landless labourers depend upon landlords or rich farmers for their livelihood and where the traditional caste equations have a potential to yield economic surplus to the latter, provide ideal setting for atrocities. What impact would the new regime have on the socio-economic setting of Indian villages?

In face of it, this relationship cannot be altered till the dalits get land. Can the new regime afford this economic empowerment of the dalits? Can it, for instance, grant them land? The answer to all these questions will be in negative. Instead of talking about land reforms, the new regime will promote depeasantisation of Indian agriculture and consolidation of their holdings to start corporate farming. The capital influx in the rural areas will have natural ally in the rich farmers who have hegemonic hold over their areas. These parts will be the main beneficiaries of the improved terms of trade and capitalist development in the rural areas. The form that the new system may take will have the corporate structure of management and beneath the local vendors to provide various inputs and services.

While the rich farmers may assume the roles in this organisation as big or petty capitalist, the erstwhile landless labourers, marginal and small farmers shall together constitute the vast army of jobseekers. Although in notional terms the dalits might get rid of the old relationships, in reality they will still be dependent on their upper caste employers and certainly far more vulnerable than before.

With regards to impact of the economic Reforms on the caste system, the optimists and protagonists rely upon an old rhetoric of contradiction between feudalism and capitalism. The problem of annihilation of castes subsumes the change in the economic structure of the society in favour of the dalits and simultaneously a massive cultural movement to cleanse the minds of people of the caste notions and implant in its place the attitude of scientificism and virtue of liberty, equality and fraternity. Having seen that far from striving for economic equality, the Reforms are going to accentuate the existing inequalities, we can just examine its attitude towards the caste system. Will the Reforms promote the cultural movement for social equality? Does it have the wherewithal or motivation to catalyse struggles against the caste system?

The answers to these questions will also have to be in negative. The old rhetoric that capitalism will completely displace feudalism evokes positive expectations in some people about the prowess of the Reforms to annihilate castes. They would argue that the unbridled capitalism inherent in the Reforms is not compatible with any feudal structure and hence, implementation of the latter should remove these last blots of the caste system.

This simplistic thumb rule does not seem to be entirely validated by the developmental experience in India. The capitalism in India did not have to sprout through the bedrock of contradictions of feudalism as in Western Europe. It was planted in the fertile soil of the Indian feudalism. It has grown here on its nutrients.

The caste institution has defied the classical mould of feudalism by possessing many unique features, the most important being its resilience and adaptability.

What we experience in the mysterious growth of casteist politics today in India is precisely this ability of caste to adapt to changing times. The vast army of unemployed created by the developmental dynamics of the economic Reforms will need appropriate instruments for being controlled. The history bears ample testimony to the fact that whenever the people tended to come together with a common identity, the ruling classes have deftly used the time-tested weapon of castes to divide them.

Caste with its divisive potential will never be abandoned by any iniquitous regime. Its resilience may diffuse its contours but in its essence the caste would coexist with the Reforms. Privatisation and free market components of the Reforms are certainly impacting very adversely on the job situation. Many resources for public consumption shall also be scarce, as they would be produced in private enterprises for profits. They would be beyond the reach of common people. The impact of the Reforms in terms of increasing inequality has been established beyond doubt. Therefore, it can be inferred that the Reforms are potentially incapable to alleviate the pain of dalit masses. In sum, the atrocities on the dalits not only shall continue but may also be increased on account of the Reforms.

Socio-Cultural Suppression

Privatisation, which is the pivotal component of the Economic Reforms, will eliminate the very basis of the reservation policy in its present form. Since, the Reforms envisage minimalist role for the State, the space for the public domain and therefore for the reservations shall be greatly constricted. Reservation policy that represented the strategic response of liberal bourgeoisie to the aspirations of the dalit movement not quite unlike that of the colonial State at the time of its inception, was never swallowed by the civil society as rightful share of the dalits.

Its response initially reflected feudal magnanimity but once the first generation of the dalits started pouring out of the university portals into the job markets and claimed their share of pie, the reaction reflected feudal ferocity. The cunning of upper caste dominated State apparatus was evident in full measure in the manner the circulars proclaiming this policy were issued. Their convoluted language facilitated the unwilling bureaucracy to thwart it to the possible extent and judiciary to be labour over several years on what should have been so evident. The broad statistic on the implementation of this policy is enough to reveal the extent of prejudice of the State machinery as well as the civil society.

One of the provisions of the policy states that a dalit candidate qualifying without any concession should not be placed in the reserved seat, implying thereby that the percentage representation of the dalits in services or the educational institutions would be more than its prescribed value. But, over the five decades of implementation of the reservation policy it refuses to reach even the prescribed levels confirming the casteist notion still prevalent in society that the dalits are intrinsically an inferior specie. Despite this vile attitude of the establishment the reservations by far has been the sole contributor to advancement of the dalits. Privatisation is meant to directly hit it.

The benefits of the reservation policy to the dalit community have been more indirect than direct. Directly it benefited a few but indirectly it has created hope for advancement in the entire dalit population. This hope is already faded even when not much of privatisation has happened so far.

Their ideological amount is proving insufficient to resist it. There is a visible alienation, hopelessness and dejection setting in among them, which is getting manifested in increasing lumpenisation and criminalisation of dalit youth. This trend portends doom not only for the dalits but also for the entire oppressed people thirsting for some radical change. For, no radical change is possible in this country without dalit participation. The dalit consciousness formed over centuries of struggle is getting obliterated by the contemporary compulsions created by the Reforms. This phenomenon will catapult dalit masses back onto the vicious spiral of backwardness and fortify reactionary regimes in the similar proportion. This irrevocable loss would prove dearest to the dalits. While privatisation might set in slowly, the free market that it engenders much before could hit the dalits really harder through the legitimacy it grants to the base instincts against any emancipation project. For, the likely victims of the privatisation is still a miniscule part of the dalit population but the impact of these social would engulf entire dalit population.

Howsoever base the individual conviction might have been, the yesteryears had nearly forbidden them from surfacing openly. But, now the emergent free market is not only permitting but also promoting the vilest and venomous discourse against the dalits and the minorities. The vehemence with which the reservations or any kind of subsidy or any positive discrimination are derided today has a qualitatively distinctive edge. It is interesting to note that there is not yet a dalit voice raised against this fascist hegemony. It would indeed be difficult for the dalits to resist this onslaught. The emergence of right wing politics to national prominence is merely a corollary or consequence of this transformation. Social consequences of the economic miseries associated with these Reforms are indeed ominous for the dalits.

On one side they shall be subject to increasing popularization and on the other stand in competition with the multitude of masses in the job market. Increasing tendency of businesses to downsize, virtual abolition of the reservation system through privatisation, the strategies of flexibilisation and informalisation of labour; corporatisation and depeasantisation of farming etc. will release vast numbers of people to the job market. The resident caste prejudices in such situations will certainly get activated to the detriment of the dalits.

6

A Modern Day Manu

INDEPENDENCE

The new Viceroy Mountbatten studied the situation, went to London and returned to declare his Plan on 3/6/1947. There would be two Central govts, two Constituent Assemblies & plebiscites for Sylhet & North West Frontier Province (NWFP in short). Gandhi & Nehru threw their whole weight & forced the All India Congress Committee to accept division of the country. The truth seeker in Gandhi who had considered Pakistan a sin was dominated by the politician in him, the Socialists were neutral & the Hindu Sabhaites rattled in vain. At this juncture Travancore & Hyderabad declared that they would be independent when India became a Dominion on 15/8/1947. BRA advised them against the move.

In Delhi BRA riveted the attention of the Indian govt on the work of the boundary commission & said, 'If my fears come true & the boundary drawn by the commission is not a natural one, it needs no prophet to say that its maintenance will cost the Govt of India very dearly & it will put the safety / security of the people of India in jeopardy. I hope that the defence department will bestir itself & do its duty before it is too late'. This shows the heart of a patriot and yet the author of the Thoughts on Pakistan had preached that geographical conditions were not decisive in modern world technique! The British Parliament passed the Indian Independence Act on 15/7/1947. Because Bengal was partitioned many members lost their seats in the Constituent Assembly, BRA was one of them. He was now chosen by the Bombay Legislative Congress Party to fill the vacancy caused by Dr M R Jaykar. India's first Cabinet was to be formed. BRA was asked by Nehru whether he would join as Minister for Law, promised that a later stage he would be given the portfolio of Planning or Development. The Congress now desired rapprochement with BRA, BRA too forgot the past bickering, BRA agreed.

On August 29 the Constituent Assembly appointed a Drafting Committee with N Madhav Rao, Syed M Saadulah, Sir Alladi K, T T Krishnamachari & two others as members with BRA as its Chairman. It was a great achievement. Inspite of being Law Minister BRA kept close contact with the developments of Siddharth College, in a speech there he impressed upon youths the need for cultivating the art of speaking. In the first week of October BRA told a meeting of SC youths that independence had come so suddenly that he did not have a clear line of action before them at the moment. He stressed need for keeping the SC Federation in tact.

Results of Partition

Meanwhile the consequences of partition gave terrible shocks to the whole nation. 'The number of wounded & murdered is for a city like Delhi colossal'. BRA had proposed partition with transfer of populations of Hindus & Muslims from their respective zones to avoid civil war. Savarkar was prepared to face a civil war in order to preserve the unity of India but the Congress accepted partition plus massacres & with secular zest ridiculed the idea of transfer of population as they done with the idea of Pakistan till the dawn of Pakistan. Their policy worsened the plight of Hindus who were in the zone of Pakistan. Thus BRA's prophecy & fears were borne out to a letter!

The Untouchables being Hindus had to share the same fate. Jogendranath Mandal, law & labor member of Pakistan, who had asked the SC in Pakistan to look upon Jinnah as their savior was now rudely shaken from his dream. BRA was terribly upset, he complained that SC were not being allowed to come to India and were being forcibly converted to Islam, this was the case in Hyderabad state too. BRA advised his people, 'I would like to tell the SC who happen today to be impounded inside Pakistan to come to India by such means as may be available to them. Two is that it would be fatal for the SC to out their faith in Muslims or the Muslim League. It has become a habit with SC to look upon Muslims as their friends simply because they dislike the Hindus. This is a mistaken view'. He warned the SC of Hyderabad not to side with the Nizam and bring disgrace upon the community by siding with one who was the enemy of India. The whole nationalist press rang with praise for BRA.

During the past two months the Congress ministry of Bombay passed the Temple Entry Bill as a result of which the famous temple of Vithoba at Pandarpur, Kalaram Temple at Nasik amongst others were thrown open to SC Hindus. It was no mean achievement. BRA was busy with drafting the Constitution. How he worked & why he was called the Chief Architect of the Constitution can be seen from T T krishnamachari's speech excerpts, 'The burden of drafting the Constitution fell on BRA and I have no doubt that we are grateful to him for having achieved this task in a manner that is commendable'.

The terrific shocks of Partition were coming one after another. People showed profound disbelief in Gandhism. The Congress leaders were also chilled in their beliefs. Tandon declared that the Gandhian doctrine of non-violence was responsible for the division of India. 24 hours before the dawn of freedom people had stoned Gandhi's house in Calcutta. And Gandhi's fast started on 3/1/1948 for the reinstatement of the Muslims in their houses in Delhi, restoration of some mosques, five other reasons & as a sequel the Govt of India was forced to pay Pakistan 55 crores rupees had been loudly decried.

Amidst this confusion Godse shot dead Gandhi. While the world was shocked BRA did not react. Hard facts mentioned above & the old bitterness had not cooled down. He did not utter publicly a syllable on his tragedy nor did he issue any statement. In end February 1948 BRA completed the Draft Constitution & submitted it to the President of the Constituent Assembly.

Marriage + Constitution - After completing the drafting work BRA came to Bombay for treatment. He felt the need for a companion who would take care of him in his old age. In the hospital he met Dr Savita Kabir. Although he had resolved not to marry he now wanted an educated lady who knew cooking & was a medical practioner. As it was not possible to find such a lady among the SC he chose a Saraswat Brahmin lady. He married her on 15/4/1948.

In a speech in April 1948 he said that political power was the key to social progress & the SC could achieve their salvation if they captured power by organizing themselves into a third party & held the balance of power between the Congress & Socialists. He said that he had joined the Congress govt but not the Congress. He asked his followers to keep the SC organization in tact, as the Congress would be ruined in a couple of years.

In a Memorandum submitted to the Linguistic Commission on 14/10/1948 he said, 'A linguistic province produces what democracy needs, namely social homogeneity, & makes democracy work better than it would in a mixed province. There is no danger in creating linguistic provinces but danger lies in creating such provinces with the language of each province as its official language'. The latter would lead to creation of provincial nationalities. That would lead to the break up of India, it might end becoming Europe. BRA had presented an irrefutable case for a single official language for the Centre & States in the Constituent Assembly but none listened. He visualized a unitary Maharashtra province, said that Maharashtra & Bombay were interdependent.

BRA's great book, Untouchables was published. He said that Untouchables were broken men since those poor men could not give up beef eating & Buddhism they were treated as untouchables. He traces the origin of untouchability to 400 AD & said that is born out of the struggle for supremacy between Buddhism & Brahmanism. This book showed that BRA had the power of language & strength of thought and wielded a powerful pen. His writings had a peculiar fragrance of simplicity & directness.

The Draft Constitution was before the public for six months. As the last day dawned BRA introduced it on 4/11/1948 to the Constituent Assembly. In a grand, lucid & elaborate speech he brought out its salient features, the whole Assembly listening to him as one man. Replying then to the charges that there was nothing new in the Constitution, he said, 'More than a 100 years have rolled since the first constitution was drafted. Fundamentals of constitutions across the world are similar. That the constitution has produced a good part of the provisions of the Govt of India Act of 1935, I make no apologies. There is nothing to be ashamed of in borrowing. It involves no plagiarism'.

BRA praised - The whole Assembly paid tributes to BRA. On 12/11/1948 Article 11 was adopted declaring the abolition of Untouchability amidst great acclamation. BRA urged his people that progress of the community would depend on how they advanced in education. A battle royal was fought on the question of the national language, and Hindi with the Nagari script was declared to be the national language of India by a majority of one vote only. As Chairman of the Drafting Committee BRA had to explain in the Assembly many knotty points & niceties of law. He described Article 32 which defines the powers of Parliament & Supreme Court in respect of fundamental rights, as the very soul of the Constitution and the very heart of it. BRA worked hard inspite of ill health.

Not all members were pleased with the form of the Constitution. A member said that it had reduced the Provinces to the status of municipalities. Another felt that it had discarded the idea of decentralization propagated by Gandhi. Another thought that it had not provided for the ban on cow slaughter.

Amidst loud applause he rose on 25/11/1949 to reply to the debate on the third reading of the Constitution. Looking to the future of the country he observed, 'What perturbs me is the fact that India has lost her independence by the infidelity & treachery of her own people. In the invasion of Sind by M Kasim, the military commanders of King Dahir accepted bribes & refused to fight on the side of their king.

It was Jaichand who invited M Ghori to invade India & fight Prithiviraj Chauhan & promised him the help of himself / Solanki kings. When Shivaji was fighting the Mughals, the other Maratha noblemen & Rajput kings were fighting battles on the side of the Mughal emperors. When the British were fighting the Sikh rulers, their principal commandment sat silent & did not help save the Sikh kingdom. In 1857 when a large part of India had declared a war of independence against the British, the Sikhs stood & watched as silent spectators. Will history repeat itself?'

He then turned to the ways of maintaining democracy. He said that the first thing to do was to hold fast to the constitutional methods of achieving their social & economic objectives & abandon the methods of civil disobedience, non cooperation & satyagraha, for those methods were nothing but the grammar of anarchy. Another danger he felt arose from hero worship. The third things people must do to safeguard Indian democracy was that they must not be content with pure political democracy & they must make it a social & economic democracy. In the end he appealed to the Indians to be a nation in the social & psychological sense of the word by discarding castes which brought about separation in social life & created jealousy and antipathy between caste & caste. The House listened to his forty-minute speech spellbound, punctuating it with cheers. Newspapers published his speech with great joy & pride.

On 26/11/1949 the Constituent Assembly adopted the Constitution. In his concluding speech Dr Rajendra Prasad as President of the Assembly said, 'Sitting in the chair & watching the proceedings from day to day I have realized that nobody else could have with what zeal & devotion the Members of the Drafting Committee & esp its Chairman have worked. He has not only justified his selection but added luster to the work he has done'.

THE ROLE OF BABASAHEB AMBEDKAR

The presence of a picture of Dr.Ambedkar in all Buddhist viharas and at all Buddhist functions seems to set the Indian Buddhists apart from the main Buddhist tradition. The inclusion of 'Babasaheb' Ambedkar as an object of reverence is the most visible innovation in the practice of contemporary Buddhists in India. The Buddha and Babasaheb in plaster, stone, poster-art and painting, in song and drama and story, seemingly of near-equal importance, rarely one without the other, are continual evidence that contemporary Indian Buddhism proudly combines its own tradition with that of the main Buddhist tradition. Ambedkar is neither worshipped nor prayed to nor, of course, is the Buddha. No puja is performed, no navas (vows) are made to either figure, so their functions are not those of a Hindu god.

But at every occasion, both figures are garlanded, the Buddha first; incense is lit; and Bhagwan Gautam Buddha and Parampujya Dr.Babasaheb Ambedkar are addressed before the speaker acknowledges the Chairman of the function and 'Brothers and Sisters'. Efforts have been made to place Dr.Ambedkar in the traditional Buddhist framework.

Some Buddhists acknowledge Dr.Ambedkar as Boddhisatva in recognition of his role in bringing modern Indian converts into Buddhism, *i.e.* as a saviour. This use has been justified by, at least, one traditionally trained Thervada Buddhist bhikshu. Other Buddhists reject the Bodhisatva concept as Mahayana Buddhism, which they see as inferior to the rational, non-supernatural, humanity-centered religion they believe the Buddha taught. Another broadly accepted way of honouring Ambedkar is to add the diminutive of his first name, Bhimrao, to the list of refuges, *i.e* Bhimam sarnam gachchami, so that the 'Three Jewels' become four:

1. I go for refuge to the Buddha
2. I go to refuge to the Dhamma (doctrine)
3. I go to refuge to the Sangha (order of monks)
4. I go for refuge to Ambedkar.

These efforts to honour Dr.Ambedkar within the framework of the Buddhist tradition are an affront to some outside the conversion movement. Those who understand the importance of Dr.Ambedkar in the earlier struggle for political, social and religious rights are more charitable in accepting the continuing homage paid to him. That homage can best be understood by reference to the Indian tradition of the Guru (teacher or master) a concept most explicit in Hinduism but also found in heterodox sects and in secular life in India.

The use of the term 'Bodhisatva', the inclusion of Ambedkar as a refuge, is an attempt to use Buddhist concepts for the basic Indian idea of the need for a teacher to show the way to religious insight and personal freedom. The old practice of guru-shishya (master-pupil) is often expanded in modern India to a generalized acceptance of the importance of one special person-parent, teacher, ideal, hero—as a chief inspiration in life. The key is that the guru figure is the one who brings his disciple into self-realization, into freedom, *i.e.* the man who 'saves' him. Ambedkar himself claimed that he had three gurus: The Buddha, the fifteenth century iconoclastic saint-poet Kabir, and the nineteenth century radical social reformer, Mahatma Jotiba Phule. In turn, his followers feel that he has been responsible for almost all the educational, social and political progress in their lives and in addition has shown them the way to a religion which is both honourable and honoured, a religion which negates the religious concepts that made them untouchables in the eyes of society. Many feel that Ambedkar has quite literally saved them, and often highly educated Buddhists feel more strongly about Ambedkar as guru than those who have not benefited so much from the movement.

Ambedkar is by no means a guru in the way that Maharshi Mahesh Yogi or Bhagwan Shree Rajneesh or any of the many contemporary cult figures are gurus. He is a guru in a less specific but totally Indian way. One's guru does not need to be saintly in character or religious in profession; he needs only to be the one who points towards enlightenment. The picture of Dr.Ambedkar, usually clad in a blue business suit, a book in his hand, a fountain pen in his pocket, placed beside the picture of the yellow-robed Buddha, makes clear the very human sort of guru he was.

One of the many contemporary songs to folk tunes or film music by Buddhist singing groups illustrates the combination of social and religious enlightenment Ambedkar represents:

- He gave us the conversion at Nagpur
- He threw his light in the darkness
- He never was the slave of anyone
- He showed us the way of Buddha
- He gave us salvation

The importance of this concept is also expressed in a more sophisticated way by Namdev Dhasal, a political radical and a poet of the new Dalit school of literature, which is briefly composed of educated Buddhists. In this context from one of Dhasal's poems, 'they' refers to the forefathers of today's ex-untouchables; 'fakir' is used in Marathi for a Muslim saint and Dhasal has used it here probably to avoid a reference to Hinduism: Turning their backs to the sun, they journeyed through centuries;

- Now, now, we must refuse to be pilgrims of darkness
- After a thousand years we were blessed

- with a sunflower-giving fakir;
- Now, now, we must like sunflowers turn our face to the sun.

Whether he is called Bodhisatva, a refuge, a guru or a fakir, Ambedkar is honoured as the one who in his lifetime showed the way and who continues after his death to be seen as the wisest and most inspiring of men.

The Vihara-Meeting place for Buddhists

The new buildings dedicated to the Buddhist religion in Maharashtra as well as the old buildings converted to Buddhist use are called Viharas, the technical term for the residence of the Buddhist monks. The words for temple in Marathi, deul and mandir are studiously avoided, and the only term for a gathering place in the old Buddhist tradition seemed to be vihara. The need of today's Buddhists, however, is not so much living quarters for bhikshus as a meeting place for the laity, a place where the image of the Buddha can be kept, the community can gather for lectures on Buddhism or for vandana and children can be instructed. As in the case of other lay elements in Buddhist structure, there was no living model for the place of gathering of the Buddhist community available in India, and so the multipurpose vihara came into being. The vihara is most often a plain rectangular structure, embellished, where possible, with architectural detail from the most accessible models of Buddhist structures: the caves of Ajanta and the Stupa of Sanchi. These buildings are newly built whenever the Buddhists of some locality have the money and the cooperative spirit to create a symbol of their newly accepted faith.

In many villages, the caudi (community hall) of the old Maharwada (the quarters of the Mahar, somewhat removed from the village proper), does double service as community meeting room and center for Buddhist activities. I have seen few Hindu temples converted to Buddhist use, probably because few were completely in the hands of those Mahars who converted. No one has undertaken the immense amount of travelling over Maharashtra and in the cities of the Buddhist conversion elsewhere to record the presence of viharas, nor is there any organizational record, since the building of a Buddhist center is an entirely local matter.

The ones I have seen range from a small community shrine, large enough only to accommodate a statue of the Buddha, in the slums of Delhi, to a large building with an elaborate stupa on top in Pulgaon, Maharashtra, where Buddhists constitute a large, economically secure, factory-worker community.

Most viharas serve the Buddhist community in several ways, Daily or weekly vandana, memorial services and meetings for religious observances are held in the viharas, although few are large enough to accommodate all Buddhists in the locality and great occasions require that a pavillion be erected near the vihara. Many viharas are used for educational and social as well as religious purposes.

In some, there are rooms for visiting or resident bhikshus. Others combine a room for the image of the Buddha with a room for a pre-school or a kindergarten. Such a vihara was dedicated in Wardha in May 1976. Residents of the area, many of them casual labour on the railway, collected money for some twenty years and then built a small building.

The lower room is a balwadi (children's school) dedicated to Mahatma Phule; underneath a Sanchi like dome, is a small room dominated by a Buddha image brought from Thailand and a photograph of Dr.Ambedkar, with quotations from both the Pali scripture and Dr.Ambedkar painted on the walls. The vihara of Buddhists today is not an imitation of a Hindu temple.

There is no pujari or ritual priest, there is no stream of individual worshippers paying homage to the image. The vihara serves chiefly as a symbol of the community's faith and as a center for the community to gather as Buddhists. And since knowledge is seen as a Buddhist virtue, both Buddhist and secular education can easily be combined with its religious function.

ONE PERSON, ONE VALUE

When Dr B R Ambedkar rose to speak in the Constituent Assembly on November 25, 1949, it was evident that several issues of social equity and justice that had dominated the drafting of the Indian Constitution had remained unresolved. Ambedkar hinted at this in as many words: "On January 26, 1950, we are going to enter into a life of contradictions. In politics we will have equality and in social and economic life we will have inequality. In politics, we will be recognising the principle of one man-one vote and one vote-one value. In our social and economic life, we shall by reason of our social and economic structure, continue to deny the principle of one man-one value." This hint at continued exclusion in various spheres of social existence in this country came from a man who arguably made the most important contribution to the intellectual and institutional foundations of modern India. Ambedkar had warned: "If we continue to deny it (equality) for long, we will do so only by putting our political democracy in peril. We must remove this contradiction at the earliest possible moment or else those who suffer from inequality will blow up the structure of political democracy which this Assembly has labouriously built up."

But six decades later, millions of dalits continue to be denied the most basic of human rights – to be treated as equals. Women, the other victims of the 'shastras', are excluded in their own homes and society. Other excluded sections include the adivasis, the denotified tribes, religious minorities, the differently abled, and sexual minorities, to mention just a few. Though caste-based discrimination is less intense today, there is empirical evidence that untouchability persists, as the article in this issue by Sukhadeo Thorat illustrates. In rural India, restrictions on temple entry, access to drinking water sources, segregated seating arrangements in classrooms and so on are still the order of the day. In urban India – and even in the Indian diaspora — where caste distinctions seem to have blurred, the notional sense of untouchability remains pervasive even while adjusting to modern living. Even when concessions are made to dalits, in education and jobs for example, they are perceived as favours and not rights. Intellectual discussions on caste-based reservations are largely confined to their impact on merit. The two are seen as incompatible by the privileged castes. The strange thing is that India is so diverse. Over the centuries people of all major religions of the world—Hinduism, Islam, Christianity, Sikhism, Buddhism, Jainism, Zoroastrianism, and Bahaism — have lived in India. According to B S Guha's classification, people of six racial stocks live in India, and according to the 1971 census there are 1,652 languages spoken as mother-tongue across the country. The Mandal Commission alone lists 3,743 castes in addition to around 1,000 Scheduled Castes.

Despite this diversity we see widespread exclusion. Our lessons on India's 'unity in diversity' seem to be forgotten the moment we leave school, though the slogan popularised by Jawaharlal Nehru is still recalled at moments of national pride. If we analyse the nature of exclusion in Indian society we will find exclusion on the basis of cultural heterogeneity — as seen in the recent outburst against North Indians in Mumbai; on the basis of faith — the most glaring example of which is the exclusion of Muslims and more recently of Christians; and on the basis of gender. Sex-selective abortion is the latest, most frightening form of exclusion. According to Unicef India loses 7,000 girls every day through abortion. The British medical journal *Lancet* estimates that 10 million female foetuses have been aborted in the past two decades in India.

It is important to understand that social and economic exclusion has more to do with group identity than income, productivity or merit of individuals in the group. Unlike members of privileged groups, who may be excluded from education or work due to individual lack of income, low merit or poor skills, members of excluded groups are denied opportunities due to their identity as members of a certain social group. Experts have long pointed out that few of the debates on poverty in India have questioned the links between poverty and social discrimination. But the big question is the extent to which social exclusion causes economic deprivation and thus poverty. National Sample Survey (NSS) data reveals that the Scheduled Castes (dalits) and Scheduled Tribes (adivasis) are particularly disadvantaged. Average per capita income of SC/STs at an all-India level is about one-third lower than other groups. Headcount poverty in 1999/2000 was 16% among non-deprived groups, 30% for minorities (Muslims), 36% for SCs and 44% for STs.

NSS data also encapsulates gender differences. Census data shows female literacy increasing from 35% to just over 50% between 1991 and 2001, but the disparity between men and women in 2001 was still about 25 percentage points, and has only marginally declined since 1991. Health indicators, including maternal mortality, also highlight the considerable disadvantages women face. It is in this context that the struggle of 26-year-old Sumathi T N, a postgraduate in Arts, gains importance.

Sumathi dared not reveal her dalit identity while employed as a teacher at a local school in Tumkur, a district town some 70 km from India's Silicon Valley, Bangalore. "I used to see how they treated the dalits; not letting them enter hotels or households and even beating them up if they dared to do so. I thought it was safer to say I was not a dalit," she told our contributor. Sumathi had to quit her job after her caste identity was accidentally revealed to her colleagues and it took a while to come to terms with the fact: "... I learned about dalit history and culture and realised the importance of accepting my identity and fighting for my rights. I am not ashamed or afraid of my being dalit any more."

This issue 'Against Exclusion' is about the struggles of many such individuals and groups. There is Moghubai from a nondescript village in Jharol block, Rajasthan, where widows are branded witches for any misfortune from a child getting chicken pox to a cow that has stopped giving milk. There are Tamil Nadu's approximately 300,000 transgenders or *aravanis* who have fought for and won major concessions including the introduction of a 'third gender' on ration cards and social visibility and acceptance as mediapersons and television anchors. There are the IT companies that are increasingly employing persons with disability, not as a token CSR gesture but because it makes good business sense to do so.. And there are the girls of the Meo Muslim community, who are finally getting an education thanks to Vinodkumar Kanathia, who chucked up his job as a bank manager to set up a series of schools in Mewat region of north India. "I was shocked by the vast disparities between Gurgaon and Mewat, located hardly 40 km of each other. If the yuppie crowd inside the plush malls of Gurgaon symbolise the new India, the toiling daughters of the impoverished Meos in Mewat are rude reminders of the uneven growth policies of a booming Indian economy," says Kanathia. Their stories emphasis what Ambedkar had warned, that equality cannot be denied for long.

AMBEDKAR'S VIEW OF INDIAN RELIGION

A large part of Ambedkar's writings had a direct bearing on Hinduism, most of which remained unpublished and in the initial draft form during his lifetime. In these studies, which he undertook mainly from the second half of the 1940s, Ambedkar argued that Buddhism, which attempted to found society on the basis of reason and morality, was a major revolution, both social and ideological, against the degeneration of the Aryan society.

It condemned the varna system and gave hope to the poor, the exploited and the women. It rallied against sacrifices, priestcraft and superstition. The Buddhist Sangha became the platform for the movement towards empowering and ennobling the common man.

However, Brahminism struck back against the revolution through the counter-revolution launched by Pushyamitra. Here, Ambedkar deployed a specific terminology employed to explain mainstream European transitions of nineteenth and twentieth centuries and he felt that the corresponding explanation was appropriate for India too, although the periods in question were wide apart.

For Ambedkar, literature, which legitimized and instituted the counter-revolution, was Smriti literature in general and Manusmriti in particular. It gave birth to the principle of assigning human beings to social roles, reduced the Shudra to servitude and condemned women to ignominy.

On the contrary, the governing principle during the Vedic period for assigning social roles was varna, the principle of worth, which allowed wide mobility although it ordered society hierarchically. The trajectory of social transformation that Ambedkar traced was divided into the following phases: the Vedic society and its degeneration into Aryan society; the rise of Buddhism and the social and moral transformation it set into motion; and finally, the counter-revolution and the rise of Brahminism.

Ambedkar found that the Hindu scriptures do not lend themselves to a unified and coherent understanding. There are strong contentions built into them within and across trends and traditions. There are cleavages within the Vedas; the Upanishadic thought is in contentions with the Vedic thought; Smriti literature argues against Sruti literature; sometimes the Vedas are considered lower than the Shastras; gods are pitted against one another; and tantra is tallied against Smriti literature.

The icons of Hinduism such as Rama and Krishna have little to recommend them, in that there is nothing morally elevating about them. Further, Ambedkar generally tended to suggest a later date to the central texts of Hinduism as compared to other Indian scholars.

He did not comment much on the Upanishads, and compared to the rest of the Hindu literature, is relatively favourably disposed towards them. As late as 1936, Ambedkar felt that Hinduism could be redrafted on the basis of Upanishadic thought. For Ambedkar, the Gita is a post-Buddhist text.

It is primarily a defence of karma-kanda, i.e., religious acts and observance, by removing the excrescence which was grown over it. The Gita advances a set of philosophical arguments to save Brahminism in the context of the rise of Buddhism and the inability of the former to defend itself by a mere appeal to the rituals and practices of the Vedas. He finds that the Gita defends the position of Jaimini's Minamsa against Badarayan's Brahmasutras.

Ambedkar developed a new interpretation of Buddhism which made commentators label it "Ambedkar's Buddhism". His magnum opus, The Buddha and His Dhamma highlights the central issues that concerned him throughout his life and demarcates his view sharply from that of his adversaries.

The work contains the central teachings of the Buddha along with a commentary built into it. The commentary transposes the Buddha's teachings to the present and suggests its contemporary relevance with respect to the problems that confront humanity. He saw Buddhism as an ideology that engages with the world, privileging the poor and exploited.

Ambedkar repeatedly asserted that Buddha has a social message. Further, he constructed Buddhism in opposition to Hinduism arguing that if there are some traces of Hinduism in Buddhism, they could be attributed to Brahminical interpolations. Ambedkar also upheld the superiority of Buddhism over other religions, particularly Islam and Christianity.

AMBEDKAR'S VIEW OF INDIAN CASTE

Ambedkar's understanding of caste and the caste system underwent certain significant changes over the period of his writings. Initially, he had argued that the characteristic of caste was endogamy, superimposed by exogamy in a shared cultural ambience. He suggested that evils such as sati, child marriage and prohibition on widow remarriage were the outcome of caste.

Further, if a caste closed its boundaries, other castes were also forced to follow the suit. The Brahmins closing themselves socially first gave rise to the system of castes. Ambedkar continued to emphasize the endogamous characteristic of caste but roped in other features such as the division of labour, absence of inter-dinning and the principle of birth, which he had earlier largely absorbed within endogamy.

He also found that the caste name is an important feature, which keeps inequality in the normative anchor of the caste system. Graded inequality restricts the reach of equality to members of the caste at the most. Ambedkar thought that caste is an essential feature of the Hindu religion.

Although a few reformers may have denounced it, for the vast majority of Hindus breaking the codes of caste in a clear violation of deeply held religious beliefs. He found Gandhi subscribing to caste initially and later opposing it but upholding varna instead. Gandhi's conception of varna is the same as that of caste, that is, assigning social agents on the basis of birth, rather than worth.

It led to upholding graded inequality and the denial of freedom and equality, social relations that cannot beget community bonds. The solution that Ambedkar proposed was the annihilation of caste. He suggested inter-caste marriage and inter-dinning for the purpose although the latter by itself is too weak to forge any enduring bonds.

Further, he felt that hereditary priesthood should go and it should remain open to all the co-religionists endowed with appropriate qualifications as certified by the state. Ambedkar, however, felt that these suggestions would not be acceptable to Hindus. After the early 1930s he gave up any hope of reforming Hinduism except for a belief while with the Hindu Code Bill which was, in a way, the continuation of the agenda he had set for himself in the 1920s.

AMBEDKAR'S VIEW OF INDIAN UNTOUCHABILITY

Ambedkar's engagement with untouchability, as a researcher, intellectual and activist, is much more nuanced, hesitant but intimate as compared to his viewpoint on caste, where he is prepared to offer stronger judgements and proffer solutions. However, with untouchability, there is often a failure of words. Grief is merged with anger.

He often exclaims how an institution of this kind has been tolerated and even defended. He evinces deep suspicions about the bona fides of others in terms of their engagement with it. He distinguished the institution of untouchability from that of caste, though the former is reinforced by the latter, and Brahminism constituted the enemy of both.

He felt that it was difficult for outsiders to understand the phenomena. He thought human sympathy would be forthcoming towards alleviating the plight of the untouchables, but at the same time anticipated hurdles to be crossed - hurdles made of age-old prejudices, interests, religious retribution, the burden of the social pyramid above and the feeble resources that the untouchables could muster.

He found that the colonial administration did little to ameliorate the lot of the untouchables. He argued that the track-record of Islam and Christianity, in this regard, is not praiseworthy either, although they may not subscribe to untouchability as integral to their religious beliefs.

Ambedkar felt that untouchables have to fight their own battle and if others are concerned about them, then, such a concern has to be expressed in helping them to fight rather than prescribing solutions to them. He discussed attempts to deny the existence of untouchables and to reduce the proportion of their population in order to deny them adequate political presence.

He resorted to comparison with what he called the parallel cases, such as the treatment meted out to slaves and Jews but found the lot of the untouchables worse than theirs. He argued that in spite of differences and cleavages, all untouchables share common disadvantages and treatment from caste Hindus: they live in ghettos; they were universally despised and kept outside the fold.

He maintained a graphic account of the course of the movement of the untouchables, although this was much more specific about the movement in the Bombay Presidency. He threw scorn at the Gandhian attempt to remove untouchability and termed it as a mere facade aimed at buying over the untouchables with kindness.

He presented voluminous empirical data to defend such a thesis, and suggested his own strategies to confront untouchability, warning untouchables not to fall into the trap of Gandhism. He exhorted them to fight for political power. Although he did not find the lot of untouchables better among Christians and Muslims, he felt that they had a better option as they did not subscribe to untouchability as a religious tenet. Ambedkar was also deeply sensitive to insinuations offered by others to co-opt untouchables within their political ambit.

Ambedkar rarely went into the question of the origin of untouchability in history. He rebutted the suggestion that race has anything to do with it, and did not subscribe to the position that caste has its basis in race either. However, in one instance, he proposed a very imaginative thesis that untouchables were broken men living on the outskirts of village communities who, due to their refusal to give up Buddhism and beef-eating, came to be condemned as untouchables.

He did not repeat this thesis in any central way later to the fold either.

It has to be noted that the thesis was proposed when Ambedkar was fighting for the recognition that untouchables were a separate element in India and, therefore, should be constitutionally evolved with appropriate safeguards, while the colonial administration and Gandhian leadership were prepared to recognize only the Muslims and Sikhs as distinct communities.

7

Ambedkar and Social Justice

SOCIAL JUSTICE AND SOCIETY

Just Society through a Model Society (Sangha) of Just People: The vision of an awakened society led the Buddha to set in motion the Wheel of the Dhamma. The Buddha set in motion the wheel of the Dhamma when he awakened five disciples in Sarnath. According to Dr. Ambedkar, the Buddha organized the Bhikku Sangha to make this just society a living reality and to set a model for the society to imitate.

But the blessed Lord also knew that merely preaching the Dhamma to the common man would not result in the creation of that ideal society based on righteousness. An ideal must be practical and must be shown to be practicable. Then and then only people strive after it and realize it. To create this striving, it is necessary to have a picture of a society working on the basis of the ideal and thereby proving to the common man that the ideal was not impracticable but on the other hand realizable. The Sangha is a model of a society realizing the Dhamma preached by the blessed Lord. (BAWS XI, 434)

According to Dr. Ambedkar, the code of the bhikkhu, the patimokkha, was formulated to make the sangha an ideal society. Thus, the bhikkhu must always be seen as subordinate to and enfolded into the sangha or ideal society. The training of a bhikkhu/bhikkhuni is aimed at making him/her a perfect citizen of the ideal society. In another sense, the rules of the monastic are not meant for making a perfect being, but for creating a servant of the society who will be committed to end suffering and living the ideals of Liberty, Equality and Fraternity. The monastic should not be indifferent to the suffering of lay people.

She/he must fight for establishing an ideal society.

Since the Buddha established the sangha in order to lay the foundation of an awakened society, he preached his Dhamma to all without distinction, to monastic as well as to lay people. Ambedkar felt there was no difference between the monastic and a lay person as far as the practice of the Dhamma goes. The distinction, however, is in the degree of involvement in the preaching and propagating of the Dhamma, essentially of time and commitment. Monastics are the full-timers, having neither the worldly responsibilities of marriage nor private property. On the other hand, lay persons are the part-timers, ensconced in worldly duties. As the full-timers have no private property, the part-timers have had to support them with dana. The part-timers have mainly given alms, and provided abodes and robes to the full-timers. The Buddha put in place these dependencies, which are also freedoms, as a check and balance mechanism to ensure that the full-timers should not betray the mission. The part-timers could complain to the larger sangha about the misconduct of any of the full-timers. Thus, the bond of alms between monastic and lay person was instrumental in the successful spread of the Dhamma.

However, this bond of alms was taken to extremes when the lay emperor Ashoka supported and interfered in the matters of sangha. The history of this disappearance of Buddhism in India is the history of the gradual weakening of this bond of alms and the disappearance of the nucleus of the Buddhist society, the monastic sangha. How could any teaching survive with the destruction of its organization and propaganda base? Buddhism eventually disappeared, because although the lay sangha strove hard, they could not give their best energies and could not organize themselves effectively.

Despite his often strong criticisms, Dr. Ambedkar did not wish to do away with the monastic sangha. On the contrary, he saw the sangha as having an important role in the awakened society. His ideal society was the Buddhist Sangha. But here is a departure from the tradition. He wanted lay persons to be part and parcel of the New Sangha. With this basic view in mind, Dr. Ambedkar expressed his views on the reconstruction of the sangha to suit modern society.

Firstly, he felt that the absence of a dhamma diksha for lay followers was a grave omission. Throughout history, the bhikkhus have been initiated and organised but the lay sangha has not. Except for a few insignificant exceptions, the Dhamma is common to both. Dr. Ambedkar wanted to correct this anomaly, and so accepted the challenge to initiate his own lay followers in the Dhamma. He also suggested the creation of lay preachers who could go about and preach the Buddha's Dhamma among the people and look after the new converts to guide their practice, rather than creating newly ordained monastics or depending on foreign monastics for this purpose. He felt these lay preachers must be paid and that they could be married. He wanted to restructure the Sangha so as to fit it in the modern society. Unfortunately, Dr. Ambedkar did not live long enough to build a movement to actualize this new understanding of the role of monastics in an awakened society.

However, the British monk Sangharakshita, who met Dr. Ambedkar thrice and helped lead the neo-Buddhist movement in India after Ambedkar's death, did develop Ambedkar's basic concept further. He has integrated Ambedkar's criticisms of the bhikkhu sangha in the creation of his new orders, the British-based Friends of the Western Buddhist Order (FWBO) and the Indian-based Trailokya Buddha Mahasangha (TBM) order nurtured by Dhammachari Lokamitra. In the spirit of

Ambedkar's notion of married lay preachers who would spread the Buddha Dhamma about India, Sangharakshita has developed an intermediate form of Buddhist practitioner, called a dharmachari/charini or "dharma-farer," which dissolves the dichotomy between lay and monastic. Sangharakshita's order has sought to intensify serious training for those interested while not creating a distinction of superiority between those who choose less arduous courses. This flexibility of practice models has significantly allowed those with a high level of training to maintain a lay appearance, thereby facilitating involvement in social activities. The uniting factor of the different levels of practice is the commitment to social service within the community and the society. Sangharakshita's vision is one of a decentralized community of people sharing the same spiritual commitment without the need for ecclesiastical structure (Sponberg, 1996:90).

Dr. Ambedkar also had other concrete ideas for the creation of an awakened society based on the Buddha Dhamma. He had planned to establish a Buddhism and Religions Seminary where persons who wished to become preachers could be taught Buddhism and trained in the comparative study of other religions. He suggested the introduction of congregational worship in the Buddha Vihara every Sunday followed by a sermon. The Buddha and His Dhamma, itself, was an attempt to create a "Buddhist Bible"-a single volume work which could be a constant companion of the convert. Like the lay preacher, the Buddhist Bible represents a middle way intended to bridge the gap between the lofty ideals of monastic practice and learning and the daily needs of the larger lay sangha.

Dr. Ambedkar made many provisions to create the Dhamma as a living force in India. Besides his emphasis on the Dhamma, which he wanted to make heart of his movement, he knew the importance of social awakening and politics. After his conversion, he planned to constitute a political party, The Republican Party of India. The aim was to ensure the social, political and economic justice enshrined in the preamble of the constitution of India in order to create an ideal society. Society, according to Ambedkar, cannot do without Dhamma nor without just government.

Society has to choose one of the three alternatives. Society may choose not to have any Dhamma as an instrument of government. For Dhamma is nothing if it is not an instrument of government. This means society chooses the road to anarchy. Secondly, society may choose the police, i.e., dictatorship as an instrument of government. Thirdly, society may choose Dhamma plus the magistrate wherever people fail to observe the Dhamma. In anarchy and dictatorship liberty is lost. Only in the third liberty survives.

According to Ambedkar, the norm or the criterion for judging right and wrong in modern society is justice. Justice is ensured when the society is based on the principles of liberty, equality, and fraternity. The system of grading people as in the caste system will always lead to injustice. Ambedkar saw no solution in communism or capitalism, the two political currents dominant during his day. He found a solution in Buddhism. He said. "Man must grow materially as well as spiritually. Society has been aiming to lay a new foundation which was summarized by the French Revolution in three words, Fraternity, Liberty and Equality. The French Revolution was welcomed because of this slogan. It failed to produce equality. We welcome the Russian Revolution because it aims to produce equality. But it cannot be too much emphasized that in producing equality in society one cannot afford to sacrifice fraternity or liberty. Equality will be of no value without fraternity or liberty. It seems that the three (liberty, equality and fraternity) can coexist only if one follows the way of the Buddha" (BAWS III, 462, Italics and bracket added).

He saw the ideal society as one full of channels for conveying change taking place in one part to other parts. In an ideal society, he remarked, there should be many interests, consciously communicated and shared. There should be varied and free points of contact with other modes of association. In other words there must be social endosmosis. This is fraternity, which is only another name for democracy. Democracy is not merely a form of government. It is primarily a mode of associated living, of conjoint communicated experience. It is essentially an attitude of respect and reverence towards fellow beings. Finally, this reconstruction of the world is possible through Dhamma. Dhamma is essentially and fundamentally social. In this way, his ideal society is based on the universality of Dhamma, which consists of liberty, equality and fraternity. In the All India Radio broadcast of his speech on October 3,1954, Dr. Ambedkar clarified the usage of these terms:

Positively, my social philosophy may be said to be enshrined in three words: Liberty, Equality and Fraternity. Let no one, however, say that I have borrowed my philosophy from the French Revolution. I have not. My philosophy has roots in religion and not in political science. I have derived them from the teachings of my master, the Buddha.

The sad part of Dr. Ambedkar's movement, however, has been the lack of recognition in the entire movement of the role of Dhamma (the practice of liberty, equality and fraternity). As a result of this, the social organizations and political parties based on Ambedkar face the problems of caste and conflict. They fall asunder due to organizational problems. The success of Dr. Ambedkar's movement lies not just in education and agitation but in how effectively his followers organize themselves; that is to say how they use fraternity as a principle to make fraternity universal. Ambedkar wanted to establish universal fraternity which was not to be based on sectarian attitudes and caste prejudices. He wrote:

There are two forces prevalent in society: individualism and fraternity. Individualism is ever present. Every individual is ever asking "I and my neighbours, are we all brothers, are we even fiftieth cousins, am I their keeper, why should I do right by them?" and under the pressure of his own particular interests acting as though he was an end to himself, thereby developing a non-social and even an antisocial self.

There are many offshoots of the political party of which Dr. B. R. Ambedkar himself planned and wrote a constitution. Their main motivation is anti-Brahmanism and anti-caste. However, most of them are trapped in their own prisons of caste or the interests of their group, and therefore become antisocial. Dhamma is the way to break the prison of caste and prejudices. Dhamma is to extend fraternity both horizontally and vertically in the social structure and hence the Dhamma can help in overcoming caste identities.

In conclusion, the most unfortunate part of Dr. B. R. Ambedkar's movement was his untimely death. He died just after the great conversion movement in 1956. Most of the ideas in his mind died with him. However, he left enough material and blueprints for his millions of followers to follow and organize themselves as an ideal society to set up a model for the world. The re-entry of Buddhism to India after a gap of hundreds of years has been very dramatic. Buddhism has come back as a mass movement among the untouchables.

The success of the Buddhist movement depends on the organization of a sangha of full-timers and part-timers. This sangha must transcend caste and should not get trapped in one caste or group. It needs to integrate with the larger Indian society by breaking isolation. This sangha should exemplify liberty, equality, and fraternity to live and act in harmony within itself. There is a necessity for trained dhammasevak (servants of the Dhamma). The dhammasevak must have at the same time a strong sense of history and should be ready to go beyond the great wall of caste. The new servants of the Dhamma must passionately fight for practising and propagating liberty, equality, and fraternity. In short, Dhamma can re-ethicize Indian society but it depends on how the followers of Dr. Ambedkar understand and situate the Dhamma in the various movements organized under his name and philosophy.

Think 'The System' before Taking Action: Unlike most untouchables Ambedkar's was fortunate to receive an excellent international education. Under the protection of a local Maharaja he completed his masters at Columbia, his PhD in economics at the London School of Economics and earned a law degree in England in the 1920's. During his days at university, while being introduced to western notions of individualism, equality and democracy he had the opportunity to reflect on the caste system structuring his own society. These theoretical notions went completely opposite to the intrinsic hierarchy of Hinduism that implied a natural notion of inequality. His time abroad gave him the possibility to look at his own society with an outsider's eye, and to question the so-called harmonious social structure of India. He realised that untouchability was not a universal but a social construct that could be challenged and that 95 untouchables as Indian nationals had the duty to ask for the same rights as their co-citizens.

To illustrate the perverse nature of the caste system to his Western colleagues, Ambedkar would compare it to the class system of the West.

For him in the class system there was a possibility for upward mobility, for horizontal cooperation and for revolution. In other words, according to Ambedkar, classes were not closed units. On the other hand, a social structure based on the caste system was like a closed class unit in which upward mobility was impossible and revolution unthinkable. To him, caste was like the colour of the skin or a physical attribute: it was there to stay, the same, until death.

Thus, this intrinsic fatalism imposed by God-a supreme being-impeded untouchables aspiring to greater goals. He came to the conclusion that because untouchables were an integral element participating to the "harmony of the whole" in Hinduism, they were doomed to be subdued. Thus making this system unique in its genre, as no other religion had ever created a permanent status of untouchability:

> *"Untouchables are born impure, they are impure while they live, they die the death of the impure, and they give*

birth to children who are born with the stigma of untouchability affixed to them. It is a case of permanent, hereditary stain which nothing can cleanse".

This questioning awaked the social activist soul in Ambedkar. He embarked on a life long quest to reform his society into recognizing the unique dignity of each of its citizens.

UNTOUCHABLES' ORGANISATION AND CONVERSION

The present movement of the Untouchables has been very severely criticised. It has been said that there are several castes among the Untouchables, and every caste practices untouchability. Mahars and Mangs do not dine together. Both these castes do not touch the scavengers, and practice untouchability against them. It is therefore asked what right these people have to expect from others the non-observance of the practice of untouchability, when they themselves practice casteism and untouchability amongst themselves. The untouchables are generally advised to abolish castes and untouchability from amongst them, and then come (to the caste Hindus) for redress.

There is a little truth in this argument. But the allegations made in this against the Untouchables are absolutely false. It cannot be denied that the castes included in the (category of) Untouchables practice untouchability. But equally, it is false to say that they are in any way responsible for this crime. Casteism and untouchability originated not from the Untouchables, but from the high-caste Hindus. And if this is true, the responsibility for this age-old tradition falls on the caste Hindus and not on the Untouchables. While practising untouchability and casteism, the Untouchables merely follow the lesson taught by the caste Hindus. If this lesson is not true, the burden of its being untruthful falls on those who taught it, and not on those who learnt it. Though this reply may appear to be correct, it does not satisfy me. Though we are not responsible for the causes due to which castes and untouchability have taken root among us, it will be insane not to fight them but to allow them to continue as they are. Though we are not responsible for the introduction of untouchability and castes among us, we are surely responsible for their annihilation. And I am glad that all of us have realised this responsibility.

I am sure there is no leader among the Mahars who advocates the practice of casteism. If comparison is to be made, it will have to be made among the leaders. Compare the educated class of the Mahar community with that of the Brahmins, and one will have to admit that the educated Mahars are more eager to abolish castes. This can well be proved by facts also. Not only the educated class of Mahars, but even the uneducated and illiterate Mahars, are the protagonists (advocates) of the abolition of castes. This also can be proved. Today, there is not a single person in the Mahar community who is opposed to the inter-caste dining among the Mahars and the Mangs. I feel greatly satisfied that you have realised the necessity of the abolition of castes—for which I extend my heartiest congratulations.

But have you ever thought as to how the efforts toward the abolition of castes can be made successful? Castes cannot be abolished by inter-caste dinners or stray instances of inter-caste marriages. Caste is a state of mind. It is a disease of the mind. The teachings of the Hindu religion are the root cause of this disease. We practise casteism, we observe untouchability, because we are asked to do it by the Hindu religion in which we live. A bitter thing can be made sweet. The taste of anything can be changed. But poison cannot be made Amrit (nectar). To talk of annihilating castes is like talking of changing poison into Amrit. In short, so long as we remain in a religion which teaches man to treat man as a leper, the sense of discrimination on account of caste, which is deeply rooted in our minds, cannot go. For annihilating castes and untouchability from among the Untouchables, change of religion is the only antidote.

The Distinction between "Change in Name" and "Change in Religion"

So far, I have placed before you the points in favour of conversion. I hope this has been good food for your thoughts. Those who consider this discussion very difficult and complicated—I propose to put up (provide) simple thoughts in simple language for them.

What is there in conversion which can be called novel? Really speaking, what sort of social relations do you have with the caste Hindus at present? You are as separate from the Hindus as Muslims and Christians are. The same is (true of) their relation with you. Your society, and that of the Hindus, are two distinct groups. By (our choosing) conversion, nobody can say or feel that one society has been split up. You will remain separate from the Hindus, as you are today. Nothing new will happen on account of this conversion. If this is true, then why should some people be afraid of conversion? I, at least, do not find any reason for such fear.

Secondly, though, you undoubtedly have understood the importance of a change of name. If anybody from among you is asked about his caste, he tells it as Chokhamela, Harijan, or Walmiki, but does not say that he is a Mahar. Nobody can change a name unless certain conditions demand it. There is a very simple reason for such a change of name. An unknown (unknowing) person cannot distinguish between a touchable and an Untouchable. And so long as a Hindu does not come to know the caste of a person, he cannot have born in him the hatred of that person for being an Untouchable. The caste Hindus and Untouchables behave in very friendly ways during journeys, so long as they are unaware of their castes. They exchange betels, bidis, cigarettes, fruits, etc. But as soon as the Hindu comes to know that the person with whom he is talking is an Untouchable, a sense of hatred germinates in his mind. He thinks that he is deceived. He gets angry, and ultimately this temporary friendship ends in abuses and quarrels.

Such experiences are not new to you. Why does all this happen? The names that depict your caste are considered so filthy that even their utterance is enough to create a vomiting sensation in the heart of Hindus. Thus by calling oneself a Chokhamela instead of a Mahar, you try to deceive the people.

But you know, people are not deceived. Whether you call yourself a Chokhamela or a Harijan, people understand what you are. By your actions, you have proved the necessity of a change of name. Then what objection should there be to a change of religion? Changing a religion is like changing a name.

A change of religion, followed by a change of name, will be more beneficial to you. To call oneself a Muslim, a Christian, a Buddhist, or a Sikh, is not merely a change of religion, but is also a change of name.

That is a real change of name. This new name will have no filth attached to it. It is an overall change. No one will search for the origin of it. The change of name as Chokhamela or Harijan has no meaning at all. In this case, all the hatred, contempt, etc., attached to the original name passes to the new name. So long as you remain in the Hindu religion, you will have to change the name. (To seek change) by calling oneself a Hindu is not enough. Nobody recognises that there is a man called a Hindu. So also, calling oneself a Mahar will not serve the purpose. As soon as you utter this name, you will not be allowed to come near. So I ask you, why should you not change your name permanently by changing your religion, instead of changing to one name today and another tomorrow, and thus remaining in the state of a pendulum?

The Role of Opponents

Since the beginning of this movement of conversion, various people raised various objections to it. Let us now examine the truth, if any, in such objections. Some Hindus, pretending to be religious preachers, advise you, saying, "Religion is not a thing that can be consumed. Religion cannot be changed as we change our coat daily. You wish to leave this Hindu religion and embrace another one. Then do you think that your ancestors who clung to this religion for so long a period were fools?" Some wise men have raised this question.

I do not find any substance in this objection. A congenital idiot alone can say that one should stick to his religion because it is ancestral. No sane man will accept such a proposition. Those who advocate such an argument seem not to have read history at all. The ancient Aryan religion was called Vedic religion. It has three distinct characteristics: beef eating, drinking, and merrymaking was the religion of the day. Thousands of people followed it in India, and even now some people dream of going back to it. If the ancient religion alone is to be adhered to, then why did the people of India leave it and accept Buddhism? Why did they divorce (themselves) from the Vedic religion?

It cannot be denied that our ancestors lived in the ancient religion, but I cannot say that they remained there voluntarily. The Chaturvarnya system prevailed in this country for a pretty long time. In this system, the Brahmins were permitted to learn, the Kshatriyas to fight, the Vaishyas to earn property, and the Sudras to serve.

This way of life was the rule of the day. In those days, the Sudras had no learning, no property, and no food and clothing. Your ancestors were thus forced to live in penniless and armless (disarmed) conditions. Under these circumstances, no man with common sense can say that they accepted that religion voluntarily.

Here it is also necessary to consider whether it was possible for your ancestors to revolt against this religion. Had it been possible for them to revolt, and had they still not acted upon (the possibility), only then can we say that they had accepted this religion voluntarily. But if we try to look into the then-prevalent conditions, it will be clear that our ancestors were forced to live in that religion. Thus this Hindu religion is not the religion of our ancestors, but it was a slavery forced upon them. Our ancestors had no means to fight this slavery, and hence they could not revolt.

They were compelled to live in this religion. Nobody can blame them for this helplessness. Rather, anyone will pity them. But now nobody can force any type of slavery upon the present generation. We have all sorts of freedom. If the present generation do not avail (themselves) of such freedom and free themselves, one will have to call them, most regretfully, the most mean, slavish, and dependent people who ever lived on earth.

The Difference between Man and Animal

Only a fool can say that one should cling to one's own religion only because it is ancestral. No sane person can accept such an argument.

"You should live in the same circumstances in which you are living at present" may be worthy advice for the animals, but it can never be for man. The difference between an animal and a man is that the man can make progress, while the animal cannot. No progress can be made without change. Conversion is a sort of change. And if no progress can be made without change, *i.e.* conversion, obviously conversion becomes essential. The ancestral religion cannot be a hindrance in the path of a progressive man.

There is still one more argument against conversion. They say, "Conversion is a sort of escapism. Today a number of Hindus are bent upon improving the Hindu religion. Untouchability and caste can be eradicated with the help of these Hindu reformers. It is therefore not proper to change the religion at this juncture." Whatever opinion anybody may possess about the Hindu social reformers, I personally have a nausea for them. I have no regard for them. I have had very bitter experience of them. That those people, who live in their own caste, die in their own caste, marry in their own caste, should befool the people with false slogans, saying, "We will break the caste!", is really surprising. And if the Untouchables do not believe them, they get annoyed with them! Is it not astonishing?

When I hear the slogans shouted by these Hindu social reformers, I recollect the efforts made by the American white people for the emancipation of the American Negroes. Years ago, the condition of the Negroes in America was just the same as that of Untouchables in India. The difference between the two was that the slavery of Negroes had the sanction of the law; while that of your (people), by religion. So, some reformers were trying for abolition of the slavery of the Negroes. But can those white reformers be compared with their counterparts, the Hindu social reformers in India? The American white reformers fought battles in war with their kith and kin for the emancipation of the Negroes. They killed thousands of whites who defended the slavery of the Negro people, and also sacrificed their own blood for this cause.

When we read these chapters through the pages of history, the social reformers in India cut a very sorry figure before them. These so-called benefactors of the Untouchables of India called "reformers" need to be asked the following questions: Are you prepared to fight a civil war with your Hindu brethren, like the whites in America who fought with their white brothers for the cause of the coloured people? And if not, why these proclamations of reforms?

Now let us take the example of Mahatma Gandhi, the greatest of the Hindus who claim to fight for the cause of the Untouchables. To what extent can he go? Mahatma Gandhi, who pilots the nonviolent agitation against the British Government, is not prepared to hurt the feelings of the Hindus, the oppressors of the Untouchables. He is not willing to launch a peaceful Satyagraha against them. He is not even prepared to take legal action against the Hindus. What is the good of such Hindu reformers for us? I don't see any.

SOCIAL HIERARCHY AND THE CASTE SYSTEM

Society and Social Hierarchy

It would not be wrong if one begins the thesis with defining the word, society. Although our approach to the caste system will be more historical than sociological, this is inevitable. The very heart of the things we have learned from our past is that humans or Homo sapiens prefer to live in groups. Humans do not live alone.

They gather and form groups, which we call societies.

- A definition of society can be given as "The totality of social relationships among humans; A group of humans broadly distinguished from other groups by mutual interests, participation in characteristic relationships, shared institutions, and a common culture; an extended social group having a distinctive cultural and economic organization; The institutions and culture of a distinct self-perpetuating group. Biology A colony or community of organisms, usually of the same species."
- Where also social is defined as "animals tending to move or live together in groups or colonies of the same kind.

The science again created by human mind is sociology to cope with the problems and the questions of social groups. As the one who established the sociology as a discipline, Durkheim tells that the importance of social facts was that they constitute a domain of phenomena that fall outside the scientific purview of biology and psychology. In comparison to the phenomena studied by biology and psychology, social facts constitute a class by themselves, or sui generis, as Durkheim referred to them. Thus according to Durkheim, the study of social facts requires an autonomous scientific discipline -- namely, the discipline of sociology. What we know in certain is that as a species, human being lives in groups or what we call societies.

And the science of history is the past experiences of those societies formed by different groups of people.

As Fernand Braudel states:

- Society, scattered, can be seen every where and sometimes containing just like the air we breathe but we don't feel, it permeates and direct our whole life. Young Marx wrote, as "What is thinking in me is the society itself". Then most of the time the historian is just being charmed by the illusion that when looking to the past there are only individuals which he can judge about their responsibilities. But his real duty is not finding the 'human' that is a misused formula, but to define social groups which have responsibilities to other groups.

According to Durkheim, social facts are properties that can be attributed only to human groups and not to the human individuals who make up those groups. Ordinary language is another example of a social fact. Ordinary languages such as English, French, and Chinese are products of groups rather than of individuals. More important, languages can be attributed only to whole groups rather than to single individuals.

As Wittgenstein has demonstrated, it makes no sense to say that a single individual has a private language that only he or she can speak. So, in this thesis as suggested, try to take a photograph of a period of one of those human societies, the Indian society, a society, which has roots down to the time of the Pharaohs.

The Social Structure

After defining the word society in a basic manner, we have to define some main types of societies. Especially when the subject is the caste system, we find a timeline of civilization inside India, which was built on the mainstreams of social life; the nomadic and the sedentary. Indian civilization is one of the oldest sedentary civilizations. But just like others it was not sedentary at the beginning. And it is clear for us to see that the whole story of the formation of a social system, which we call the caste system, is at the same time the history of the formation of a new civilization.

The known predecessors of today's Hindu culture were the Aryans. Arya is an English word derived from the Vedic Sanskrit and Avestan (language of old Iran) term arya, meaning noble. They are believed to have been a nomadic society, which came to the Indian sub-continent from northwest. The migration of the Aryans to the subcontinent is dated as early as the 15th century BC. But we must acknowledge that this dating was not build on historical or archeological proofs.

In reality the whole Aryan Migration theory is based on philological proofs, tracking the similarities between the proto Indo-European languages such as Persian, Greek, Armenian to Vedic Indic, the latter which was later called Sanskrit. So it is hard to make the whole theory dependant on philological evidences and give exact dates of migration of societies. The main evidence of Aryan migrations is the warfare stories of an ancient text, which is called the "Rigveda". The manner of this scripture is mostly religious and literary and it is a very valuable historical source.

However, examining the scripture, historians believe that the geographical names used are defining the geography of northern India or the Punjab, and their fierce struggling with their enemies, the Dasas gives evidence. Until the first decades of the 20th century, the Dasas told in the Vedas had no meaning than a myth. But with the re-discovery of the Indus Valley Civilization city, called Harappa in Pakistan the late 19th century by the explorers Charles Masson and Alexander Burnes, and the archaeologist Sir Alexander Cunningham in the 1870's, we came to know that the Dasa of the Vedas could have been a reality. The word Dasa later became the usual word for 'slave'. After the re-discovery of ancient cities of an unknown culture led to the the first excavations in the early 20th century at Harappa by Rai Bahadur Daya Ram Sahni, and by R.D. Banerji at another Indus Valley city, Mohenjo-daro. Romila Thapar also mentions the possibility that the Dasas were the descendants of the Indus Valley Civilization. One of the main differences between the Aryans and the Indus Valley civilization is their way of life.

Aryans were migrants and that meant that they were probably a nomadic society. The philological links between the Iranian and Aryan languages shows us that at some time in their history Iranian and Aryan tribes were living together and than they were separated.

So we can assume that Aryans migrated into India. The nomadic character of the Aryans can also be observed with the religious ritual of horse sacrifice where horse breeding is linked to nomadic life. The other evidence, which makes one think that the Aryans were nomads that the Vedas were first born as, hymns where the society was illiterate.

It is believed that the writing down of Vedas were nearly a thousand years later from they were first composed. Before the arrival of Aryans into the subcontinent, the Indus Valley culture had already produced a scripture and literal civilization. So it would be right to think that the Aryans were a semi-nomadic society at the very beginning of their arrival into India. On the other hand the Indus Valley civilization was a well-developed civilization with well-established cities with a population of 50.000 individuals. They had their own scripture and operational harbors making commerce with the antique Mesopotamian cultures such as Sumerians. The pattern of a nomadic society invading a sedentary civilization in general does not match the story of Aryans and the Indus Valley civilization.

Although it is stated that some of the verses of the RigVeda points to the destruction of the cities:

- "In aid of Abhyavartin Cayamana, Indra destroyed the seed of Virasakha. At Hariyupiyah he smote the vanguard of the Vrcivans, and the rear fled frighted."-[Rg.V. XXVII.5]

The name Indra indicated here was the god in Vedic times. He was the leader of the Devas, the god of war, the god of thunder and storms, and the greatest of all warriors, the strongest of all beings. It is assumed that he was the king of the first Aryan tribes who seized ancient India. As it is also stated that the place called Hariyupiyap is the famous lost city of Harappa that indicates that the Aryans destroyed the Indus Valley civilization. But it is a statement without sufficient evidence. Most possibly the Aryans never had the chance to see the glimmering cities of the Indus Valley Civilization. What they had found was perhaps the remnants of those cities and probably people who were living just as they did in a tribal nomadic society or at least villages.

This is why for half a millennium and more was needed for the flourishing of Aryan cities and also why they were unable to inherit the famous Indus Valley script and develop a literary culture. The Aryans were the usual nomadic people who had the knowledge of horse breeding, iron casted weapons and war chariots. We can assume that after invading north India, they captured the whole native society and turned them into semi-slaves.

This process, which began with the mixture of two completely different cultures, Aryans as the invaders on the one hand, and possibly the native Dravidian, Munda speaking people as the slaves on the other, must be the very first establishment of the "Caste System". It is just adding a new group into the society whether they are slaves or not. And with the process of urbanization and the rise of civilization, this position of slavery turned into a much more meaningful concept, first religiously and then socially since a time when nobody remembered why things were like this way.

So the cause of the caste system cannot only be the Aryans but also the native people of India though in an indirect way. They were not capable to overcome the invaders and they did not have the cultural sedentary environment to swallow the large flow of Aryan speaking nomadic people. Romila Thapar also mentions this anomaly and explains the overwhelming power on the possibly civilized people with the technology of iron against the technology of copper.

The last thing to remember about the Hindu social structure is its dependence on religion. From the very beginning the Hindu society was shaped within the rules of religion, which also caused the birth of the caste system.

- However, Brahmanism had already defined the worldly authority according to the religious rules and turned the Brahmans and Kshatriyas into the very upper classes of society as a part of its caste system.

This is a brief description of the social structure of India well before the birth of Christ, which gave rise to Hindu civilization and its important part the caste system that is the subject of this study. Later on, based on this structure as suggested, try to explain the birth of caste system.

Social Hierarchy

Social hierarchy whether in the singular or the plural form, indicates the real meaning of the word society. The word "hierarchy" can be applied to the history of the societies with big population as a whole and without any effort. None of these societies grow horizontally in the means of equality. They grow vertically. Just as Braudel states and just; humans had always been a social creature, living in groups. Social groups are consisted of individuals and social groups forms social systems.

Every individual or group forming a social system is interdependent.16 This kind of social system is applicable to any kind of species besides humans, which form societies. So it is a general and a universal rule that every member of a system has to follow the rules of nature and the rules formed in time in that system. Because of this there is always a system of relations within the groups or societies. And another inevitable rule of the societies or groups is that there had always been a hierarchical system within the members of the system. There had always been individuals that were much more privileged than others. So we can say that human societies are build upon hierarchies that are unequal in its character. The inequalities can be based on gender, age, physical appearance, race or any other kind of difference that can form subgroups within the big groups.

Again as Braudel says:

- But a village is an order of grouping. Even the societies build in utopias are hierarchical in their nature. Even the Greek Gods of the Olympos live in hierarchical order. As a conclusion: there is no society without a skeleton and structure.

And as Anthony Giddens have emphasized, whether it is modern or primitive there had always been inequalities. Even in societies where there is no wealth or power differences do exist, we can observe inequalities between man and woman, young and olds and etc. Sociologists, use the term social hierarchy to define those social inequalities.

Hierarchies are inequalities between different human groups those are established and institutionalized within the society. And all of the social inequalities or to say social hierarchies takes place in a hierarchy from the most privileged to the less privileged. This means that social classes are not formed in a shape where they are all at the same level and equal, but in a vertical form where each one is above another. Classes and hierarchical systems became much more complicated during the process of alteration from first the hunter-gatherer life, than into agricultural village life and at last into sedentary life where today millions of people call groups what we call city today.

To understand this we have to take a look on the diagram which shows the percentage of the hunter-gatherer population inside the general human population. Tens of thousands of years ago the whole human population that was a few million was hunter-gatherers. It is understandable for 10 million people to be nomadic and hunter where there were endless lands unpopulated. With the rise of the population, humans began forming bigger groups and with the help of technology they have produced villages were established first. One must admit that this process of change is not linear and the same for the whole human population. It was different for each of the societies living in different parts of the world. Even if history is based on selected data, the data selected need not be entirely arbitrary.

They assume that all societies change and that in a period stretching from 2500 B.C. to A.D. 1000 Indian society and its institutions must have undergone change; it is the work of the historian to study the nature of this change. The idea of a static society is no longer reliable. As it is accepted within the social sciences that, there had always been hierarchical systems within human societies. These hierarchical systems themselves were also different from each other according to time and place. Before the formation of the hierarchical system of our modern world, which we call the class system, the main stream of social hierarchy was a little bit different. Again changing from time to place societies was divided into subclasses like the nobles and soldiers, the priests and people who had professions. The subject of this thesis which is caste system is just one of those hierarchical systems which is a famous but example. It is not very different from the others but unique enough to left its name in history.

- There was an observant Greek ambassador in India about 300 B.C., Megasthenes, whose account of the country and its people gives us our first general view of India as seen by a visitor. He observed that the people divided themselves into a number of occupationally specialized groups, that a person could only marry within his own group, and that no one could change affiliation from one group to another. Many other voyagers to India after Megasthenes

> remarked upon this distinctive social order. It regulated a large part of public and private behaviour; it was a most important concern of the people of the land. It seemed both familiar and quite unfamiliar to a visitor. It was familiar in that like tended to marry like elsewhere; sons followed their father's occupation in the voyager's homeland; a hierarchy of society and privileges of rank were not strange to anyone. What did strike observers as unfamiliar was the rigor of the social divisions, the bases on which the divisions were made, and the thoroughgoing way in which they were applied to all aspects of life.

The caste system is unique enough to become the main concept of the Hindu image world wide. As told by Mandelbaum, every individual who was interested somehow with India was stunned in the concept throughout history. But at the same time caste system is one of the hardest social systems to understand and solve especially for non-Indians like us.

As an Indian low caste member emphasizes about the caste system:

- It is a truism that an outsider cannot really know the inside story. However the outsider does posses some degree of objectivity although this it may be conditioned by his background.

Born in an illiterate society and managed to survive for nearly 3.000 years without changing its mainframe, the caste system deserves to be studied. But what makes caste system so interesting does also include many problems for the researchers. Because of illiteracy of the people in which the caste system is born much of the social system and the history of the founders of the society are still unknown. The very few evidences about the born of caste system lies mostly in the sacred books of the Hindus, the Vedas, which are literary, religious and social treatises which do not enter into the category of hard-core historical evidence.

Indian sub-continent and Indian civilization

The Geography of the Sub-Continent The Indian subcontinent is the peninsular region of larger South Asia in which the nations of India, Bangladesh, Pakistan, Sri Lanka as well as parts of Nepal, Bhutan, Myanmar and some currently controlled by China, namely Tibet are located. It is also known as the "Indian Subcontinent" and, primarily in Pakistan, as the "Indo-Pak Subcontinent". Being the only region in the world that is commonly described as a subcontinent, "The Subcontinent" is also a very common characterization and often the preferred term, especially in Pakistan.

Geologically, the notion of a subcontinent is based on the fact that this region rests on a tectonic plate of its own, separate from the rest of Asia. The southern region of the subcontinent forms an enormous peninsula, while in the north it is separated from the colder regions of China and Mongolia by the Himalaya mountain range, which also acts as a cultural and geographical barrier between it and the rest of Asia. The main character of the region we call India is that, it is quite insular from the rest of Asia.

The Himalaya mountain range as being the highest geographical boundaries all over the world cuts the whole subcontinent from Asia. While the north of the subcontinent is impossible to pass, western direction is also not so friendly, where there are deserts in the west and again mountains as high as 3000 meters in the northwest where famous Khaybar Pass to be found. There is also the famous Indus river and its branches dividing the western planes.

On the East the other famous river of India, the Ganges, pours into the Indian Ocean, forming an enormous Delta where modern Bangladesh is founded. Being nearly 10 million square kilometers, India is as big as Europe. We have to admit again that considering the geographical isolation and the largeness India is more like a continent than Europe. The subcontinent shows an isolated position not only in geography but also in history. Although beginning with the known history of Aryan invasions, there had always been migrations from the northwest into the subcontinent; still India is a more isolated part of the old world than other places like Mesopotamia or Europe.

As we have said India is a very huge country. And it contains every kind of climate from dry deserts to the rain forests and cold and high mountains surrounded by a big and warm ocean. It has all the evens for the human beings to form high-grade civilizations. For thousands of years it has been a vast country, out of the human imagination to capture and control.

When we think of the few million people populating India, ten thousands of years ago, we can assume that tribes or clans were far apart from each other, surrounded with enough and more supplies they need, preventing them to fight for sources. When we take into consideration that the Indus Valley Civilization -as it can be understood from its name- was a river civilization.

Rivers are the other main geographical factors that shaped the destiny of the subcontinent. They provided the tribes with an environment where they were able to produce their own crops, just like cities built in Mesopotamia. The most famous and biggest of these rivers are the Indus which in the northwest region of subcontinent, and Ganges in the northern region of the subcontinent. Both of these mega rivers are born from the Himalayan mountain range. The remnant sites of the Indus Valley civilization are all found near the main and secondary branches of the Indus river. And as some historians state the Aryan culture spread to the east following the river Ganges, before it spread all over the subcontinent.

It is logical not for us today, but also for the ancient man, to settle around the endless sources of those great rivers. Southern India was also suitable with its endless plains for the humans to spread. Within these geographical situation the ecosystem allowed humans to reach big numbers and through out the whole history India had always contained a great portion of the whole human population as it is today. And as Romila Thapar states that,

- "It also led tho the recognition of the fact that an area as large as the Indian sub-continent will show evidence of regional variations in the cultural pattern and this historical change in the sub-continent need not to be identical nor occur simultaneously."

The Caste System

Description

The title we use here seems problematic, because it is a fact that the caste system, considering its old age, is a really complicated social system with its four castes and hundreds of sub-castes.

The 'caste' as a definition is not a native one but a description that was used first by the Portuguese who appeared on the subcontinent from the end of the 15th century. It is just a mispronunciation of the Indian word 'Jat', which means class divided according to professions. After the decline of the Portuguese naval power; other Europeans filled the gap and the British who arrived to India much later after the Portuguese also used the word caste.

The British used the word Caste instead of Jat and Varna, which is the classical word used to denote caste and which means, "colour" in Sanskrit. Just as other social researches the first investigations on the ancient Indian society and the Europeans made its structure. Their approach was likely to be related with their interpretations with the supremacy of Western culture. Especially after they understood that Sanskrit was very essence of the Indo-European languages. And it turned into a tool for the approval of the racist supremacy of Indo-European nations that were also speaking versions of the same languageations that were also speaking versions of the same language.

In Keshab Chunder Sen's words:

- The Aryans it was argued were implicitly superior to the non- Aryans as they were the initial conquerors that have founded civilizations in Europe and Asia. In India, the arrival of the Aryans was associated with the compilation of the Rig Veda and this was believed to be the bedrock of Indian civilization, the excavation of the Indus civilization not as yet having taken place. By the late nineteenth century, the fallacy of equating language with race had been clearly demonstrated. Nevertheless, the theory remained established in European thought with reference to India. It also became acceptable to the new middle-class elite in India as it could call itself Aryan, differentiate itself from the lower castes believed to be non-Aryan and even seek a connection with the British rulers who represented European aryandom.

So, since the birth of nationalism in the 18th century in Europe, Aryandom as Mr. Keshab defines had become the center for the new ideologies of supremacy of the West, which also legalized the patronage of the West over the rest of the world.

- In reality there are two concepts that has to be understood to have an idea on the whole caste system, which are "Jat" and "Varna". As in most of the societies of the world, so in India, profession is inherited from father to the son. And so in India there developed families, who professed the same family profession for generation in which, the son continued his father's profession. Later on as these families became larger, they were seen as communities or as they are called in Indian languages, Jat. The Indians use the word 'Jat' for any community who has something common like religion, language, origin, similar geographical background and so on. At the same time they also use the word 'Jat' for Varna. Different families who professed the same profession developed social relations between them and organized as a common community, meaning Jat. Sometimes in English the word caste is used for Varna and the word sub-caste for Jat.

As regards the structure of the Hindu society, it comprised four varnas or orders, functionally differentiated -the Brahmana, acting as the custodian of the sacred lore and performing priestly function; the Kshatriya responsible for governance and maintenance of peace; the Vaishya, engaged in agriculture, industry and trade and the Sudra rendering general services to the whole community. This is the functional definition of the caste system.

The main division in the caste system is the varna of the people. Varna, means colour in the Sanskrit. Basic caste is called varna, or "colour" Subcaste, or jâti, "birth, life, rank," is a traditional subdivision of varna. And the question which comes into mind is if the varna division had something to do with the skin colour of the ancient Indians. And after varna, the society is divided into "Jat"s. Varna is the most famous division of the caste system that is divided into four castes, which are the Brahmans, the Kshatriyas, the Vaisyas and the Shudras. And there is another group that is not included in this division, which is called "the untouchables". Or to say the ones who are outcastes.

Although they are called outcastes, it can be thought as if they are a little portions of the society that had been excluded from the society. But today there are hundreds of millions of outcastes in the Indian society. We do not know the skin colour of the Aryans of the 15th century B.C., but it can be assumed that the colour of the native people were much more darker than the Aryans. Aryans classified the native people as Dasas and put them into the lowest class of society to be used in the labour. Even today the people who are called Shudras and untouchables are estimated as much as 150 million in populations and most of them have darker skin colours. In the

"Laws of Manu" –which are estimated to be written in the 4th century B.C.—the differences between the Shudras, untouchables and the upper castes are well described:

- "But he who does not (worship) standing in the morning, nor sitting in the evening, shall be excluded, just like a Shudra, from all the duties and rights of an Aryan."

There are various theories trying to explain the caste system in their own point of view. One can be called the biological theory which claims that all existing things, animated and unanimated, inherent three qualities in different apportionment. Sattva qualities include wisdom, intelligence, honesty, goodness and other positive qualities. Rajas include qualities like passion, pride, valor and other passionate qualities. Tamas qualities include dullness, stupidity, lack of creativity and other negative qualities. People with different doses of these inherent qualities adopted different types of occupation.

According to this theory the Brahmans inherent Sattva qualities. Kshatrias and Vaisias inherent Rajas qualities and the Shudras inherent Tamas qualities. A man who is in search of the understanding of the caste system will come to an end where he understands that although the caste system is a very strict social hierarchy which limits the social mobility is also a system that has endless exceptions. This kind of relation is similar to the one between the order and chaos, an endless loop just like the Hindu belief of life, a circle that has no beginning and no end.

The Beginning

To understand the establishment of the caste system which is nearly 3.000 years old, we must first understand the social environment it was build in. As we have mentioned before what we know about ancient India during the 3rd and 2nd millenniums A.D. is limited. But what we know for sure is that there existed a great civilization in northern India before the questionable migration of Aryans during the 1500 B.C. A civilization that was as developed as other civilizations like Sumers or Egyptians of its age.

Social hierarchy is a concept that we can observe in every society from the most primitive to the most advanced, and which means the Indus Valley Civilization had to have a social hierarchy of its own. We can only make assumptions about the daily life of the ordinary people living in Harappa, Mohenjodaro or other developed cities, where we do not have solid proofs. These assumptions have to be generalizations of social and historical facts. For example the most obvious evidence about this lost cultures is the remnant of their cities itself.

So we can assume that they were a developed and sedentary culture, but not nomadic or underdeveloped. So we have to build our assumption over other observations about other urban societies that we know better. Another thing we know is the fact that 2.500 A.D. was a time where currency and money were unknown even to the urban societies. This means that there was possibly no exchange tool for the goods to change hands. And what is more possible that goods were exchanged with other goods. Exchange mechanisms of a society are the basic factor that affects the daily life. Without money or something similar, the main exchange instrument must be the exchange of goods and services. In an economic structure like this one, it must be important what profession did the individuals had concerning the goods or services they were able to present to the economy.

- In old times, there was no concept of money or cash. People produced things and bartered (traded) them for other goods and services. A producer or trader belonging to Vaishya would include people such as farmer producing grains and milk etc., blacksmith (Lohar) making iron implements, leather-worker (Charmar or Chamar, charm meaning leather) manufacturing shoes, and so on. Thus, for subsistence,

> a Brahmin would do worship (puja) in a 'Vaishya' farmer's house and get grains and milk in return. Similarly, a Chamar would exchange shoes for food items from a farmer, iron implements from a Lohar, and so on. Similarly, a 'Shudra' servant might work or help in a farmer's field for food in return. If he were to help a Lohar, then a Lohar would provide him with food items. Moreover, all these people would give a share of their goods (produced) and services to the Kshatriya (tribal chief) for administration of Visha (tribe or society). Society was basically managed through bartering system.

As Dr. Sharma states in his article, social hierarchy in the pro-money societies had to be very important. But we have to admit that it should not have happened so easily. It is questionable that people were giving their goods and services to the tribal chief because of the administrative service he was offering. First of all, in the pro-Aryan society we have no proof of castes like Kshatriya, Brahmin or Vaishya.

They were all names used in the Aryanic tribal and nomadic society and in a nomadic society distinction of professions should not be as advanced as in an urban society. But it can be true for an urban society like the Indus Valley Civilization to have a social hierarchy based on professions.

As it is known caste system consists of the infamous castes the Brahmins (priests), Kshatriyas (the rulers), the Vaishyas (people with profession), Shudras (people doing low-level and dirty jobs), and again as you can see this division is a division of profession in reality. And there are hundreds, perhaps thousands of sub-castes again mainly defined with the job done. Yet we have to make a second distinction between the first three castes (Brahmins, Kshatriyas, Vaishyas) and the last one (Shudras). Because Shudras are not accepted as Aryans from the very first Vedas chanted in the second millennium B.C..

They are not noble in the meaning. The first three castes are called as twice-borns that as suggested, explain later. It looks like that Shudra caste is an implementation of the non-Aryanic population into the Aryanic society and legalizing the bad conditions dictated over them as the conquered and an explanation why they are low. Although the caste system is based on the Brahmanic religious myths, it is not unusual for a human society to have a social hierarchy like the caste system.

First of all this division of ruler, priest and people depending on mainly professions, can be observed almost in every society of its time to the time of modernization where we were introduced with the classes as the social hierarchy. From the very early civilizations like the Sumerians and Egyptians to the comparatively modern societies like the Ottomans or the pre-enlightenment Europe this social division was usual. Because of this the travellers who made their way to India, beginning from the antique Greek and Roman times, to the Chinese, Muslims and colonial European powers were not surprised to see a social structure like this. What they were surprised of was the strict inter-caste rules that prohibited the social mobility in an unseen way. One of the biggest scholars of his time, the 10th century Al- Biruni is one of those, who describes the Indian caste system and depending on the antique customs which are later forgotten. He also mentions that antique social hierarchy was based on the distinction of professions.

When we turn back to the roots of the caste system and its link with the Indus Valley civilization, we have look for evidences. First of all it must be proved that the migrating and occupying Aryan tribes must have come face to face with those cities of Harappan culture. There are some theories that the Indus Valley civilization was destroyed by the invading Aryans, which we had talked about previously in the first stage. But there is no solid proof for that theory to be proved. And we have to underline that this theory of Aryans destroying the Indus Valley civilization is put forward by the famous Indian character of the 20th century Dr. Ambedkar, who was one of the founders and leaders of the "Dalit Movement" which demanded equal rights with the upper castes.

The decline and disappear of the Indus Valley civilization still has to be proved. So we can assume that the theory that Indus Valley people and the Aryans never met before. When the Aryans first invaded the continent the Dasas they fought were other native people, perhaps the descendants of the Indus Valley civilization but not themselves. Whatever the truth is we can guess that at least there should be some remnants of the Indus Valley civilization when the Aryans came and in some way they must be in contact where two cultures effect each other. Although the glamorous cities were deserted, the knowledge produced in those cities must somehow prevail. But this fact does not give us the extent of the cultural interaction and also does not mean that caste system had its roots inside the Indus Valley civilization.

Rhys Davis also thinks likely, telling us:

- It is a common error, vitiating all conclusions as to the early history of India, to suppose that the tribes, with whom the Aryans, in their gradual conquest of India, came into contact, were savages. Some were so. There were hill tribes, gypsies, and bands of hunters in the woods. But there were also settled communities with highly developed social organization, wealthy enough to excite the cupidity of the invaders, and in many cases too much addicted to the activities of peace to be able to offer.

As we have explained there are different theories trying the give meaning to the caste system. One of them was biological theory or lets' better call it biological approach. And there are religious-mystical theories. The religious theory explaining how the four Varnas were founded, but they do not explain how the Jats in each Varna or the untouchables were founded.

According the Rig Veda, the ancient Hindu book, the primal man - Purush - destroyed himself to create a human society.

The different Varnas were created from different parts of his body. The Brahmans were created from his head; the Kshatrias from his hands; the Vaishias from his thighs and the Shudras from his feet. The Varna hierarchy is determined by the descending order of the different organs from which the Varnas were created. Other religious theory claims that the Varnas were created from the body organs of Brahma, who is the creator of the world. Al-Biruni had also his own theory about the creation of the caste system, which also seeks the roots of this social system not inside the Hindu society, but somewhere else.

- If a new order of things in political or social life is created by a man naturally ambitious of ruling, who by his character and capacity really deserves to be a ruler, a man of firm convictions and unshaken determination, who even in times of reverses is supported by good luck, in so far as people then side with him in recognition of former merits of his, such an order is likely to become consolidated among those for whom it was created, and to continue as firm as the deeply rooted mountains. It will remain among them as a generally recognised rule in all generations through the course of time and the flight of ages. If, then, this new form of state or society rests in some degree on religion, these twins, state and religion, are in perfect harmony, and their union represents the highest development of human society, all that men can possibly desire.
- The kings of antiquity, who were industriously devoted to the duties of their office, spent most of their care on the division of their subjects into different classes and orders, which they tried to preserve from intermixture and disorder. Therefore they forbade people of different classes to have intercourse with each other, and laid upon each class a particular kind of work or art and handicraft. They did not allow anybody to transgress

the limits of his class, and even punishend those who would not be content with their class.

- All this is well ilustrated by the history of the ancient Chosroes (Khusrau), for they had created great institutions of this kind, which could not be broken through by the special merits of any individual nor by bribery. When Ardashin bin Babak restored the Persian Empire, he also restored the classe or castes of the population in the following way:
  - The first class were the knights and princes,
  - The second class were the monks, the fire-priests, and the lawyers,
  - The third class were the physicians, astronomers and other men of science,
  - The fourth class were the husbandmen and artisans.
- And within these classes there were subdivisions, distinct from each other, like the species within a genus. All institutions of this kind are like a pedigree, as long as their origin is remembered; but when once their origin has been forgotten, they become, as it were, the stable property of the whole nation, nobody any more questioning its origin. And forgetting is the necessary result of any long period of time, of a long succession of centuries and generations.
- Among the Hindus institutions of this kind abound. We Muslims, of course, stand entirely on the other side of the question, considering all men as equal, except in piety; and this is the greatest obstacle which prevents any approach or understanding between Hindus and Muslims.

Like human beings, food also inherent different dosage of these qualities and it affects its eater's intelligence. The Brahmans and the Vaisias have Sattvic diet, which includes fruits, milk, honey, roots and vegetables. Most of the meats are considered to have Tamasic qualities. Many Shudra communities eat different kinds of meat (but not beef) and other Tamasic food. But the Kshatrias who had Rajasic diet eat some kinds of meat like deer meat that is considered to have Rajasic qualities.

Many Marathas who claim to be Kshatrias eat mutton. The drawback of this theory is that in different parts of India the same food was sometimes qualified to have different dosage of inherent qualities. For example there were Brahmans who eat meat that is considered Tamasic food. Another explanation of the caste system is a social historical theory explains the creation of the Varnas, Jats and of the untouchables, which we have mentioned before.

According to this theory, the caste system began with the arrival of the Aryans in India. Before the Aryans there were other communities in India of other origins, where Negrito, Mongoloid, Austroloid and Dravidian are among them. The Negritos have physical features similar to people of Africa. The Mongoloid have Chinese features. The Austroloids have features similar the aboriginals of Australia. The Dravidians originate from the Mediterranean and they were the largest community in India.

When the Aryans arrived in India their main contact was with the Dravidians and the Austroloids. The Aryans disregarded the local cultures. They began conquering and taking control over regions in north India and at the same time pushed the local people southwards or towards the jungles and mountains in north India. All these religious, biological, or socio-historical theories contain a piece of truth inside. We must be sure that just like every action made by man, the formation of caste system also has to be religious, social, biological and even economical faces. As we know from the Vedas that Aryans were fierce enemies of the native Indians, which they won a certain victory against this ended with enslaving. Aryans had a simple social hierarchy within them. But when they turned out to be conquerors of a massive land, leaving no serious threat to their hegemony, they became something much more than nomadic tribes.

They found a land to rule. So just as it is said in the socio-historical approach, the remnant population of the Aryan invasion was enslaved. Slavery was not an uncommon concept in those times where most of the world economies were dependent on slave labour. Four hundred years before the Aryans invaded India, a society called Amorites captured the ancient Sumerian lands and established the Babylonian Empire. At the time of Aryan invasion they were in charge of the ruling of the Mesopotamia with a glamorous and developed city life.

And the Babylon society was also had a social hierarchy of its own composed of classes called:

- Awilu (a free person of upper class)
- Mushkenu, (a free person of middle or lower class)
- Wardu, (a slave)
- Babylonian society was well differentiated. At the basis of it lay the slave population, the necessary condition of all economic activity in antiquity. Slaves were employed upon the farms, by the manufacturers and in the temples. The sources of the supply were various. War furnished many; others had fallen from the position of free laborers; still others were purchased from abroad, or were children of native bondsmen. Rich private owners or temple corporations made a business of hiring them out as laborers. They were humanely treated; the law protected them from injury; they could earn money, hold property, and thus purchase their freedom. Laws exist which suggest that young children could not be separated from their slave-parents in case of the sale of the latter.

Most of the communities that were in India before the arrival of the Aryans were integrated in the Shudra Varna or were made outcast depending on the professions of these communities. Communities who professed nonpolluting jobs were integrated in Shudra Varna. And communities who professed polluting professions were made outcasts.

The Brahmans are very strict about cleanliness. In the past people believed that diseases can also spread also through air and not only through physical touch. Perhaps because of this reason the untouchables were not only disallowed to touch the high caste communities but they also had to stand at a certain distance from the high castes.

- But in India the acceptance of the ideology of the ruling categories by the general population was ensured by a neat integration of religion into the social structure. The cleverly contrived theory of cycles of rebirth, with the possibility of birth in a higher caste being linked to faithfully carrying out one's duties as per caste rules. The fatalistic acceptance of the membership of a particular caste as a result of deeds in past life. The pseudo-religious practices of untouchability and endogamy which segregated one caste from another, apart from the various social privileges and also laws as provided in our Dharmashastras drilled into the minds of people that caste is a pre-ordained and hereditary institution which has divine sanction.

The Aryans organized among themselves in three groups. The first group was of the warriors and they were called Rajayana, later they changed their name Rajayana to Kshatria. The second group was of the priests and they were called Brahmans. These two groups struggled politically for leadership among the Aryans. In this struggle the Brahmans got to be the leaders of the Aryan society. The third group was of the farmers and craftsmen and they were called Vaisia. The Aryans who conquered and took control over parts of north India subdued the locals and made them their servants. In this process the Vaisias who were the farmers and the craftsmen became the landlords and the businessmen of the society and the locals became the peasants and the craftsmen of the society.

In order to secure their status the Aryans resolved some social and religious rules that allowed only them to be the priests, warriors and the businessmen of the society. For example take Maharashtra. Maharashtra is in west India. This region is known by this name for hundreds of years. Many think that the meaning of the name Maharashtra is in its name, Great Land. But there are some who claim that the name, Maharashtra, is derived from the Jat called Mahar who is considered to be the original people of this region. In the caste hierarchy the dark skinned Mahars were outcasts. The skin colour was an important factor in the caste system. The meaning of the word "Varna" is not class or status but colour.

- Associated with each varna there is a traditional colour. These sound suspiciously like skin colours; and, indeed, there is an expectation in India that higher caste people will have lighter skin—although there are plenty of exceptions (especially in the South of India). This all probably goes back to the original invasion of the Arya, who came from Central Asia and so were undoubtedly light skinned. The people already in India were quite dark, even as today many people in India seem positively black. Apart from skin colour, Indians otherwise have "Caucasian" features --narrow noses, thin lips, etc.—and recent genetic mapping studies seem to show that Indians are more closely related to the people of the Middle East and Europe than to anyone else. Because Untouchables are not a varna, they do not have a traditional colour.

Between the outcasts and the three Aryan Varnas there is the Shudra Varna who are the simple workers of the society. The Shudras consisted of two communities. One community was of the locals who were subdued by the Aryans and the other were the descendants of Aryans with locals. In Hindu religious stories there are many wars between the good Aryans and the dark skinned demons and devils. The different Gods also have dark skinned slaves.

There are stories of demon women trying to seduce good Aryan men in deceptive ways. There were also marriages between Aryan heroes and demon women. Many believe that these incidences really occurred in which, the gods and the positive heroes were people of Aryan origin. And the demons, the devils and the dark skinned slaves were in fact the original residence of India whom the Aryans coined as monsters, devil, demons and slaves. Later on the Aryans who created the caste system, added to their system non-Aryans. Different Jats who professed different professions were integrated in different Varnas according to their profession. Other foreign invaders of ancient India - Greeks, Huns, Scythains and others - who conquered parts of India and created kingdoms, were integrated in the Kshatria Varna (warrior castes). But probably the Aryan policy was not to integrate original Indian communities within them and therefore many aristocratic and warrior communities that were in India before the Aryans did not get the Kshatria status.

So at first just like it is else where on earth, the conquered people must have been enslaved. But what makes the difference between the Aryanic society and Mesopotamia or other places of world is the legalization of the slavery. In Babylon slavery was a judicial subject that had strict rules, but only related with the state and the judiciary system. But in ancient Aryans it did not work this way. Most probably, because of the illiteracy of the nomadic Aryan tribes that had no scripture and eventually a written code system had only their religion to explain and define things. This situation caused the birth of a social system described earlier in the religious theory, which placed the conquered people in the context of a religious myth.

As we have said it is believed that Shudras were created from the feet of the primal man, Purush. And as Al-Biruni indicates in a time of a millennium and a half, as the social foundation of a system was completely forgotten and where only an illiterate mythology of religion were left, the separation of caste system became rock hard. And it took three more millenium before the low castes began asking questions about their position. In short, Shudras and untouchables were the slaves of the society; unfortunately who had no judicial rights who began to believe a religion that did not want them.

SOCIAL DEMORALIZATION

How does the living dialogue become a religious issue or a theological issue? It is because a breakdown of this dialogue results in the spread of demoralization within society. Ambedkar's work is a great study of the colossal effects or the tremendous ill effects that flow from the absence of a living dialogue within a given society. Ambedkar saw the widespread poverty in India as linked to the lack of a spiritual framework capable of generating enthusiasm among the people to attempt to better themselves. Thus, like Hayek, who saw the possibility of a movement within society as a necessary component of its life and growth Ambedkar saw that the presence of enthusiasm in the population as a necessary condition of growth, including economic growth. Ambedkar attributed the reason for the lack of enthusiasm as the realization that the possibilities for movement within society did not in fact exist.

The caste system of India was in fact a system that outlawed such movement. It was not just a question of lack of opportunity that the caste system had created but the lack of any possibility for hope. The ideologies of inequality and injustice leave no room for the development of enthusiasm, he said. He demonstrated this view with an example. "As soon as a Brahmin women conceives, she thinks of the High Court whether any post of Judge has fallen vacant but when a Dalit woman becomes pregnant she cannot think of any thing better than a sweeper's post under the municipal committee."

He spoke of such lack of enthusiasm as a disease.

> *"Now, what saps the enthusiasm in man? If there is no enthusiasm, life becomes a drudgery-a mere burden to be dragged. Nothing can be achieved if there is no enthusiasm.*

Why does one lose enthusiasm? Main reason for this lack of enthusiasm on the part of a man is that an individual loses hope to get an opportunity to elevate oneself. Hopelessness leads to lack of enthusiasm. The mind in such cases becomes diseased."

In fact, in all his writings and work, Ambedkar treated Indian society as a diseased society (he often used the word sick), due to thousands of years of the practice of the caste system.

This astute politician who held the Law Minister's post in Nehru's Cabinet and contributed a great deal to the discussion of all vital political issues of his time did not hesitate to state that India's loss of freedom time and again which resulted in India being subject to foreign domination was caused by this diseased condition of the Indian mind, and due to the operation of the caste system:

"*It is because our country as a whole never stood against the enemy. It was always a small section of the society and whoever over-powered it became the victor. This was mainly due to the pernicious caste system of the Hindus.*"

This analysis differs greatly from the analysis of many nationalists in India, and outside of the causes of the paralysis of the Indian mind. No one really argues seriously that there is no such paralysis. The differences of opinion relate to the reasons causing this paralysis. The nationalists argue that the paralysis was due to foreign invasion and foreign domination. Ambedkar's position is that the foreign domination itself became possible due to the deep division among the people who are humanly divided, without any hope of coming together. There was no source to draw from when fighting a foreign element. Caste, notionally accepted as the foundation of society nullified the possibility of a common front to fight against outsiders' invasions and domination.

The invaders once in power used this deep internal division to maintain their power and to exploit India's resources. The group that had the natural leadership of the country was the Brahmins and they could not call the low castes to a common fight. Any physical act of solidarity would require holding common meetings and discourses. However, such physical contact would pollute the higher caste and make them impure. How could any strategy be developed or carried out without physical contact? Castes distanced groups of people physically. In this, caste was worse than slavery. The slaves often lived in the houses of their masters and helped in the household work. Slaves were sometimes even allowed to get some education, so that they could be more useful to the master. This is not so within the caste system. Low caste persons were to be kept in their low positions and not allowed to participate in any social activity. The low castes had to be avoided and not be touched in any way. That is how the terms such as touchable and untouchable came into use.

Ambedkar demonstrated the depth of this physical aspect of caste:

> *"I would like to tell you some of the reminiscence of my childhood. There was a Maratha women employed in my school. She was herself quite illiterate but observed untouchability and avoided touching me. One day, I remember, I was very thirsty. I was not allowed to touch the water tap. I told my master that I wanted to drink water. He called the peon and asked him to turn on the tap and I drank water. Whenever the peon was absent I had to go without water. Thirsty, I had to return home and then only I could quench my thirst."*

Ambedkar thus provided a tremendous study of how a society and the individuals within it go through a fundamental metamorphosis when it become organically incapable of what Grundtvig would have called a living dialogue. Ambedkar did not see caste as the only source from which such a negative change can take place; The same result can happen when the concentration in society is making wealth or getting enriched.

He wrote:

> "*You know the proprietors of mills. They appoint managers in the mills who extract work from labour. The proprietors remain so much engrossed in their work that they have little time to develop their minds. While they accumulate wealth and become economic giants they remain mental dwarfs." Perhaps this aspect may apply to the situation of the West in present times. Perhaps, the West too needs to wake up from decadence of this type and address its own spiritual crisis.*"

It is also a well known fact of the contemporary situation in most Third World countries that the impact of international relationships combined with internal factors have created a situation of destitution, which in turn has increased demoralization within many societies. Such demoralization often leads to internal warfare or ethnic, tribal and local conflicts. In fact, the area of conflict has now shifted from the international arena to local theatres of horror. Can these be resolved purely by physical rebuilding only? Are not the issues relating to internal inspiration irrelevant, when objective conditions prevent internal communication?

The related matter is about debt renunciation. Should not the first world countries consult their own internal sources of inspiration when considering these matters? Are policies that are followed on these matters based on the traditions of enlightenment of their countries or are they based on narrow considerations unworthy of great peoples? Should these matters be left purely to bureaucrats or must they become matters of living dialogue based on the inspirational sources of the Western traditions? Grundtvig's writings on the issues relating to neighbouring countries of his time showed enlightened views. He often opposed actions which would lead to loss of freedom or enslavement of peoples. Such deprivation of freedom and enslavement contradicted the Christian "Anskuelse." If the Economic policies pursued by the West create conditions of deep poverty and demoralization among the Third World countries is that not a matter of fundamental importance to the peoples of First World Countries?

It is in this context that Grundtvig's theology of the human as the precondition for the Christian needs to be looked at. Hinduism has created a conception of gods and a conception of holy life at the cost of destroying the human foundation of their society. This destruction was not only seen as irrelevant but also as necessary for Brahmins to achieve oneness with god. It was a conception of holiness and perfection which demanded deprivation of the humanity of most of the human beings living in Indian society. It was the inhumanity that was implied in adherence to caste that made Ambedkar look for outside inspiration. This he found in Buddhism. Buddha, Ambedhar said, was the only person who had the courage not only to condemn caste but also to espouse a promote new religious principles on the basis of the common humanity of everyone. Ambedkar wrote "The fundamental principle of Buddhism is equality. Of all Bhikkhus who joined the order in the time of Lord Buddha, about 75% of the Bhikkus belonged to the Brahmin caste and the remaining 25% were Sudra. Even then Buddhism was called the religion of the Sudra."

Here Ambedkar quotes from Buddha.

> *"O Bhikkhus, you belong to different castes and have come from various lands. Just as the great rivers when they have fallen into the great ocean lose their identity, just so brethren, O, brethren, do these four castes, Brahmins, Kshatriyas, Vaishyas, Sudra when they begin to follow the doctrine and discipline as propounded by the Tathagatta, they renounce different names of castes and rank and become members of one and same society."*

To have a common identity it was necessary to lose caste identity, which was an identity based on the superiority of some and the inferiority of others. Ambedkar's attempt to rediscover a basis to end the disease of the Indian mind led him to Buddhism which was once a powerful tradition in India. Grundtvig found the source of inspiration for democratic ideals in a reinterpretation of the local Lutheran tradition and bringing in the radical idea that the human, or the folk life was the precondition for spirituality. If the precondition was absent, the other had no ground to grow. Ambedkar was pointing to an historical example where the precondition had been killed. His was an attempt to indicate a way to recreate a similar precondition.

Grundtvig's conceptions about Nordic mythology and Christian "Anskuelse" may be compared with Ambedkar's views on the original tradition of Buddhism as a source of inspiration. In describing the work on Buddhism he said, "We have started this movement to develop and educate our minds." Explaining the need for religion among the poor as a need arising for hope, Ambedkar referred to a German professor of his, Professor Winternitz.

> *"The Watergang Rabelan Depth, was the book which he recommended and by which I was much inspired. 'It is only the poor, he said who need religion. 'Hope is the spring of action in life. Religion affords hope. Therefore, mankind finds solace in the religion, and that is why the poor cling to religion."*

Here it must be noted that Buddhism is not a religion but the reference here is to Dhamma. The term poor is more to the term ordinary people used by Grundtvig and religion more to "Anskuelse," used by Grundtvig.

To those who had not turned to Buddhism, but remained within Hinduism but wanted Hinduism to change, Ambedkar made the following suggestion:

> *"You must give a new doctrinal basis to your Religion-a basis that will be in consonance with Liberty, Equality and Fraternity, in short, with Democracy."*

Though he said this to a group of Hindus who considered themselves to be enlightened and wanted a fundamental change, he himself did not seem to have believed in this option. A few months before this meeting he had announced that though he was born a Hindu he would not die a Hindu.

In this very text of the prepared speech-Annilation of Caste-for this meeting where the above mentioned words were to be spoken, he mentioned, "I shall not be in your fold for long." He spent the subsequent 20 years, the last years of his life, in a very extensive historical studies of India's past and preparing his people to look in a different direction for inspiration.

8

Political Career of Ambedkar

In 1935, Ambedkar was appointed principal of the Government Law College, Mumbai, a position he held for two years. Settling in Mumbai, Ambedkar oversaw the construction of a house, and stocked his personal library with more than 50,000 books. His wife Ramabai died after a long illness in the same year. It had been her long-standing wish to go on a pilgrimage to Pandharpur, but Ambedkar had refused to let her go, telling her that he would create a new Pandharpur for her instead of Hinduism's Pandharpur which treated them as untouchables. Speaking at the Yeola Conversion Conference on October 13 near Nasik, Ambedkar announced his intention to convert to a different religion and exhorted his followers to leave Hinduism.

He would repeat his message at numerous public meetings across India In 1936, Ambedkar founded the Independent Labour Party, which won 15 seats in the 1937 elections to the Central Legislative Assembly. He published, The Annihilation of Caste in the same year, based on the thesis he had written in New York. Attaining immense popular success, Ambedkar's work strongly criticised Hindu orthodox religious leaders and the caste system in general. Ambedkar served on the Defence

Advisory Committee and the Viceroy's Executive Council as minister for labour. With What Congress and Gandhi Have Done to the Untouchables, Ambedkar intensified his attacks on Gandhi and the Congress, hypocrisy.

In his work Who Were the Shudras?, Ambedkar attempted to explain the formation of the Shudras, *i.e.*, the lowest caste in hierarchy of Hindu caste system. He also emphasised how Shudras are separate from Untouchables. Ambedkar oversaw the transformation of his political party into the All India Scheduled Castes Federation, although it performed poorly in the elections held in 1946 for the Constituent Assembly of India.

In writing a sequel to Who Were the Shudras? in 1948, Ambedkar lambasted Hinduism in The Untouchables: A Thesis on the Origins of Untouchability: The Hindu Civilization.... is a diabolical contrivance to suppress and enslave humanity. Its proper name would be infamy. What else can be said of a civilization which has produced a mass of people.... who are treated as an entity beyond human intercourse and whose mere touch is enough to cause pollution?

CASTE AND THE INSTITUTIONALIZATION OF DEMOCRACY: THE MOMENT OF POLITICS

Notwithstanding their faith in the scientific value of the classical anthropological theorizing, the encounter of social scientists, the social anthropologists and political scientists, working on India during the post independence period produced very different accounts of caste. Even when they worked with evolutionist models of social change, they recognized the tremendous resilience that caste was showing on the ground. Caste could enter the "modern" institutions, such as democracy, and survive or could even find a new life for itself.

The rise of non-Brahmin movements in southern and western Indian provinces provoked Ghurye to argue that their attack on Brahmin dominance did not necessarily mean the end of caste. These mobilizations generated a new kind of collective sentiment, "the feeling of caste solidarity" which could be "truly described as caste patriotism". M. N. Srinivas developed this point further in his writings during the late 1950s.

Focusing specifically on the possible consequences of modern technology and representational politics, both of which were introduced by the colonial rulers in India, he argued that far from disappearing with the process of modernization, caste was experiencing a "horizontal consolidation".

Commenting on the impact of modern technology on caste, he wrote:

- The coming in of printing, of a regular postal service, of vernacular newspapers and books, of the telegraph, railway and bus, enabled the representatives of a caste living in different areas to meet and discuss their common problems and interests. Western education gave new political values such as liberty and equality. The educated leaders started caste journals and held caste conferences.

Funds were collected to organize the caste, and to help the poorer members. Caste hostels, hospitals, co-operative societies etc., became a common feature of urban social life. In general it may be confidently said that the last hundred years have seen a great increase in caste solidarity, and the concomitant decrease of a sense of interdependence between different castes living in a region.

Similarly, the introduction of certain kinds of representational politics by the British helped in this process of horizontal consolidation of caste.

- The policy which the British adopted of giving a certain amount of power to local self governing bodies, and preferences and concessions to backward castes provided new opportunities to castes. In order to be able to take advantage of these opportunities, caste groups, as traditionally understood, entered into alliances with each other to form bigger entities.

However, this was not a one-way process. The caste system too was undergoing a change. The horizontal solidarity of caste, which also meant a kind of 'competition' among different castes at the politico-economic plane, eventually weakened the vertical solidarity of caste. This process received a further impetus with the introduction of democratic politics after India's independence. Encountered with the question of change in caste order, Louis Dumont too followed Srinivas and speculated on similar lines. Castes, he argued, did not disappear with the process of economic and political change, but its logic was altered. He described this process as change from "structure" to "substance".

This substantialization of caste indicated:

- ...the transition from a fluid, structural universe in which the emphasis is on interdependence and in which there is no privileged level, no firm units, to a universe of improbable blocks, selfsufficient, essentially identical and in competition with one another, a universe in which the caste appears as a collective individual (in the sense we have given to this word), as a substance.

These attempts at theorizations of the changing realities of caste openedup many new possibilities for looking at the dynamic relationship of caste with the democratic political process.

Thus by 1960s sociologists and political scientists began to talk about caste and politics in a different language. Discussions shifted from a predominantly moral or normative concern about the corruption that caste brought into democratic political process to more empirical processes of interaction between caste and politics. The gradual institutionalization of democratic politics changed caste equations. Power shifted from one set of caste groups, the so-called ritually purer upper castes, to middle level "dominant castes". The democratic politics also introduced a process of differentiation in the local levels of power structure.

As Beteille reported in his study of a village in Tamil Nadu during late 1960s:

- ...a vast body of new structures of power has emerged in India since Independence. Today traditional bodies such as groups of caste elders (which are functionally diffuse) have to compete increasingly with functionally specific structures of power such as parties and statutory panchayats.

However, this differentiation did not mean that these new structures were free of caste. Caste soon entered in their working but the authority of these institutions had to be reproduced differently. Though traditional sources of power continued to be relevant, introduction of universal adult franchise also made "numbers" of caste communities in a given local setting critical.

Power could be reproduced only through mobilizations, vertically as well as horizontally. This also gave birth to a new class of political entrepreneurs. Over the years some of them have begun to work successfully without confining their political constituency to a single caste-cluster, thus undermining the logic of caste politics.

PARTITION OF BENGAL (1905)

The decision to effect the Partition of Bengal was announced in July 1905 by the Viceroy of India, Lord Curzon. The partition took effect in October 1905 and separated the largely Muslim eastern areas from the largely Hindu western areas. Indians were outraged at what they recognise as a "divide and rule" policy, where the colonisers turned the native population against itself in order to rule, even though Curzon stressed it would produce administrative efficiency. The partition animated the Hindus and led the Muslims to form their own national organisation. Bengal was reunited in 1911.

Background

The province of Bengal had an area of 189,000 miles and a population of nearly 8 crores (80 million). Eastern Bengal was almost isolated from the western part by geography and poor communications. In 1836, the upper provinces were placed under a lieutenant governor, and in 1854 the Governor-General-In-Council was relieved of the direct administration of Bengal. It was hard to manage a province as large as Bengal with this large population.

Partition

Partitioning Bengal was first considered in 1903. There were also additional proposals to separate Chittagong and the districts of Dhaka and Mymensingh from Bengal and attaching them to the province of Assam. The government officially published the idea in January 1904, and in February, Lord Curzon made an official tour to eastern districts of Bengal to assess public opinion on the partition. He consulted with leading personalities and delivered speeches at Dhaka, Chittagong and Mymensingh explaining the government's stand on partition. The idea was opposed by Henry John Stedman Cotton, Chief Commissioner of Assam 1896-1902. The Partition of Bengal in 1905 was made on October 16 by Viceroy Curzon. Partition was promoted for administrative reasons: Bengal was as large as France but with a significantly larger population. Curzon decided The eastern region was neglected and under-governed. By splitting the province, an improved administration could be established in the east where, subsequently, the population would benefit from new schools and employment opportunities. However, other motives lurked behind the partition plan. Bengali Hindus were in the forefront of political agitation for greater participation in governance; their position would be weakened, since Muslims would now dominate in the East. Hindus tended to oppose partition, which was more popular among Muslims. What followed partition, however, stimulated an almost national anti-British movement that involved non-violent and violent protests, boycotts and even an assassination attempt against the Governor of the new province of West Bengal.

The new province would consist of the state of Hill Tripura, the Divisions of Chittagong, Dhaka and Rajshahi (excluding Darjeeling) and the district of Malda incorporated with Assam province. Bengal was to surrender not only these large eastern territories but also to cede to the Central Provinces the five Hindi-speaking states. On the western side it was offered Sambalpur and five minor Oriya-speaking states from the Central Provinces. Bengal was left with an area of 141,580 square miles (366,700 km) and population of 54 million, of which 42 million were Hindus and 12 million Muslims. The new province was named Eastern Bengal and Assam with Dhaka as its capital and subsidiary headquarters at Chittagong. Its area would be 106,540 square miles (275,940 km) with a population of 31 million, where 18 million were Muslims and 13 million Hindus. The governor would deal with a Legislative Council, a Board of Revenue of two members, and the jurisdiction of the Calcutta High Court would be left undisturbed. The government pointed out that Eastern Bengal and Assam would have a clearly demarcated western boundary and well defined geographical, ethnological, linguistic and social characteristics. The partition took effect on October 16, 1905.

Political crisis

Partition sparked a major political crisis along religious lines. Hindu resistance exploded as the Indian National Congress began the *swadeshi* movement that included boycotting British goods, terrorism, and diplomatic pressure. The Muslims in East Bengal hoped that a separate region would give them more control over for education and employment, but they instead lost ground. In 1906, Rabindranath Tagore wrote *Amar Shonar Bangla* as a rallying cry for proponents of annulment of Partition; in 1972, it became the national anthem of Bangladesh. Opposition was supported by Sir Henry John Stedman Cotton who had been Chief Commissioner of Assam, but Curzon was not to be moved. Later, Cotton, now Liberal MP for Nottingham East coordinated the successful campaign to oust the first lieutenant-governor of East Bengal, Sir Bampfylde Fuller. Due to these political protests, the two parts of Bengal were reunited in 1911. A new partition which divided the province on linguistic, rather than religious, grounds followed, with the Hindi, Oriya and Assamese areas separated to form separate administrative units. The administrative capital of British India was moved from Calcutta to New Delhi as well. In 1919, separate elections were established for Muslims and Hindus. Before this, many members of both communities had advocated national solidarity of all Bengalis. Now, distinctive communities developed, with their own political agendas. Muslims, too, dominated the Legislature, due to their overall numerical strength of roughly twenty eight to twenty two million. Nationally, Hindus and Muslims began to demand the creation of two independent states, one to be formed in majority Hindu and one in majority Muslim areas with most Bengali Hindus now supporting partitioning Bengal on this basis.

The Second Partition

In 1947, Bengal was partitioned for the second time, solely on religious grounds, as part of the Partition of India following the formation of the nations India and Pakistan. East Bengal became East Pakistan, and in 1971 became the independent state of Bangladesh after a successful war of independence with West Pakistan in the partition of Bengal congress leaders also supported this revolt.

ROUND TABLE CONFERENCES AND GANDHI

Meanwhile, the Indian Freedom Movement had gained momentum under the leadership of Mahatma Gandhi. In 1930, a Round Table Conference was held by the British Government in London to decide the future of India. Baba Saheb represented the 'untouchables'. He said there:-The Depressed Classes of India also join in the demand for replacing the British Government by a Government of the people and by the people... Our wrongs have remained as open sores and have not been righted although 150 years of British rule have rolled away. Of what good is such a Government to anybody?" The British had done nothing to alleviate the status of the depressed classes. He declared that India must have a minimum of Dominion Status. He pressed for a separate electorate for the depressed classes. Soon a second conference was held, which Mahatma Gandhi attended representing the Congress Party.

Baba Saheb met Gandhi in Bombay before they went to London. Gandhi told him that he had read what Baba Saheb said at the first conference. Gandhi told Baba Saheb he knew him to be a real Indian patriot. At the Second Conference, Baba Saheb asked for a separate electorate for the Depressed Classes-Hinduism, "he said-has given us only insults, misery, and humiliation." A separate electorate would mean that the 'untouchables' would vote for their own candidates and be allotted their votes separate from the Hindu majority. Baba Saheb was made a hero by thousands of his followers on his return from Bombay-even though he always said that people should not idolise him.

News came that separate electorates had been granted. Gandhi felt that separate electorates would separate the Harijans from the Hindus. The thought that the Hindus would be divided pained him grievously. He started a fast, saying that he would fast unto death. The Mahatma's Fast: Gandhiji felt that separate electrorates would only separate the Harijans from the Hindus. The very thought that the Hindu would be divided pained him much. He started a fast against separate electorates. He said he would fast unto death in necessary. There was anxiety in the country because of Gandhiji's fast. Many Congress leaders went to Ambedkar to save Gandhiji.

"Muslims, Christians and Sikhs have obtained the right of separate electorates. Gandhiji did not fast to oppose them. Why should Gandhiji fast to oppose Harijans getting separate electorates?" questioned Ambedkar. "If you are unwilling to give the 'untouchables' separate electorates, what other solution is there? It is essential to save Gandhiji. But just to save him I am not prepared to give up the interests of the backward classes," he declared. He said, reserve a larger number of seats for the untouchables' than the British have given; then I will give up the claim for separate electorates." Only Baba Saheb could save Gandhi's life-by withdrawing the demand for separate electorates. At first he refused, saying it was his duty to do the best he could for his people-no matter what. Later he visited Gandhi, who was at that time in Yeravda jail. Gandhi persuaded Baba Saheb that Hinduism would change and leave its bad practices behind. Finally Baba Saheb agreed to sign the Poona Pact with Gandhi in 1932. Instead of separate electorates, more representation was to be given to the Depressed Classes. However, it later became obvious that this did not amount to anything concrete.

In the Prime of His Life: Baba Saheb had by this time collected a library of over 50,000 books, and had a house named Rajgriha built at Dadar in north Bombay to hold it. In 1935 his beloved wife Ramabai died. The same year he was made Principal of the Government Law College, Bombay. Also in 1935 a conference of Dalits was held at Yeola. Baba Saheb told the conference:-We have not been able to secure the barest of human rights... I am born a Hindu. I couldn't help it, but I solemnly assure you that I will not die a Hindu." This was the first time that Baba Saheb stressed the importance of conversion from Hinduism for his people-for they were only known as 'untouchables' within the fold of Hinduism.

During the Second World War, Baba Saheb was appointed Labour Minister by the Viceroy. Yet he never lost contact with his roots-he never became corrupt or crooked. He said that he had been born of the poor and had lived the life of the poor, he would remain absolutely unchanged in his attitudes to his friends and to the rest of the world. The All-India Scheduled Castes Federation was formed in 1942 to gather all 'untouchables' into a united political party.

Architect of the Constitution

After the war Baba Saheb was elected to the Constituent Assembly to decide the way that India-a country of millions of people-should be ruled. How should elections take place? What are the rights of the people? How are laws to be made? Such important matters had to be decided and laws had to be made. The Constitution answers all such questions and lays down rules. When India became independent in August 1947, Baba Saheb Ambedkar became First Law Minister of Independent India. The Constituent Assembly made him chairman of the committee appointed to draft the constitution for the world's largest democracy. All his study of law, economics, and politics made him the best qualified person for this task.

A study of the Constitutions of many countries, a deep knowledge of law, a knowledge of the history of India and of Indian Society-all these were essential. In fact, he carried the whole burden alone. He alone could complete this huge task. On July 15, 1947, the British Parliament passed the act of Indian Independence and on August 15, 1947, India became free. The Constituent Assemble of Independent India appointed a Drafting Committee with Dr. Ambedkar as its Chairman to draft the Constitution of India. Dr. Ambedkar was also invited to join the Cabinet as the Minister of Law. Ambedkar toiled over the Constitution while he took care of his ministry. In February 1948, Dr. Ambedkar presented the Draft Constitution before the people of India. After completing the Draft Constitution, Baba Saheb fell ill.

At a nursing home in Bombay he met Dr. Sharda Kabir and married her in April 1948. On November 4, 1948 he presented the Draft Constitution to the Constituent Assembly, and on

November 26, 1949 it was adopted in the name of the people of India. On that date he said: I appeal to all Indians to be a nation by discarding castes, which have brought separation in social life and created jealousy and hatred." Later Life-Buddhist Conversion: In 1950, he went to a Buddhist conference in Sri Lanka. On his return he spoke in Bombay at the Buddhist Temple. In order to end their hardships, people should embrace Buddhism. I am going to devote the rest of my life to the revival and spread of Buddhism in India." Why did he choose Buddhism?: Ambedkar told his friend Dattopant Thengadi: "I am in the evening of my life. There is an onslaught of ideas on our people from different countries from the four corners of the world. In this flood our people may be confused. There are strong attempts to separate the people struggling hard, from the main life-stream of this country and to attract them towards other countries. This tendency is fast growing. Even some of my colleagues who are disgusted with 'untouchability', poverty and inequality are ready to be washed away by this flood. What about the others? They should not move away from the main stream of the nation's life; and I must show them the way. At the same time, we have to make some changes in the economic and political life. That is way I have decided to follow Buddhism." There is a way of life which has come down as a steady stream in India for thousand of years. Buddhism is not opposed to it. The backward people must rebel against the injustice done to them; they must wipe it out. But 'untouchability' is a problem of the Hindu Society. To solve this, a path which does not harm the culture and the history of Bharat must be followed. This is the basis of his resolution.

He did not believe in the theory that Aryans came from a different land and that they defeated the Dasyus' (the Dravidians) of this country. There is no foundation for this in the Vedas. The word 'Arya' appears some 33 or 34 times in the Vedas. The word has been used as an adjective meaning 'the noble' or 'the elder'. It is said in the Mahabharata that 'Dasyus' can be found in all 'varnas' (castes) and 'ashramas' (stage of life). In this way Ambedkar used to support this view. On 14th October 1956 at a big function in Nagpur, Ambedkar, with his wife, embraced Buddhism. In May 1956, on Buddha's Anniversary, Dr. Ambedkar announced that on October 14 he would embrace Buddhism. With him his wife and some three lakh followers also converted to the faith. When asked why, Dr. Ambedkar replied, "Why can't you ask this question to yourself and... your forefathers...?"

For the next five years Baba Saheb carried on a relentless fight against social evils and superstitions. On October 14, 1956 at Nagpur he embraced Buddhism. He led a huge gathering in a ceremony converting over half a million people to Buddhism. He knew that Buddhism was a true part of Indian history and that to revive it was to continue India's best tradition. 'Untouchability' is a product only of Hinduism. Bhim was an average student.

He became fond of gardening and, whenever he could, he bought saplings and with great devotion nurtured them to full growth. While studying in Satara, many of his classmates left for good jobs in Bombay. He too wanted to go to Bombay and get a job and become independent. He realized that if he ever were to be successful, he would have to concentrate more on his studies. He became interested in reading. He read not just the prescribed books in school but any book in general. His father was too pleased when he digressed from school books but he never said "no" when Bhim wanted a book.

Fight against Untouchability

As a leading Dalit scholar, Ambedkar had been invited to testify before the Southborough Committee, which was preparing the Government of India Act 1919. At this hearing, Ambedkar argued for creating separate electorates and reservations for Dalits and different religious communities. In 1920, he began the publication of the weekly Mooknayak (Leader of the Dumb) in Mumbai. Attaining popularity, Ambedkar used this journal to criticize orthodox Hindu politicians and a perceived reticence in the Indian political community to fight caste discrimination. His speech at a Depressed Classes Conference in Kolhapur impressed the local state ruler Shahu IV, who shocked orthodox society by dining with Ambedkar and his untouchable colleagues. Ambedkar exhorted his Mahar community to abandon the idea of sub-castes, and held a joint communal dinner in which the principle of segregation was abandoned. Upon his return from Europe, Ambedkar established a successful legal practise, and also organised the Bahishkrit Hitakarini Sabha (Group for the Wellbeing of the Excluded) to promote education and socioeconomic upliftment of the depressed classes. In the same vein, he was highly critical of the practice of untouchability in Indian Muslim Society, lending credence to the view that he was not exclusively against Hindus or Hinduism, but was speaking of reforming social evils.

In his illustrious publication "Pakistan and the Partition of India", he writes that, while Islam speaks of "brotherhood", the practice of slavery and caste discrimination were rampant in Muslim society in South Asia, such as the Ashraf/Ajlaf caste divide and the severe discrimination against the Arzal castes or Dalit Muslim untouchables. With the help of Shahu Maharaj of Kolhapur, a sympathizer of the cause for the upliftment of the depressed classes, Bhimrao started a fortnightly newspaper, the Mooknayak (Leader of the Dumb) on January 31, 1920. The Maharaj also convened many meeting and conferences of the "untouchables" which Bhimrao addressed. Impressed by Ambedkar, the Maharaj declared at a meeting, "You have found your saviour in Ambedkar. I am confident he will break your shackles." In July 1924, Ambedkar founded the Bahishkrut Hitkarini Sabha.

The aim of the Sabha was to uplift the downtrodden socially and politically and bring them to the level of the others in the Indian society. The Sabha aimed at scrapping the caste system from the Hindu religion. The Sabha started free school for the young and the old and ran reading rooms and libraries. Dr.

Ambedkar took the grievances of the "untouchables" to court and gave them justice. Soon he became a father-figure to the poor and downtrodden and was respectfully called "Baba Saheb." On March 19-20, 1927 a conference of the depressed classes was held at Mahad. Ten thousand delegates attended, workers and leaders attended. Baba Saheb condemned the British for banning the recruitment of "untouchables" into the military.

He declared: "No lasting progress can achieved unless we put ourselves through a threefold process of purification. We must improve the general tone of our demeanour, re-tone our pronunciation and revitalize our thoughts. I, therefore, ask you now to take a vow to renounce eating carrion, the... flesh of... animals, from this moment....Make an unflinching resolve not to eat the thrown away crumbs. We will attain self-elevation only if we learn self-help, regain our self respect and gain self-knowledge."

On December 25 of the same year, thousands responded to Ambedkar's call. Speaker after speaker spoke, passions rose and the vast gathering waited for the satyagraha to begin with intense anticipation. The satyagraha was deferred when the matter was referred to the court. At the end of conference, a copy of the Manusmruti, the age-old code of the Hindus that gave rise to the caste system, was ceremoniously burnt. In a thundering voice, Ambedkar demanded in its place a new smruti, devoid of all social stratification. This act sent shockwaves through the nation. On October 13, 1935, at a conference at Nasik, Dr. Ambedkar reviewed the progress made on the condition of the "untouchables" in the decade since Ambedkar started his agitation. Ambedkar declared that their efforts had not borne the kind of results he had expected. He then made a fantastic appeal to the "untouchables." He encouraged them to forsake the Hindu religion and convert to a religion where they would be treated with equality.

The nation was shocked. The British Government agreed to hold elections on the provincial level in 1937. The Congress,

Muslim League and Hindu Mahasabha started gearing up for the elections. Dr. Ambedkar set up the Independent Labour Party in August 1936 to contest the elections in the Bombay province. On February 17, 1937, Ambedkar and many of his candidates won this a thumping majority. Around the same time, the Chavdar Taley water dispute which was referred to the Bombay High Court in 1927 finally handed down its verdict in favour of the depressed classes.

The Constituent Assemble adopted the Draft Constitution as the Constitution of India on November 26, 1949 with all its 356 Articles and eight Schedules and Article 11 which abolished untouchability in all forms. A Legacy Marking Indian Sociopolitical History: Ambedkar's legacy, as a sociopolitical reformer, has been long-lasting on modern India. In post independence India his sociopolitical thought has acquired respect across political spectrum and influenced various spheres of life like socioeconomic, education and Government policies of affirmative action by socioeconomic and legal incentives. Ambedkar organized untouchable political parties and social organizations, and served in the legislative councils of British India.

He would intensify his criticism of orthodox Hindu society, as well as his criticism of slavery and exclusivism in Islam. Despite this, his reputation as a scholar led to his appointment as free India's first law minister, and chairman of the committee responsible to draft a constitution. Ambedkar's work would guarantee political, economic and social freedoms for untouchables and other ethnic, social and religious communities of India. His polemical condemnation of Hinduism and attacks on Islam would make him unpopular and controversial, although his conversion to Buddhism sparked a revival in interest of Buddhist philosophy in India. In 1926, he became a nominated member of the Bombay Legislative Council. By 1927 Dr. Ambedkar decided to launch active movements against untouchability. He did begin with public movements and marches to open up & share public drinking water resources to which until then untouchable communities had no access; also he put up a struggle for entry in Hindu Temples which was not allowed by upper caste communities.

Poona Pact

Ambedkar had become one of the most prominent untouchable political figures of the time. He had grown increasingly critical of mainstream Indian political parties for their perceived lack of emphasis for the elimination of the caste system. Ambedkar criticized the Indian National Congress and its leader Mahatma Gandhi, whom he accused of reducing the untouchable community to a figure of pathos. Ambedkar was also dissatisfied with the failures of British rule, and advocated a political identity for untouchables separate from both the Congress and the British. At a Depressed Classes Conference on August 8, 1930 Ambedkar outlined his political vision: "...Safety of the Depressed Classes hinged on their being independent of the Government and the Congress" both: "We must shape our course ourselves and by ourselves... Political power cannot be a panacea for the ills of the Depressed Classes. Their salvation lies in their social elevation. They must cleanse their evil habits. They must improve their bad ways of living.... They must be educated.... There is a great necessity to disturb their pathetic contentment and to instill into them that divine discontent which is the spring of all elevation."

Born in a class considered low and outcast. Dr. Ambedkar fought untiringly for the downtrodden. The boy who suffered bitter humiliation became the first Minister for Law in free India, and shaped the country's Constitution. A determined fighter, a deep scholar, human to the tips of his fingers. We Need Dharma-But Casteism Should Go: 'Undouchablity' is a branch of casteism; until casteism is wiped out 'untouchability' will not go-this was Ambedkar's firm belief.

He argued that to wipe out casteism, political power was very necessary. He believed that Dharma was essential for men. But he revolted against those who, in the name of Dharma, treated some of their fellowmen like animals. Many people criticised him. Some newspapers also wrote against him. There were many occasions when his life was in danger. Also, Ambedkar knew from his own experience that even a bright man could not come up in life vacuse of casteism. People give his cast importance and make him powerless. Ambedkar fought casteism. He was disgusted to find how difficult it was to secure justice and to find how many men were still narrow-minded. He even said that it would be better to give up the Hindu Dharma itself. Muslim and Christian priest and missionaries learnt about this declaration; they tried very hard to attract Ambedkar. They met and assured him that the 'untouchables' who changed their religion would be given equal status in their society.

SPEECH ON ROUND TABLE CONFERENCES

Dr. B. R. Ambedkar: Mr. Chairman, my purpose in rising to address this conference is principally to place before it the point of view of the depressed classes, whom I and my colleague, Rao Bahadur Srinivasan, have the honour to represent, regarding the question of constitutional reform. It is a point of view of 43,000,000 people, or one-fifth of the total population of British India.

The depressed classes form a group by themselves, which is distinct and separate from the Mohammedans, and, although they are included among the Hindus, they in no sense form an integral part of that community. Not only have they a separate existence, but they have also assigned to them a statute which is invidiously distinct from the status occupied by any other community in India. There are communities in India, which occupy a lower and subordinate position; but the position assigned to the depressed classes is totally different.

It is one which is midway between that of the serf and the

slave, and which may, for convenience, be called servile with this difference, that the serf and the slave were permitted to have physical contact, from which the Depressed Classes are debarred. What is worse that this enforced servility and bar to human intercourse, due to their untouchability, involves, not merely the possibility of discrimination in public life, but actually works out as a positive denial of all equality of opportunity and the denial of those most elementary of civic rights on which all human existence depends. I am sure that the point of view of such a community, as large as the population of England or of France, and so heavily handicapped in the struggle for existence, cannot but have some bearing on the right sort of solution of the political problem, and I am anxious that this Conference should be placed in possession of that point of view at the very start.

The point of view I will try to put as briefly as I can. It is this that the bureaucratic form of Government in India should be replaced by a Government, which will be a Government of the people, by the people, and for the people. This statement of the view of the depressed classes I am sure will be received with some surprise in certain quarters. The tie that bounds the Depressed Classes to the British has been of a unique character. The Depressed Classes welcomed the British as their deliverers from age long tyranny and oppression by the orthodox Hindus. They fought their battles against the Hindus, the Mussalmans and the Sikhs and won for them this great Empire of India.

The British, on their side, assumed the role of trustees for the depressed classes. In view of such an intimate relationship between the parties, this change in the attitude of the depressed classes towards British Rule in India is undoubtedly a most momentous phenomenon. But the reasons for this change of attitude are not far to seek. We have not taken this decision simply because we wish to throw in our lot with the majority. Indeed, as you know, there is not much love lost between the majority and the particular minority I represent. Ours is an independent decision. We have judged of the existing administration solely in the light of our own circumstances and we have found it wanting in some of the most essential elements of a good Government.

When we compare our present position with the one, which it was our lot to bear in Indian society of the pre-British days, we find that, instead of marching on, we are only marking time. Before the British, we were in the loathsome condition due to our untouchability. Has the British Government done anything to remove it? Before the British, we could not enter the temple. Can we enter now? Before the British, we were denied entry into the Police Force. Does the British Government admit us in the Force? Before the British, we were not allowed to serve in the Military. Is that career now open to us? To none of these questions can we give an affirmative answer. That the British, who have held so large a sway over us for such a long time, have done some good we cheerfully acknowledge. But there is certainly no fundamental change in our position. Indeed, so far as we were concerned, the British Government has accepted the social arrangements as it found them, and has preserved them faithfully in the manner of the Chinese tailor who, when given an old coat as a pattern, produced with pride an exact replica, rents, patches and all. Our wrongs have remained as open sores and they have not been righted, although 150 years of British rule have rolled away.

We do not accuse the British of indifference or want of sympathy. What we do find is that they are quite incompetent to tackle our problems. If the case was one of indifference only it would have been a matter of small moment, and it would not have made such a profound change in our attitude. But what we have come to realise on a deeper analysis of the situation is that it is not merely a case of indifference, rather it is a case of sheer incompetence to undertake the task. The depressed classes find that the British Government in India suffers from two very serious limitations.

There is first of all an internal limitation, which arises from the character, motives, and interests of those who are in power. It is not because they cannot help us in these things but because it is against their character, motives and interests to do so. The second consideration that limits its authority is the mortal fear it has of external resistance. The Government of India does realise the necessity of removing the social evils which are eating into the vitals of Indian society and which have blighted the lives of the downtrodden classes for so many years.

The Government of India does realise that the landlords are squeezing the masses dry, and the capitalists are not giving the labourers a living wage and decent conditions of work. Yet it is most painful thing that it has not dared to touch any of these evils. Why? Is it because it has no legal powers to remove them? No. The reason why it does not intervene is because it is afraid that its intervention to amend the existing code of social and economic life will give rise to resistance. Of what good is such a Government to anybody? Under a Government, paralysed between two such limitations, much that goes to make life good must remain held up. We must have a Government in which the men in power will give their undivided allegiance to the best interest of the country. We must have a Government in which men in power, knowing where obedience will end and resistance will begin, will not be afraid to amend the social and economic code of life which the dictates of justice and expediency so urgently call for. This role the British Government will never be able to play, It is only a Government which is of the people, for the people and by the people that will make this possible.

These are some of the questions raised by the Depressed Classes and the answers which in their view these questions seem to carry. This is therefore the inevitable conclusion which the Depressed Classes have come to: namely, that the bureaucratic Government of India, with the best of motives, will remain powerless to effect any change so far as our particular grievances are concerned. We feel that nobody can remove our grievances as well as we can, and we cannot remove them unless we get political power in our own hands. No share of this political power can evidently come to us so long as the British Government remains as it is. It is only in a Swaraj constitution that we stand any chance of getting the political power into our own hands, without which we cannot bring salvation to our people.

There is one thing, Sir, to which I wish to draw your particular attention. It is this, I have not used the expression Dominion Status in placing before you the point of view of the Depressed Classes. I have avoided using it, not because I do not understand its implications nor does the omission mean that the depressed classes object to India's attaining Dominion Status. My chief ground for not using it is that it does not convey the full content of what the Depressed Classes stand for. The Depressed Classes, while they stand for Dominion Status with safeguards, wish to lay all the emphasis they can on one question and one question alone. And that question is, how will Dominion India function? Where will the centre of political power be? Who will have it? Will the Depressed Classes be heirs to it?

These are the questions that form their chief concern. The Depressed Classes feel that they will get no shred of the political power unless the political machinery for the new constitution is of a special make. In the construction of that machine certain hard facts of Indian social life must not be lost sight of. It must be recognised that Indian Society is a gradation of Castes forming an ascending scale of reverence and a descending scale of contempt-a system which gives no scope for the growth of that sentiment of equality and fraternity so essential for a democratic form of Government. It must also be recognised that while the intelligentsia is a very important part of Indian society, it is drawn from its upper strata and although it speaks in the name of the country and leads the political movement, it has not shed the narrow particularism of the class from which it is drawn. In other words what the Depressed Classes wish to urge is that the political mechanism must take account of and must have a definite relation to the psychology of the society for which it is devised. Otherwise you are likely to produce a constitution which, however symmetrical, will be truncated one and a total misfit to the society for which it is designed.

There is one point with which I should like to deal before I close this matter. We are often reminded that the problem of the Depressed Classes is a social problem and that its solution lies elsewhere than in politics. We take strong exception to this view. We hold that the problem of the Depressed Classes will never be solved unless they get political power in their own hands. If this is true, and I do not think that the contrary can be maintained, then problem of Depressed Classes is I submit eminently a political problem and must be treated as such. We know that political power is passing from the British into the hands of those who wield such tremendous economic, social and religious sway over our existence.

We are willing that it may happen, though the idea of Swaraj recalls to the mind of many of us the tyrannies, oppressions and injustices practised upon us in the past and fear of their recurrence under Swaraj. We are prepared to take the inevitable risk of the situation in the hope that we shall be installed, in adequate proportion, as the political sovereigns of the country along with our fellow countrymen. But we will consent to that on one condition and that is that the settlement of our problems is not left to time. I am afraid the Depressed Classes have waited too long for time to work its miracle. At every successive step taken by the British Government to widen the scope of representative Government the Depressed Classes have been systematically left out. No thought has been given to their claim for political power. I protest with all the emphasis I can that we will not stand this any longer. The settlement of our problem must be a part of the general political settlement and must not be left over to the shifting sands of the sympathy and goodwill of the rulers of the future. The reasons why the

Depressed Classes insist upon it are obvious. Every one of us knows that the man in possession is more powerful than the man who is out of possession.

Everyone of us also knows that those in possession of power seldom abdicate in favour of those who are out of it. We cannot therefore hope for the effectuation of the settlement of our social problem. If we allow power to slip into the hands of those who stand to lose by settlement unless we are to have another revolution to dethrone those, whom we today help to ascend the throne of power and prestige. We prefer being despised for too anxious apprehensions, than ruined by too confident a security, and I think it would be just and proper for us to insist that the best guarantee for the settlement of our problem is the adjustment of the political machine itself so as to give us a hold on it, and not the will of those who are contriving to be left in unfettered control of that machine.

What adjustments of the political machine the Depressed Classes want for their safety and protection I will place before the Conference at the proper time. All I will say at the present moment is that, although we want responsible Government, we do not want a Government that will only mean a change of masters. Let the Legislature be fully and really representative if your Executive is going to be fully responsible.

I am sorry Mr. President. I had to speak in such plain words. But I saw no help. The Depressed Classes have had no friend. The Government has all along used them only as an excuse for its continued existence. The Hindus claim them only to deny them or, better still, to appropriate rights. The Mohammedans refuse to recognise their separate existence, because they fear that their privileges may be curtailed by the admission of a rival. Depressed by the Government, suppressed by the Hindu and disregarded by the Muslim, we are left in a most intolerable position of utter helplessness to which I am sure there is no parallel and to which I was bound to call attention.

Regarding the other question, which is set down for discussion, I am sorry it was decided to tag it on to a general debate. Its importance deserved a session for itself. No justice can be done to it in a passing reference. The subject is one in which the Depressed Classes are deeply concerned and they regard it as a very vital question. As members of a minority, we look to the Central Government to act as a powerful curb on the provincial majority to save the minorities from the misrule of the majority. As an Indian, interested in the growth of Indian nationalism, I must make it plain that I am a strong believer in the Unitary form of Government and the thought of disturbing it I must confess does not please me very much. This Unitary Government has been the most potent influence in the building up of the Indian nation. That process of unification, which has been the result of a unified system of Government, has not been completed and I should be loathed to withdraw this most powerful stimulus in the formative period and before it has worked out its end.

However, the question in the form in which it is placed is only an academic question and I shall be prepared to consider a federal form, if it can be shown that in it local autonomy is not inconsistent with central unity. Sir, all that I, as a representative of the depressed classes, need say on their behalf I have said. May I crave your indulgence to permit me as an Indian to say a word or two generally on the situation, which we have to meet. So much has been said regarding its gravity that I shall not venture to add a word more to it, although I am no silent spectator of the movement.

What I am anxious about is to feel whether we are proceeding on right lines in evolving our solution. What that solution should be rests entirely upon the view that British delegates choose to take. Addressing myself to them I will say, whether you will meet the situation by conciliation or by applying the iron heel must be a matter for your judgement for the responsibility is entirely yours. To such of you as are particular to the use of force and believe that a regime of

Letters de Cachet and the Bastille will ease the situation, let me recall the memorable words of the greatest teacher of political philosophy, Edmund Burke. This is what he said to the British nation when it was faced with the problem of dealing with the American colonies:

> *"The use of force alone is but temporary. It may endure for a moment, but it does not remove the necessity of subduing again; a nation is not governed which is perpetually to be conquered. The next objection to force is its uncertainty. Terror is not always the effect of force, and an armament is not a victory. If you do not succeed, you are without resource; for conciliation failing, force remains, but force failing, no further hope of reconciliation is left. Power and authority are sometimes bought by kindness, but they can never be begged as alms by an impoverished and defeated violence. A further objection to force is that you impair the object by your very endeavours to preserve it. The thing you fought for (to wit the loyalty of the people) is not the thing you recover but depreciated, sunk, wasted and consumed in the contest."*

The worth and efficacy of this advice you all knew. You did not listen to it and you lost the great continent of America. You followed it to the lasting good of yourself and the rest of the Dominions that are with you. To such of you as are willing to adopt a policy of conciliation I should like to say one thing. There seems to be prevalent an impression that the Delegates are called here to argue for and against a case for Dominion Status and that the grant of Dominion Status will be dependent upon which side is the victor in this battle of wits.

With due deference to all who are sharpening their wits, I submit that there can be no greater mistake than to make the formula of logic govern so live an issue. I have no quarrel with logic and logicians. But I warn them against the disaster that is bound to follow if they are not careful in the selection of the premises they choose to adopt for their deductions.

It is all a matter of temper whether you will abide by the fall of your logic, or whether you will refute it, as Dr. Johnson did the paradoxes of Berkeley by trampling them under his feet. I am afraid it is not sufficiently realised that in the present temper of the country, no constitution will be workable which is not acceptable to the majority of the people.

The time when you were to choose and India was to accept is gone, never to return. Let the consent of the people and not the accident of logic be the touchstone of your new constitution, if you desire that it should be worked.

9

Father of India's Constitution

Upon India's independence on August 15, 1947, the new Congress-led government invited Ambedkar to serve as the nation's first law minister, which he accepted. On August 29, Ambedkar was appointed Chairman of the Constitution Drafting Committee, charged by the Assembly to write free India's new Constitution. Ambedkar won great praise from his colleagues and contemporary observers for his drafting work. In this task Ambedkar's study of sangha practice among early Buddhists and his extensive reading in Buddhist scriptures were to come to his aid. Sangha practice incorporated voting by ballot, rules of debate and precedence and the use of agendas, committees and proposals to conduct business. Sangha practice itself was modelled on the oligarchic system of governance followed by tribal republics of ancient India such as the Shakyas and the Lichchavis. Thus, although Ambedkar used Western models to give his Constitution shape, its spirit was Indian and, indeed, tribal.

Granville Austin has described the Indian Constitution drafted by Dr. Ambedkar as 'first and foremost a social document.' ... 'The majority of India's constitutional provisions are either directly arrived at furthering the aim of social revolution or attempt to foster this revolution by establishing conditions necessary for its achievement.' The text prepared by Ambedkar provided constitutional guarantees and protections for a wide range of civil liberties for individual citizens, including freedom of religion, the abolition of untouchability and the outlawing of all forms of discrimination Ambedkar argued for extensive economic and social rights for women, and also won the Assembly's support for introducing a system of reservations of jobs in the civil services, schools and colleges for members of scheduled castes and scheduled tribes, a system akin to affirmative action. India's lawmakers hoped to eradicate the socio-economic inequalities and lack of opportunities for India's depressed classes through this measure, which had been originally envisioned as temporary on a need basis. The Constitution was adopted on November 26, 1949 by the Constituent Assembly.

Ambedkar resigned from the cabinet in 1951 following the stalling in parliament of his draft of the Hindu Code Bill, which sought to expound gender equality in the laws of inheritance, marriage and the economy. Although supported by Prime Minister Nehru, the cabinet and many other Congress leaders, it received criticism from a large number of members of parliament. Ambedkar independently contested an election in 1952 to the lower house of parliament, the Lok Sabha, but was defeated. He was appointed to the upper house, of parliament, the Rajya Sabha in March 1952 and would remain a member until his death.

EVOLUTION OF THE CONSTITUTION

Acts of British Parliament before 1935

After the Indian Rebellion of 1857, the British Parliament took over the reign of India from the British East India Company, and British India came under the direct rule of the Crown. The British Parliament passed the Government of India Act of 1858 to this effect, setting up the structure of government in India. It established in England the office of the Secretary of State for India through whom Parliament would exercise its rule, along with a Council of India to aid him.

It also established the office of the Governor-General of India along with an Executive Council in India, consisting of high officials of the British Government. The Indian Councils Act of 1861 provided for a Legislative Council consisting of the members of the Executive council and non-official members.

The Indian Councils Act of 1892 established provincial legislatures and increased the powers of the Legislative Council. These acts increased the representation of Indians in the government, however their power remained limited. The Government of India Acts of 1909 and 1919 further expanded participation of Indians in the government.

Government of India Act 1935

The provisions of the Government of India Act of 1935, though never implemented fully, had a great impact on the constitution of India. Many key features of the constitution are directly taken from this Act. The federal structure of government, provincial autonomy, bicameral legislature consisting of a federal assembly and a Council of States, separation of legislative powers between the center and provinces are some of the provisions of the Act which are present in the Indian constitution.

The Cabinet Mission Plan

In 1946, British Prime Minister Clement Attlee formulated a cabinet mission to India to discuss and finalize plans for the transfer of power from the British Raj to Indian leadership as well as provide India with independence under Dominion status in the Commonwealth of Nations.

The Mission discussed the framework of the constitution and laid down in some detail the procedure to be followed by the constitution drafting body. Elections for the 296 seats assigned to the British Indian provinces were completed by

August 1946. The Constituent Assembly first met and began work on 9 December 1946.

Indian Independence Act 1947

The Indian Independence Act, which came into force on 18 July 1947, divided British Indian territory into two new states: India and Pakistan, which were to be dominions under the Commonwealth of Nations until their constitutions were in effect. The Constituent Assembly was divided into two for the separate states. The Act relieved the British Parliament of any further rights or obligations towards India or Pakistan, and granted sovereignty over the lands to the respective Constituent Assemblies.

When the Constitution of India came into force on 26 January 1950, it repealed the Indian Independence Act. India ceased to be a dominion of the British Crown and became a sovereign democratic republic. 26 November 1949 is also known as National Law Day.

CONSTITUENT ASSEMBLY

The Constitution was drafted by the Constituent Assembly, which was elected by the elected members of the provincial assemblies. Jawaharlal Nehru, C. Rajagopalachari, Rajendra Prasad, Sardar Vallabhbhai Patel, Maulana Abul Kalam Azad, Shyama Prasad Mukherjee and Nalini Ranjan Ghosh were some important figures in the Assembly. There were more than 30 members of scheduled classes.

Frank Anthony represented the Anglo-Indian community, and the Parsis were represented by H. P. Modi. The Chairman of the Minorities Committee was Harendra Coomar Mookerjee, a distinguished Christian who represented all Christians other than Anglo-Indians. Ari Bahadur Gururng represented the Gorkha Community.

Prominent jurists like Alladi Krishnaswamy Iyer, B. R. Ambedkar, Benegal Narsing Rau and K. M. Munshi were also members of the Assembly. Sarojini Naidu and Rajkumari Amrit Kaur were important women members. The first president of the Constituent Assembly was Sachidanand Sinha later, Rajendra Prasad was elected president of the Constituent Assembly. The members of the Constituent Assembly met for the first time in 1946 on 9 December.

Drafting

In the 14 August 1947 meeting of the Assembly, a proposal for forming various committees was presented. Such committees included a Committee on Fundamental Rights, the Union Powers Committee and Union Constitution Committee. On 29 August 1947, the Drafting Committee was appointed, with Dr Ambedkar as the Chairman along with six other members. A Draft Constitution was prepared by the committee and submitted to the Assembly on 4 November 1947.

The Assembly met, in sessions open to the public, for 166 days, spread over a period of 2 years, 11 months and 18 days before adopting the Constitution. After many deliberations and some modifications, the 308 members of the Assembly signed two hand-written copies of the document on 24 January 1950. Two days later, the Constitution of India became the law of all the Indian lands. Constitution of India has undergone 94 amendments in less than 60 years since its enactment.

STRUCTURE

The debate on the 'basic structure' of the Constitution, lying somnolent in the archives of India's constitutional history during the last decade of the 20th century, has reappeared in the public realm. While setting up the National Commission to Review the Working of the Constitution, the National Democratic Alliance government (formed by a coalition of 24 national and regional level parties) stated that the basic structure of the Constitution would not be tampered with.

Justice M.N. Venkatachalaiah, Chairman of the Commission, has emphasised on several occasions that an enquiry into the basic structure of the Constitution lay beyond the scope of the Commission's work. Several political parties—notably the Congress (I) and the two Communist parties which are in the opposition—have made it clear that the review exercise was the government's ploy to seek legitimacy for its design to adopt radical constitutional reforms thus destroying the basic structure of the document.

Much of the public debate has been a victim of partial amnesia as even literate circles of urban India are unsure of the ramifications of this concept, which was hotly debated during the 1970s and 1980s. The following discussion is an attempt to chart the waters of that period rendered turbulent by the power struggle between the legislative and the judicial arms of the State.

According to the Constitution, Parliament and the state legislatures in India have the power to make laws within their respective jurisdictions. This power is not absolute in nature. The Constitution vests in the judiciary, the power to adjudicate upon the constitutional validity of all laws. If a law made by Parliament or the state legislatures violates any provision of the Constitution, the Supreme Court has the power to declare such a law invalid or ultra vires.

This check notwithstanding, the founding fathers wanted the Constitution to be an adaptable document rather than a rigid framework for governance. Hence Parliament was invested with the power to amend the Constitution.

Article 368 of the Constitution gives the impression that Parliament's amending powers are absolute and encompass all parts of the document. But the Supreme Court has acted as a brake to the legislative enthusiasm of Parliament ever since independence.

With the intention of preserving the original ideals envisioned by the constitution-makers, the apex court pronounced that Parliament could not distort, damage or alter the basic features of the Constitution under the pretext of amending it. The phrase 'basic structure' itself cannot be found in the Constitution.

The Supreme Court recognised this concept for the first time in the historic Kesavananda Bharati case in 1973. Ever since the Supreme Court has been the interpreter of the Constitution and the arbiter of all amendments made by Parliament.

The pre-Kesavanada position

Parliament's authority to amend the Constitution, particularly the chapter on the fundamental rights of citizens, was challenged as early as in 1951. After independence, several laws were enacted in the states with the aim of reforming land ownership and tenancy structures. This was in keeping with the ruling Congress party's electoral promise of implementing the socialistic goals of the Constitution [contained in Article 39 (b) and (c) of the Directive Principles of State Policy] that required equitable distribution of resources of production among all citizens and prevention of concentration of wealth in the hands of a few. Property owners—adversely affected by these laws—petitioned the courts.

The courts struck down the land reforms laws saying that they transgressed the fundamental right to property guaranteed by the Constitution. Piqued by the unfavourable judgements, Parliament placed these laws in the Ninth Schedule of the Constitution through the First and Fourth amendments (1951 and 1952 respectively), thereby effectively removing them from the scope of judicial review. [Parliament added the Ninth Schedule to the Constitution through the very first amendment in 1951 as a means of immunising certain laws against judicial review.

Under the provisions of Article 31, which themselves were amended several times later, laws placed in the Ninth Schedule—pertaining to acquisition of private property and compensation payable for such acquisition—cannot be challenged in a court of law on the ground that they violated the fundamental rights of citizens. This protective umbrella covers more than 250 laws passed by state legislatures with the aim of regulating the size of land holdings and abolishing various tenancy systems.

The Ninth Schedule was created with the primary objective of preventing the judiciary-which upheld the citizens' right to property on several occasions-from derailing the Congress party led government's agenda for a social revolution.] Property owners again challenged the constitutional amendments which placed land reforms laws in the Ninth Schedule before the Supreme Court, saying that they violated Article 13 (2) of the Constitution. Article 13 (2) provides for the protection of the fundamental rights of the citizen.

Parliament and the state legislatures are clearly prohibited from making laws that may take away or abridge the fundamental rights guaranteed to the citizen. They argued that any amendment to the Constitution had the status of a law as understood by Article 13 (2).

In 1952 (Sankari Prasad Singh Deo v. Union of India) and 1955 (Sajjan Singh v. Rajasthan), the Supreme Court rejected both arguments and upheld the power of Parliament to amend any part of the Constitution including that which affects the fundamental rights of citizens. Significantly though, two dissenting judges in Sajjan Singh v. Rajasthan case raised doubts whether the fundamental rights of citizens could become a plaything of the majority party in Parliament.

The Golaknath verdict

In 1967 an eleven-judge bench of the Supreme Court reversed its position. Delivering its 6:5 majority judgement in the Golaknath v. State of Punjab case, Chief Justice Subba Rao put forth the curious position that Article 368, that contained provisions related to the amendment of the Constitution, merely laid down the amending procedure. Article 368 did not confer upon Parliament the power to amend the Constitution. The amending power (constituent power) of Parliament arose from other provisions contained in the Constitution (Articles 245, 246, 248) which gave it the power to make laws (plenary legislative power). Thus, the apex court held that the amending power and legislative powers of Parliament were essentially the same.

Therefore, any amendment of the Constitution must be deemed law as understood in Article 13 (2). The majority judgement invoked the concept of implied limitations on Parliament's power to amend the Constitution. This view held that the Constitution gives a place of permanence to the fundamental freedoms of the citizen. In giving the Constitution to themselves, the people had reserved the fundamental rights for themselves. Article 13, according to the majority view, expressed this limitation on the powers of Parliament. Parliament could not modify, restrict or impair fundamental freedoms due to this very scheme of the Constitution and the nature of the freedoms granted under it. The judges stated that the fundamental rights were so sacrosanct and transcendental in importance that they could not be restricted even if such a move were to receive unanimous approval of both houses of Parliament.

They observed that a Constituent Assembly might be summoned by Parliament for the purpose of amending the fundamental rights if necessary. In other words, the apex court held that some features of the Constitution lay at its core and required much more than the usual procedures to change them. The phrase 'basic structure' was introduced for the first time by M.K. Nambiar and other counsels while arguing for the petitioners in the Golaknath case, but it was only in 1973 that the concept surfaced in the text of the apex court's verdict.

Nationalisation of Banks and Abolition of Privy Purses

Within a few weeks of the Golaknath verdict the Congress party suffered heavy losses in the parliamentary elections and lost power in several states. Though a private member's bill-tabled by Barrister Nath Pai-seeking to restore the supremacy of Parliament's power to amend the Constitution was introduced and debated both on the floor of the house and in the Select Committee, it could not be passed due to political compulsions of the time.

But the opportunity to test parliamentary supremacy presented itself once again when Parliament introduced laws to provide greater access to bank credit for the agricultural sector and ensure equitable distribution of wealth and resources of production and by:

- Nationalising banks and
- Derecognising erstwhile princes in a bid to take away their Privy purses, which were promised in perpetuity-as a sop to accede to the Union-at the time of India's independence.

Parliament reasoned that it was implementing the Directive Principles of State Policy but the Supreme Court struck down both moves. By now, it was clear that the Supreme Court and Parliament were at loggerheads over the relative position of the fundamental rights vis-à-vis the Directive Principles of State Policy. At one level, the battle was about the supremacy of Parliament vis-à-vis the power of the courts to interpret and uphold the Constitution.

At another level the contention was over the sanctity of property as a fundamental right jealously guarded by an affluent class much smaller than that of the large impoverished masses for whose benefit the Congress government claimed to implement its socialist development programme. Less than two weeks after the Supreme Court struck down the President's order derecognising the princes, in a quick move to secure the mandate of the people and to bolster her own stature Prime Minister Indira Gandhi dissolved the Lok Sabha and called a snap poll.

For the first time, the Constitution itself became the electoral issue in India. Eight of the ten manifestos in the 1971 elections called for changes in the Constitution in order to restore the supremacy of Parliament. A.K. Gopalan of the Communist Party of India (Marxist) went to the extent of saying that the Constitution be done away with lock stock and barrel and be replaced with one that enshrined the real sovereignty of the people. The Congress party returned to power with a two-thirds majority. The electorate had endorsed the Congress party's socialist agenda, which among other things spoke of making basic changes to the Constitution in order to restore Parliament's supremacy. Through a spate of amendments made between July 1971 and June 1972 Parliament sought to regain lost ground. It restored for itself the absolute power to amend any part of the Constitution including Part III, dealing with fundamental rights.

Even the President was made duty bound to give his assent to any amendment bill passed by both houses of Parliament. Several curbs on the right property were passed into law. The right to equality before the law and equal protection of the laws (Article 14) and the fundamental freedoms guaranteed under Article 19 were made subordinate to Article 39 (b) and (c) in the Directive Principles of State Policy. Privy purses of erstwhile princes were abolished and an entire category of legislation dealing with land reforms was placed in the Ninth Schedule beyond the scope of judicial review.

Emergence of the Basic Structure Concept: the Kesavanada milestone

Inevitably, the constitutional validity of these amendments was challenged before a full bench of the Supreme Court (thirteen judges). Their verdict can be found in eleven separate judgements. Nine judges signed a summary statement which records the most important conclusions reached by them in this case.

Granville Austin notes that there are several discrepancies between the points contained in the summary signed by the judges and the opinions expressed by them in their separate judgements. Nevertheless, the seminal concept of 'basic structure' of the Constitution gained recognition in the majority verdict. All judges upheld the validity of the Twenty-fourth amendment saying that Parliament had the power to amend any or all provisions of the Constitution. All signatories to the summary held that the Golaknath case had been decided wrongly and that Article 368 contained both the power and the procedure for amending the Constitution. However they were clear that an amendment to the Constitution was not the same as a law as understood by Article 13 (2).

It is necessary to point out the subtle difference that exists between two kinds of functions performed by the Indian Parliament:

1. It can make laws for the country by exercising its legislative power and
2. It can amend the Constitution by exercising its constituent power.

Constituent Power is Superior to Ordinary Legislative Power

Unlike the British Parliament which is a sovereign body (in the absence of a written constitution), the powers and functions of the Indian Parliament and State legislatures are subject to limitations laid down in the Constitution. The Constitution does not contain all the laws that govern the country. Parliament and the state legislatures make laws from time to time on various subjects, within their respective jurisdictions.

The general framework for making these laws is provided by the Constitution. Parliament alone is given the power to make changes to this framework under Article 368. Unlike ordinary laws, amendments to constitutional provisions require a special majority vote in Parliament.

Another illustration is useful to demonstrate the difference between Parliament's constituent power and law making powers. According to Article 21 of the Constitution, no person in the country may be deprived of his life or personal liberty except according to procedure established by law. The

Constitution does not lay down the details of the procedure as that responsibility is vested with the legislatures and the executive.

Parliament and the state legislatures make the necessary laws identifying offensive activities for which a person may be imprisoned or sentenced to death. The executive lays down the procedure of implementing these laws and the accused person is tried in a court of law. Changes to these laws may be incorporated by a simple majority vote in the concerned state legislature. There is no need to amend the Constitution in order to incorporate changes to these laws.

However, if there is a demand to convert Article 21 into the fundamental right to life by abolishing death penalty, the Constitution may have to be suitably amended by Parliament using its constituent power.

Most importantly seven of the thirteen judges in the Kesavananda Bharati case, including Chief Justice Sikri who signed the summary statement, declared that Parliament's constituent power was subject to inherent limitations. Parliament could not use its amending powers under Article 368 to 'damage', 'emasculate', 'destroy', 'abrogate', 'change' or 'alter' the 'basic structure' or framework of the Constitution.

Basic Features of the Constitution according to the Kesavanada verdict

Each judge laid out separately, what he thought were the basic or essential features of the Constitution. There was no unanimity of opinion within the majority view either.

Sikri, C.J. explained that the concept of basic structure included:

- Supremacy of the Constitution
- Republican and democratic form of government
- Secular character of the Constitution
- Separation of powers between the legislature, executive and the judiciary
- Federal character of the Constitution

Shelat, J. and Grover, J. added two more basic features to this list:

1. The mandate to build a welfare state contained in the Directive Principles of State Policy
2. Unity and integrity of the nation

Hegde, J. and Mukherjea, J. identified a separate and shorter list of basic features:

- Sovereignty of India
- Democratic character of the polity
- Unity of the country
- Essential features of the individual freedoms secured to the citizens
- Mandate to build a welfare state

Jaganmohan Reddy, J. stated that elements of the basic features were to be found in the Preamble of the Constitution and the provisions into which they translated such as:

- Sovereign democratic republic parliamentary democracy
- Three organs of the State

He said that the Constitution would not be itself without the fundamental freedoms and the directive principles. Only six judges on the bench (therefore a minority view) agreed that the fundamental rights of the citizen belonged to the basic structure and Parliament could not amend it.

The minority view

The minority view delivered by Justice A.N. Ray (whose appointment to the position of Chief Justice over and above the heads of three senior judges, soon after the pronunciation of the Kesavananda verdict, was widely considered to be politically motivated), Justice M.H. Beg, Justice K.K. Mathew and Justice S.N. Dwivedi also agreed that Golaknath had been decided wrongly. They upheld the validity of all three amendments challenged before the court.

Ray, J. held that all parts of the Constitution were essential and no distinction could be made between its essential and non-essential parts. All of them agreed that Parliament could make fundamental changes in the Constitution by exercising its power under Article 368.

In summary the majority verdict in Kesavananda Bharati recognised the power of Parliament to amend any or all provisions of the Constitution provided such an act did not destroy its basic structure. But there was no unanimity of opinion about what appoints to that basic structure. Though the Supreme Court very nearly returned to the position of Sankari Prasad (1952) by restoring the supremacy of Parliament's amending power, in effect it strengthened the power of judicial review much more.

Basic Structure concept reaffirmed: the Indira Gandhi Election case

In 1975, The Supreme Court again had the opportunity to pronounce on the basic structure of the Constitution. A challenge to Prime Minister Indira Gandhi's election victory was upheld by the Allahabad High Court on grounds of electoral malpractice in 1975. Pending appeal, the vacation judge-Justice Krishna Iyer, granted a stay that allowed Smt. Indira Gandhi to function as Prime Minister on the condition that she should not draw a salary and speak or vote in Parliament until the case was decided.

Meanwhile, Parliament passed the Thirty-ninth amendment to the Constitution which removed the authority of the Supreme Court to adjudicate petitions regarding elections of the President, Vice President, Prime Minister and Speaker of the Lok Sabha. Instead, a body constituted by Parliament would be vested with the power to resolve such election disputes. Section 4 of the Amendment Bill effectively thwarted any attempt to challenge the election of an incumbent, occupying any of the above offices in a court of law.

This was clearly a pre-emptive action designed to benefit Smt. Indira Gandhi whose election was the object of the ongoing dispute. Amendments were also made to the Representation of Peoples Acts of 1951 and 1974 and placed in the Ninth Schedule along with the Election Laws Amendment Act, 1975 in order to save the Prime Minister from embarassment if the apex court delivered an unfavourable verdict.

The mala fide intention of the government was proved by the haste in which the Thirty-ninth amendment was passed. The bill was introduced on August 7, 1975 and passed by the Lok Sabha the same day. The Rajya Sabha (Upper House or House of Elders) passed it the next day and the President gave his assent two days later. The amendment was ratified by the state legislatures in special Saturday sessions. It was gazetted on August 10.

When the Supreme Court opened the case for hearing the next day, the Attorney General asked the Court to throw out the case in the light of the new amendment. Counsel for Raj Narain who was the political opponent challenging Mrs. Gandhi's election argued that the amendment was against the basic structure of the Constitution as it affected the conduct of free and fair elections and the power of judicial review.

Counsel also argued that Parliament was not competent to use its constituent power for validating an election that was declared void by the High Court. Four out of five judges on the bench upheld the Thirty-ninth amendment, but only after striking down that part which sought to curb the power of the judiciary to adjudicate in the current election dispute. One judge, Beg, J. upheld the amendment in its entirety. Mrs. Gandhi's election was declared valid on the basis of the amended election laws. The judges grudgingly accepted Parliament's power to pass laws that have a retrospective effect.

CONSTITUTION AND DR. AMBEDKAR

"Without going into the merit of constitution, however good and faultless a constitution may be, but if those who implement it are incompetent and useless, that constitution results in an evil. Similarly however defective a constitution may be, but if its executors are good the same constitution results in the good of the people", such was the view expressed by Dr. Baba Saheb Ambedkar while replying to the discussion on the Constitution on November 26, 1949.

How prophetic were his statement! The, Congress rulers during the last 40 years have made a travesty of the Constitution. They needlessly amended the original charter several times to perpetuate their single-party rule. Actually the Congress rulers have no moral right to speak on the sanctity of the Constitution.

Hindutva Challenge and Congress: In recent years the Congress has been facing a formidable challenge from the protagonists of Hindutva. It must be noted that the Hindutva challenge is to the Congress, and not to the Constitution, the judiciary or the democratic system. But a systematic Goebellsian propaganda blitzkrieg is conducted by the Congress and those whose vested interests lie in perpetuating the Congress rule and the Congress culture to present Hindutva as the worst challenge to the Constitution. The vilification campaign is joined by all those who have an eye on the main chance, and the Congress party is the highest bidder.

The Congress hangers-on have formed a Constitution Preservation committee as a part of this anti-Hindu propaganda campaign. Anything is grist for their propaganda mill. No falsehood or abuse is too base or too mean for them. They have no compunction to use shady methods. They argue: (1) The Sangh Parivar is out to scrap the Indian Constitution. (2) Its aim is to establish the system propounded by Manu. (3) If elected to power, Bharatiya Janata Party will rescind all legal provisions giving certain social rights to the dalits. (4) The dalits will again be dumped in the traditional ditch of untouchability and all the disabilities associated with it. The source of this offensive of falsehoods is far from any love for the Constitution. The whole business springs from the single-point programme of perpetuation of the Congress rule, the sole host of these parasites. Political propaganda should be matched on a political plane. Yet there is enough occasion to have a hard look at the issue in dispute, "Dr. Baba Saheb Ambedkar, Constitution and Hindutva". Let us first consider Hindutva.

Hindutva is, these days, being discussed from various angles. The dominant being the accusation that Hindutva is none else than the abuse of Hindutva for political mileage by Sangh Parivar. Even the courts of law have taken the stand that Hindutva is a religious concept. And following this, elections of several Members of Parliament and State Legislative Assemblies have been declared void. But Hindutva is not a mere religious concept. At least the Sangh Parivar does not subscribe to this view. Hindutva is a concept that is related to nationhood. The part "Hindu" in the word "Hindutva" is not used to denote a group of people following any particular way of worship. The late V.D. Savarkar has defined the word "Hindu" as "the one whose country, India, spreads between the two seas and who regards it as his fatherland and sacred land".

RSS has not defined Hindu, and Hindutva. But what the Sangh understands by these words has been amply clarified. Sangh believes Hindu to be a way of life. Guruji has stated regarding this way of life: "We have perceived the entire society as a body. It is the great social person (virat samajapurush). All men are indeed limbs and organs of the great social corpus spiritualis. Society as a mammoth humanoid body and the eternal undying spirit that dwells in that body and this realization is the specific and unique aspect of the Indian spiritual thinking. All existent objects, including all human beings are parts of that eternal existence. And that is the fount of the basic unity. Since the eternal spirit inform everyone in equal measure, the social system should be so organised as to make everyone happy. A social order where all will have equal self-interest."

Shri Guruji calls these "the principles of Hindu way of life". He further says: "The ever present principle of Hindu life, that one truth pervades in all, is the ultimate truth. That alone is the link that joins all. The selfsame truth appears in diverse forms. Therefore it is our natural duty to create all manner of scope for all to lead their life according their diverse tastes".

It should be, noted that Shri Guruji does not define Hindu-Hindutva in religious terms. He does not link Hindutva with any specific method of worship. It should be appreciated that he sheds light on the fact that the substance of Hindutva relates to the wellbeing of mankind. The Sarsanghchalak Shri Balasaheb Deoras while addressing the Maharashtra State-level camp at Tuljai declared: "The Sangh goal is to create an egalitarian society free from exploitation."

The concept of Hindutva does not imply total trust in a single scripture, neither does it strictly adhere to a single religious regimen. It does not reserve all its faith for one Prophet, nor does it profess to tailor society to the measurements given by a religious tone. Deoras has elaborated the thoughts on social system intended in Hindutva in his book Hindu Organisation and Social Equality where he says: "Untouchability should be eradicated from our society permanently, It must go lock, stock and barrel. The Hindutva of the Sangh does not accept the sense of high and low based on caste. So there is no question of Sangh justifying the present caste inequality."

The Hindutva of the RSS-is not based on any religious sect, so it has no room for religious hatred against any sect. Guruji says: "There is a deliberate attempt to create confusion around the word Hindu. Some are driven by their selfish motives to describe Hindus as opposed to Muslims, Christians, Sikhs, Jains and dalits."

They do not do this after any serious study of the issue. The Hindu thinking and the Hindu way of life have been in the world even before Islam and Christianity were yet to emerge. How could Hindus be against a religion that was not in existence, either Islam or Christianity, Sikhs, Jains, etc. are indeed under the general conceptual umbrella of Hinduism. To oppose them is a indulge in suicidal attempt to cut one's limbs. The term Hindu is never used to oppose or discriminate against any sect. The term is a positive one and could never be construed to mean anything negative.

Constitutional Idealism: While discussing the Constitution, one has to bear in mind this wider meaning of the term Hindutva. Our Constitution has three types of idealism. The political idealism, social idealism and economic idealism. The blend of these three ideals becomes the national idealism. The Constitution explains to us the objectives to be kept always before our eyes in the context of individual-society relationship.

The freedom struggle was not at all limited to political freedom only. India aimed at three kinds of freedom. The political freedom was to be followed by social and economic freedoms. The great leaders at the helm of the freedom struggle had mainly the Hindu society before, their vision. The Muslim community did not fully participate in the freedom struggle. Muslim leaders were without any big following. There was hardly any Muslim League representative in the Constituent Assembly.

The kind of political freedom the leaders in the freedom struggle had envisaged is reflected in the Constitution in the form of the fundamental rights. This freedom was not demanded by the Muslims. Because their overwhelming majority had demanded a separate land for Muslims. And the factor of social freedom in the struggle for the freedom of the country was a hundred-per-cent Hindu social reform movement. Untouchability, social inequality, traditional superstition, injustice to women, child-marriage, widow remarriage an so on and so forth were all issues of social reforms in Hindu society.

The incursion of social justice in the Constitution is the outcome of these agitations for social reforms. The demand for the country's liberation from the foreign economic yoke and all-out efforts for gaining that were the activities of Hindus. Though the Parsis like Jamshedji Tata and Dadabhoy Naoroji were at the forefront of the country's economic liberation they were different only in their manner of worship. They were in fact a factor in the all-round movement for economic emancipation carried out by Lokmanya Tilak, Mahatma Gandhi, Lalchand Hirachand in their own way. The economic ideal enshrined in the Constitution is the fruit of their efforts.

Because the ideals of political, social and economic liberaties are enshrined in the Constitution the responsibility for their fulfilment devolves on the government machinery and the citizens are granted some of these liberties in the form of the fundamental rights. All these are intended to achieve the goal of highest interests and welfare of the people, and therefore Hindutva cannot have any quarrel with these.

The noble ideals included in the Constitution, if viewed uninhibited by political considerations and those of Hindutva, would appear to have no contradictions. Hindutva does not deny individual liberty, equality and fraternity. It also does not deprive anyone of his freedom of worship.

The founding fathers of our Constitution felt that such ideals must be enshrined in our Constitution, because they were deeply impressed by Indian traditions in social thought. In this context Dr. Ambedkar's interpretation is very significant. He says: "I have not borrowed liberty, equality and fraternity from the French Revolution. I have learnt them from the teachings of Lord Buddha. To allow every person to adopt a way of worship dictated by his conscience is in the best of Hindu tradition. It is not in the Hindu tradition to oppress anyone only because he happens to worship his lord in a different manner. This has been beautifully expressed in the Mahimnastotra which says: "O Lord, you are the destination of all people reaching you by various ways, straight or crooked according to their taste as waters of various rivers flowing whichever way reach the sea." The Constitution also merely paraphrases the contents of this stotra (praise to Lord).

Social Justice : The social ideals of our Constitution are as important as the political ones. There was dual slavery in our country. One political and the other social. Under the social slavery it was mainly the scheduled castes which were trampled under the injustices by higher castes. They had no political or social rights. Their lowest state in society was determined by their birth. Great savants raised a relentless revolt against this social slavery prevalent in the Hindu society. Sages like Maharshi Dayanand, social reformers like Mahatma Phule, political leaders like Mahatma Gandhi and Swatantrya Veer Savarkar ceaselessly agitated against this social slavery. Ambedkar fought the final battle against the Hindu society. The strugglers reflected in our Constitution.

"I entered the Constituent Assembly to safeguard the interests of the dalits", said Dr. Ambedkar while explaining his purpose in joining the Constituent Assembly. He further stated: "I did not go there to draft the Constitution. But that responsibility crane upon me for certain reasons. It is a matter of pride for me to have been associated with the architects of the Constitution." Dr. Ambedkar's is the lion's share in clearly defining the social and economic ideals in our Constitution. Article 17 of the Constitution eradicates untouchability. Article 15 guarantees that no discrimination would be allowed on the basis of religion race, caste, gender or domicile. Article 16 guarantees that the State will grant equal opportunities to all citizens. And the same Article 16 makes provision for reservations for the backward people.

Political Democracy: This is a special feature of our Constitution. All adults enjoy the right to vote. All votes are of equal weightage. This right of the citizens is very important and this has invested the common man with full control on the State power. With the ballot-power the Constitution itself grants to the majority of the citizens the power to rule. To extend the right to select their rulers to the common people is politically a revolutionary measure. Politicians playing caste-card organise their parties on various caste-lines and try to acquire majority. The Ahirs, the Jats, the Rajputs, the Yadavs, the dalits and the Muslims are yoked together to present what is named as Bahujan Samaj. But this is an election strategy. Some others try to garner castes other than the Brahmins, the Kshatriyas and the Kayasthas, and try to present them as Bahujan Samaj.

But Hindutva is opposed to such fissiporous business of strengthening divisive caste sentiments through politician means because a very narrow sentiment is detrimental to national unity. The political organisation of the Indian society should be undertaken on the basis of the wide and comprehensive content of Hindutva. If caste is conceived as the basis of political activity the hallowed social ideals in the Constitution would be gathering dust in the statute. The protagonists of Hindutva in the widest ken of the term-aspire to bring a Hindu-again in the wide connotation-rule in the country.

The adult franchise granted in the Constitution is bound to result in the majority rule, *i.e.,* Hindu rule. No one can change this foregone conclusion. The limited demand of the Hindutva protagonists is that those politicians who play caste politics, who foster communal division for their politician ends and who deny the just share of the national life to the dalits and the backward sections of society should not be allowed to usurp power by formenting fissiparous, communal and caste passions. Hindutvists are not opposed to the principle of political democracy consecrated in the Constitution. Their objection and opposition is to the policies of implementing the democracy promoted by political parties with their eye on the main chance without any compunction regarding national interests.

Economic Justice: Our Constitution has vowed to render economic justice to all citizens. The directive principles laid down in the Constitution have recorded the economic goals to be achieved by the States. Article 36 to 51 comprise such directive principles, Two of them are relevant here. Article 38 enjoins on the State to establish a social system which will ensure social, political and economic justice to its citizens. Article 39 directs the State to formulate policies of distribution of physical means which will result in the greatest good of all and will provide adequate means of livelihood to all its citizens, men and women. The principle of equal remuneration for equal work should be implemented. The States should not allow centralisation of wealth and the means of-production which harm the society.

A part from these, there are other directives which have extensively discussed the responsibilities of the States regarding adult education, unemployment, children, women, etc., and how the States should execute these responsibilities. The administrators and the government are guided by these directive principles to achieve, the goals included in the preamble of the Constitution.

Bibliography

Aluwalia, B.K. & Shashi B.R.: *Ambedkar and Human Rights*, KK Publishers, New Delhi, 1981.

Anant, S. S.: *Changing Caste Hindu Attitudes Towards Harijans: A Follow Up After Four Years*, Vikas, New Delhi, 1979.

Barill, C.: *Social and Political Ideas of B.R. Ambedkar*, Aalekh Publishers, Jaipur, 1977.

Chatterjee, Partha: *Caste and Subaltern Consciousness*, Oxford University Press, Delhi, 1994.

Danda, A.K.: *Weaker Sections in Indian Villages*, Inter-India, New Delhi, 1993.

Engineer, Asghar Ali.: *Mandal Commission Controversy*, Ajanta Publications, Delhi, 1991.

Fisher, F.B.: *Touching the Untouchables, India's Silent Revolution*, MacMillan, New York, 1920.

Forrester, D.: *Caste and Christianity: Attitudes and Policies on Caste of Anglo-Protestant Missions in India*, Curzon, London, 1980.

Galanter, Marc.: *Competing Inequalities: Law and the Backward Classes in India*, University of California Press, CA, 1984.

Hardgrave, Robert L. Jr.: *The Dravidian Movement*, Popular Book Depot, Bombay, 1965.

Hocart, A. M.: *Caste*, Mathew and Co., London, 1950.

Ishwaran, K.: *Shivpur: A South Indian Village*, Routledge, London, 1968.

Jose, K.: *Constitutional Provisions for the Scheduled Castes*, Indian Social Institute, New Delhi, 1984.

Kadam, K.N.: *Dr. B.R. Ambedkar: The Emancipator of the Oppressed*, BR Publishing, Delhi, 1994.

Karve, Irawati: *Hindu Society: An Interpretation*, Sangam Press, Poona, 1961.

Khan, Mumtaz Ali: *Human Rights and the Dalits*, Uppal Publishing House, New Delhi, 1995.

Khare, R. S.: *The Untouchable as Himself: Ideology, Identity and Pragmatism Among the Lucknow Chamars*, Cambridge University Press, London, 1984.

Lal, Shyam: *Caste and Political Mobilisation: The Bhangis*, Panchsheel Prakashan, Jaipur, 1981.

Mahar, Michael J.: *The Untouchables in Contemporary India*, University of Arizona Press, Arizona, 1972.

Marriott, Mckim: *Village India: Studies in the Little Community*, The University of Chicago Press, Chicago, 1955.

Maw, Martin: *Visions of India*, Vertag Perer Lang, London, 1990.

Michael J.: *The Untouchables in Contemporary India*, University of Arizona Press, Arizona, 1972.

Naidu, A. Nagaraja: *Caste and Land in Colonial South India*, Rawat Publications, New Delhi, 1994.

Omprakash, S.: *Development of the Weaker Section: Problems, Policies and Issues*, Uppal Publishing House, New Delhi, 1989.

Paranjpe, A. C.: *Caste, Prejudice and the Individual*, Lalvani Publishing House, New Delhi, 1970.

Partha, C.: *Caste and Subaltern Consciousness*, Oxford University Press, Delhi, 1994.

Rajasekharaiah, A.M.: *B.R. Ambedkar: the Politics of Emancipation*, Sindhu Publications, Bombay, 1971.

Robbin, J.: *Dr. Ambedkar and His Movement*, Dr. Ambedkar Publishing Society, Hyderabad, 1964.

Shashi B.R.: *Ambedkar and Human Rights*, KK Publishers, New Delhi, 1981.

Silverberg, James: *Social Mobility in the Caste System in India*, Mouton Publishers, The Hague, 1968.

Suman, R.D.: *Dr. Ambedkar: Pioneer of Human Rights*, Bodhisattva Publications, New Delhi, 1977.

Varale, B.H.: *Dr. Babasaheb Ambedkarrancha Sangaki*, Shrividya Prakashan, Pune, 1988.

Viswanadhaam and Reddy, Narashima: *Scheduled Castes: A Study in Educational Achievement*, Scientific Services, Hyderabad, 1985.

Webster, John: *The Christian Dalits: A History*, Indian Society for Promoting Christian Knowledge (ISPCK), Delhi, 1994.

Yogesh, A.: *The Changing Frontiers of Caste*, National Publishing House, Delhi, 1968.

Index

P

R

S

U

V

❑❑❑